THE UNSOLD
MINDSET

THE UNSOLD MINDSET

REDEFINING WHAT IT MEANS TO SELL

———

Colin Coggins and Garrett Brown

HARPER BUSINESS

An Imprint of HarperCollins*Publishers*

HarperCollins books may be purchased for educational, business, or sales promotional use. For information, please email the Special Markets Department at SPsales@harpercollins.com.

FIRST EDITION

Designed by Kyle O'Brien

Library of Congress Cataloging-in-Publication Data:
Names: Coggins, Colin, author. | Brown, Garrett (Professor of
  entrepreneurship), author.
Title: The unsold mindset : redefining what it means to sell / Colin
  Coggins & Garrett Brown.
Description: First edition. | New York, NY : Harper Business, [2022] |
Identifiers: LCCN 2022013537 (print) | LCCN 2022013538 (ebook) | ISBN
  9780063204904 (hardcover) | ISBN 9780063204911 (ebook)
Subjects: LCSH: Selling. | Customer relations.
Classification: LCC HF5438.25 .C646 2023 (print) | LCC HF5438.25 (ebook)
  | DDC 658.85--dc23/eng/20220526
LC record available at https://lccn.loc.gov/2022013537
LC ebook record available at https://lccn.loc.gov/2022013538

23 24 25 26 27 LBC 5 4 3 2 1

Colin: For my boys, Liam and Caleb.

Garrett: Dammit, you stole my thunder! It's for *my* boys, Cooper and Brady.

Colin: Fine. For *our* boys.

Contents

Authors' Note

Before we get started, some quick housekeeping items . . .

First, *The Unsold Mindset* has been shaped by our experiences interacting with thousands of sales professionals *and* professionals who sell over many years. Some we sat down with to interview formally, some we worked with on our teams or through engagements with our clients. Still others we met at speaking events, on airplanes, at parties, bars, universities, or just about anywhere else we figured out a way to shoehorn selling into a conversation. Because many of these conversations were held in confidence, or with people who didn't know we'd be using their stories and experiences in a book someday, we feel a responsibility to protect their confidentiality. To that end, we've occasionally changed details like names of people, companies, and locations. We've done our best to be as accurate as possible, but in cases where we were recalling a story from someone we could no longer track down or communicate with, we filled in minor details for continuity, provided they did not alter the material point of the story.

Second, a very random thing we learned while writing a book about selling is that the proper way to write the plural of the word *no* is either *nos* or *noes*. These both look extremely weird to us, and as you'll soon see, this book is all about being *unsold* on what you are expected to do, so we decided to use an apostrophe and go with *no's* instead. We're obviously huge rebels for breaking this rule.

Lastly, the selling each of us do every day (and we *all* sell every day) takes countless forms. Because of this variety, putting labels on the people we're selling to can be difficult. In this book, we call these people buyers, prospects, customers, or clients. The terms are meant to be interchangeable.

Okay, that's it. Now on to the good stuff!

THE UNSOLD
MINDSET

Who Are the Unsold?

Before the first class of each new semester, there's always a moment when we look at each other, shake our heads in disbelief, and smile. There's something about watching a fresh group of students file into class for the first time—their energy is contagious. They are the next generation of executives, creators, and world leaders, and it excites us that they don't yet realize the role selling will play in their journey. But our real reason for sharing that incredulous smile is more self-serving. We know, standing together at the front of our classroom, that we're seconds away from being in that rare, special place where what we're good at and what we love doing converge. Where we're somehow getting paid for something we'd do for free. It's in those moments we're at our best, and much of what we'll do in that classroom for the rest of the semester will be about showing these students how to reach and sustain *that* mindset.

As class begins, we watch our students cautiously sizing up the room, wondering what they signed up for. The syllabus says they've enrolled in "Sales Mindset for Entrepreneurs" at the University of

Southern California's Marshall School of Business, but by the looks on their faces, they're not entirely sure what that means. *Is this a sales class? Is it a mindset class? What the hell is a mindset class anyway?*

In addition to not knowing exactly what they'll be learning, they also have no idea who they'll be learning from. Most of them have never been taught by two professors at the same time, let alone by an odd couple like us. We don't sound like professors (our language can get a bit spicy), we don't act like professors (zero slide decks, ever), and we *definitely* don't look like professors (unless the image of a professor you have in your head is wearing T-shirts, hoodies, and Nikes). The minute we start talking, it's obvious we're also very different from each other. One of us personifies logic, the other emotion. One is a clear extrovert, the other takes some time to get warmed up in front of an audience. When we start teaching, though, it's in those same dissimilarities they'll start to recognize one of the most important lessons they'll learn over the course of the semester: *There isn't one right way to succeed. In life, or in sales.*

That lesson is important because the makeup of our class reflects an even greater diversity, with students from many majors and backgrounds, each with unique aspirations. A third of our class is there to learn how to sell ideas; they're future founders, marketers, engineers, and creatives. A third are trying to learn how to sell themselves; they want to get hired or promoted, build meaningful relationships, and lead people. The last third are the future sales professionals. They want to learn how to sell products and services; normally they've got a job lined up after graduation or know someone making a lot of money in sales, and they want to do that, too. If any of them thought they were signing up for a typical sales class that would teach them how to "build rapport," "handle objections," or "ask for the close," they find out very quickly that that is *not* what we teach. Instead, our class is about to spend sixteen weeks finding out that the greatest salespeople aren't successful because of what they *do*, they're successful because of what they *think*.

· · ·

Our journey to understanding the mindset of great sellers started with two questions. The first is similar to what Daniel Pink asks in chapter three of his book *To Sell Is Human*: **"What's the first thing you think of when you hear the word 'salesperson'?"** We've asked this more times than we can remember, not just to our students, but to salespeople and non-salespeople alike, and almost everyone answers without a heartbeat of hesitation. *Pushy, manipulative, sleazy, dishonest,* and *annoying* are among the most common responses. If we're talking to someone more magnanimous, they might say *persistent, extroverted, relentless,* or *smooth-talking*, but the subtext is the same: We. Don't. Like. Salespeople.

Or so it seemed. Answers to a second question we ask just as frequently paint a different picture: **"Who is the greatest salesperson you know?"** For years, we've asked this at the end of every conversation we've had with some of the greatest sellers, leaders, and change agents on the planet. Some answer with a person they literally know, others call to mind a public figure. Some point to visionaries who sell ideas on a global scale, others to hometown heroes who sold their way out of challenging situations. Some name bona fide influencers with millions of followers, others name people with private accounts and no desire to chase "blue check" status. In *every* case, however, the answer was someone the person respected and admired.

The more we thought about it, the more these responses failed to add up. How could all these people look up to the greatest salesperson they know and simultaneously offer cringeworthy stereotypes of the "salespeople" we all hate? We couldn't leave it alone—we needed to understand the discrepancy. We wanted to know how some people could be put on a pedestal for something for which others are stigmatized.

We started reaching out to some of these much-admired sellers to ask them about their approaches to selling and, of course, find out the greatest salespeople *they* knew. As we followed the thread, we found ourselves speaking to CEOs, trial lawyers, doctors, world-renowned artists, Insta-famous bartenders, decorated army generals, professional athletes, business school deans, news anchors, musicians, actors, and entrepreneurs of so many different stripes we lost count.

The variety of people others regarded as "the best salesperson" was mind-blowing. General Stanley McChrystal (whom you'll meet in chapter 2) told us the best salesperson he knows is Major General David Grange, a "remarkable soldier" and charismatic leader who had the ability to inspire his troops by leading them to do incredible things others would not have been able to pull off, like the time he led a division chin-deep into the waves at Normandy. Jon Wexler, former vice president of Global Entertainment and Influencer Marketing at Adidas, GM of Yeezy, head of influencer marketing at Shopify, and now executive director at Fanatics Collectibles, said, "Kanye is the best salesperson I've ever met, hands down." Former Los Angeles Dodgers general manager Fred Claire reminisced about Vin Scully's incredible ability to "sell a mental picture." Two people we spoke to knew Steve Jobs personally, world-renowned oncologist Dr. David Agus (chapter 6) and legendary investor Keith Rabois (a member of the so-called PayPal Mafia that also includes Elon Musk and Peter Thiel), and both said Jobs was undoubtedly the best salesperson they had ever known.

As different as all these incredible people we spoke with were, when we asked them about their own approaches to selling, we were struck by how remarkably similar they sounded to one another. What could chef and TV personality Roy Choi, NBA superagent Alex Saratsis, and CEO of MasterClass David Rogier have in common besides American Express Black cards? Only their entire approach to selling! The more people we interviewed, the more we found their answers echoing. They were saying the same things, but in their own words. What's even more interesting is that they had no idea. With each new person we interviewed, whenever we'd tell them that their views and approaches mirrored those we'd heard from other incredible sellers, they would have moments of epiphany. Even though they hadn't always been doing these things with a specific intention, they suddenly understood why they're so successful at selling, and why they love it so much. It was as if these exceptional sellers belonged to the same secret society, abided by the same core principles, but their secret was so well kept they didn't even know their society existed.

We call these people "The Unsold," and they exhibit a distinct mindset. They are unsold on who they are *supposed* to be, how they are *supposed* to act, and what they are *supposed* to think. They're unsold on who the world *expects* a salesperson to be. They are unsold on the stereotypes around selling and people who sell. They're unsold on the idea that selling can't be an engaging, creative, fulfilling pursuit. And, most importantly, they're unsold on the belief that being a good *person* and a good *salesperson* are mutually exclusive.

The Unsold Mindset empowers people to show up as the opposite of a stereotypical salesperson, and it's not because of the conversations they have with their customers, it's because of the conversations they have with *themselves*. The mindset of a great seller mirrors the mindset of a great person—the lessons we can learn from the Unsold Mindset aren't just lessons about how to sell better, they are lessons about how to live better lives. We decided to share our discoveries because they didn't just change the way we think about selling, they changed the way we think about ourselves, and we hope they'll do the same for you.

• • •

Before we dig into what we found, let us back up for a second and talk about *why* all this matters so much to us. Neither of us grew up dreaming about careers in sales—in fact, quite the opposite—yet we're two longtime sales practitioners who have held just about every sales role you can imagine. How did *that* happen?

As is the case for many young people trying to get a foot in the door and start a career, the availability (and potential lucrativeness) of sales jobs attracted us. Colin grew up with a deep disdain for selling *and* salespeople, a sentiment most likely passed down from his mom, who wasn't a big fan of the pain and uncertainty that came with having a traveling salesman for a dad (Colin's grandfather). After graduating from the University of California, Santa Barbara, Colin set out to find his dream job in entertainment public relations, but his luck and his savings ran out at about the same time, forcing him to choose between moving back in with his parents or taking the first job he could find, selling "fractional vacation ownership" (he still won't admit they were timeshares). He never moved back home.

After graduating from the University of Southern California, Garrett followed in his dad's footsteps and went off to law school. Three years later he was working as a lawyer representing startups. He hated practicing law but loved the companies he was working with, so he left his firm and took a job at a startup selling sponsorships for online games because it was the first job he was offered and he needed the health insurance. We'll get into some of the stories about how and why we ended up falling in love with selling in the pages that follow, but it's not an exaggeration to say that our decision to embrace the profession changed the trajectory of our lives in the best way possible.

Years later, when Garrett was chief revenue officer of enterprise software security startup Bitium, he needed to bring on someone with experience scaling a fast-growing sales team. Colin, by then a seasoned technology sales leader, walked in the door and it was love at first sight! Even though it would be some time before we identified the Unsold Mindset, we immediately bonded over the fact that we refused to take a traditional approach to sales, and an initial meeting scheduled for thirty minutes turned into a deep two-hour conversation about how we could build something special by breaking every sales rule and stereotype we could think of. Colin joined Bitium as senior vice president of sales soon after.

A funny thing happened in the years that followed: Our plan to create a sales culture founded on doing the opposite of what others expected actually worked, and in the scenario anyone who's ever worked at a startup dreams of, Bitium was acquired by Google. After the acquisition, it seemed like everyone was interested in how our scrappy little team was able to pull it off. By then, we had a much deeper understanding of the Unsold Mindset and were excited about teaching it to other people, so we started our own company, Agency18. In addition to working with companies, we were asked to speak at conferences, lead discussions at corporate events, and guest lecture at universities globally. Those who invited us were expecting to hear a couple of typical sales executives discussing things like vertical segmentation and go-to market strategies, and instead they found two close friends with wildly contrasting styles and approaches telling them to *stop* doing what they were expected to do.

The responses from our audiences surprised us. People would line up after our events to tell us some version of the same two things; either "Until today I never knew why I was good," or "Until today I never knew why I wasn't good." Realizing that we could have an impact on the way sellers *and* buyers view selling, it became our mission to pay it forward, motivating as many people as possible to adopt an Unsold Mindset and destigmatize sales for good.

Several of our talks were guest lectures at universities, including USC, and one day the executive director of USC's Greif Center for Entrepreneurship, Helena Yli-Renko, called us to say she was excited about the responses to our content and wondered if we'd consider developing a class for students. Selling is critical to success in entrepreneurship, she told us, and sales was woefully undertaught at business schools. *Hell yes*, we said! We leapt at the chance. "Sales Mindset for Entrepreneurs," to our knowledge the only sales *mindset* class at the higher education level, was born.

As we developed the class, we boiled down the Unsold Mindset into nine core precepts, and in the pages that follow we devote a chapter to each. The thought of standing in front of the most unforgiving demographic out there, college students, also prompted us to do a whole lot of research; we needed to be able to show *why* the Unsold Mindset works. We quickly found ourselves drawn to some unexpected branches of psychological literature, and it was so illuminating we haven't stopped researching since. While many of the studies done on sales have focused on how to use psychological techniques to "influence" people into buying, we tapped into an entirely different body of work. Some of it highlights *why* those with an Unsold mind think the way they do, some sheds light on the practical and mental challenges of traditional sales, and much of it reveals how people from all walks of life and career paths overcome these challenges with things like creativity, learned optimism, and agency.

Even though the core ideas of each chapter are unique, each with its own set of habits, practices, and methods, they also reinforce one another. You'll see how the authentic mindset described in chapter 1 underpins the pathologically optimistic mindset of chapter 4, how the practice of intentional ignorance described in chapter 2 reinforces the Same Team mindset of chapter 6, and so on. The Unsold Mindset consists of all these concepts, together.

• • •

Whether or not you have "sales" in your job title, you'll see a piece of yourself in the Unsold and gain valuable lessons from the way they think and approach life and sales. When we saw how powerful the effect of what we were teaching was for our class, our clients, and our audiences, we knew we had to write this book. There's a pressing need for all of us to enjoy selling and flourish in it. We all sell, after all.

For those in traditional sales jobs, finding a healthier way to sell is critical. One study we found revealed that two thirds of salespeople reported that they were either close to or already experiencing burnout.

People in sales are also particularly vulnerable to developing mental health issues like anxiety, depression, and addiction, so finding a way to sell more and be happier doing it isn't just a luxury, it's critical.

For those who are not sales professionals by trade but are required to sell every day (which is pretty much everyone else), the anxiety caused by selling can be overwhelming, and reluctance toward selling can cause them to miss out on opportunities to become more successful both personally and professionally.

Our mission is to change the way people think about selling by changing the way they think about themselves. We know from experience that when selling is done the right way for the right reasons, it can effect real change. It can change circumstances, change thoughts, and change lives, all for the better. Call us naïve, but we truly believe that if everyone approached selling with just a little more of an Unsold Mindset, the sales profession could shed its stereotype and be as respected as every other profession that serves others and contributes to society.

We don't know what led you to pick up this book, but we know you're our people and we're excited to be on this journey with you.

CHAPTER ONE

You Can't "Act" Authentic

nside a dimly lit room on the outskirts of Moscow, Alex sat down at a table for dinner. On the other side of the table a member of the Russian mob sat between two hulking bodyguards in dark suits. The tone of the conversation was friendly enough, but a gun was placed conspicuously on the table in front of each henchman, a reminder of who was in charge. Before long, shots of vodka appeared in front of each man. Alex didn't feel comfortable declining, so he drank. The glasses were refilled, emptied, and filled again throughout the meal, and Alex went shot-for-shot with the menacing Russians.

As dinner was winding down, the conversation finally shifted to the business at hand. Alex, a twenty-four-year-old aspiring sports agent, had flown from the United States to the other side of the world in hopes of signing a client, a relatively unknown Russian basketball prospect who had a real shot at getting drafted to the NBA. The men sitting across from him were "representing the prospect's interests," and would ultimately decide who his agent would be.

When it came time for his pitch, Alex told us, he did what he thought a good agent should do; he sold the dream. Hard. Acting like the image of a superagent he had in his mind, he painted a tantalizing picture of the high-flying life the Russian player would enjoy as a wildly successful NBA superstar. He talked about the glamour of playing professional basketball; about money, luxury, all-star teams, record-breaking contracts, and other perks reserved for only the most elite stars. Was it possible the young Russian player would make it to those rarefied heights? Sure. Was it likely? Not at all. But Alex was on a roll, emboldened by the vodka. He found himself saying whatever it took to board the long flight home with a deal.

When he finished talking, the Russians seemed pleased. "If you can do all of that for us," the mobster said, "I'm willing to shake your hand right now." Alex gripped his chair, dizzy from the vodka and the thrill of the moment. This was huge. The Russian player would be his first client, launching the career he'd dreamed of. "But," the mobster continued, "we know your address. We know who your girlfriend is. We know where you work. If anything goes wrong, we will come find you."

Suddenly, elation turned to dread. Alex's authenticity was being put to the test. What had he done? Why had he sold so hard? He wanted this deal more than anything, but was he willing to bet his life on the picture he'd painted? His future wife's life? *No fucking way*, he thought to himself. He went home without a deal, but with the peace of mind that he might, literally, have dodged a bullet.

Today, Alex Saratsis is one of the most powerful agents in sports. He successfully negotiated one of the biggest contracts in NBA history to date for his client Giannis Antetokounmpo. He's revered by many in the business for his unorthodox-yet-genuine style, very much exemplifying the Unsold Mindset. When someone told him he was "the nicest dickhead they ever met," he took it as a compliment, knowing he'd earned that reputation by being his authentic self. These days, he's done with putting on any kind of persona; he prefers to tell it exactly how it is, as tough as that might sometimes be. In one interview, he recalled when the parents of a young player who was a long shot for making the second round of the NBA draft asked Saratsis about branding he would do for their son. His response was "I'm sorry, with all due respect, your son needs to make sure he gets on an NBA roster before we even have this kind of discussion." This is a far cry from the performance he put on in Russia so many years earlier.

Alex doesn't want to play a role; he wants to be himself. That's what we all want. But showing up as our authentic selves can be hard in any situation, especially when we find ourselves in a position where we need to sell.

From a young age, we feel pressure to present ourselves in ways that aren't authentic to us, making us feel unappreciated for who we truly are. We're worried our hair is too long or short, too straight or curly; our pants are a little too baggy or skinny or the wrong brand; we don't want people to find out we think rom coms should have their own Oscar category (Colin), we think the Oxford comma should be federal law (Garrett), or we think Taylor Swift is somehow underrated (Garrett *and* Colin . . . but mostly Garrett); and on and on. When it comes to work, from the moment we interview for a position, we feel the need to put on a persona. That might mean playing the always upbeat, nothing-ruffles-me type, the no-worries-from-me "yes" person, or the smartest-one-in-the-room character. Hopefully over time, though, we get comfortable enough with colleagues to show more and more of our genuine selves; rolling up our sleeves once in a while to let that tattoo we've been hiding breathe a little, expressing a dissenting view, or asking for help when we need it.

But when it comes to doing what we need to do to sell, like making calls to prospects, meeting with clients or managers, giving presentations inside or outside of the company, or even in non-traditional sales situations like selling ourselves in job interviews, raising money for charity, or asking for a raise, we feel like we have to put on a persona. It's a big reason many people hate selling so much. We feel we've got to be "on" in super-confident, hyper-polished, upbeat and happy, true seller form. The cultural expectation runs deep in our collective unconscious. If we're introverted, we're *supposed to* act like an extrovert. If we're nervous, we're *supposed to* hide it or we'll seem weak. If a customer is unsure about buying, we're *supposed to* be able to close that deal anyway.

People with an Unsold Mindset use a different playbook, and they don't care what the book says they're supposed to do. They don't care if their unwillingness to play a part costs them a deal from time to time. They don't care if "it's always been done that way." They know that in the long run, they'll succeed if they stay real. And being real *matters* to them; they've realized that it is enormously rewarding to show up as the person we really are, in any situation.

It sounds so simple—*be authentic*—but it's said a lot and practiced much less, especially when people sell. Who could be blamed? The cultural messaging that selling is all about phoniness and manipulation is pervasive.

The Seller You Never Wanted to Be

How many depictions of selling in books, movies, and on TV are of thoughtful, genuine, collaborative, problem-solving contributors to society? Almost none. People selling are almost always portrayed as either unctuous flatterers, smooth-talking sharks, or aggressive arm twisters. The main character in the cult sales classic *Boiler Room,* about a group of twenty-something "stock jocks" who sell bogus investments to vulnerable targets, reflects that he had more integrity when he worked in gambling. "Looking back, the casino was the most legitimate business I had running," he says wistfully. "I looked my customers in the eye and I provided a service they wanted. Now I don't even look my customers in the eye and I push them something they never asked for." In *Glengarry Glen Ross,* Alec Baldwin, as the character Blake, spews the stereotype to a beleaguered real estate sales team: "Only one thing counts in life: get them to sign on the line that is dotted!" Then there's the hilariously hapless auto parts salesman Tommy, played by Chris Farley, in *Tommy Boy:* "All right, now it's sales time," his boss preps him, "so remember, we don't take no . . ." Tommy struggles to complete the sentence, "No shit from anyone . . . Um, we don't take no prisoners . . . Oh yeah . . . We don't take 'no' for an answer!" That doesn't even account for *actual* selling that fuels the stereotypes, from the steady stream of "but wait, there's more!" infomercials, to hollering salespeople on car lots surrounded by those floppy (creepy?) arm-waving inflatable tube people, to clothing store attendants with a serious case of commission breath stalking us from rack to rack.

Sales trainings and books about selling are also crammed with advice about how to inauthentically win people over and convince them to buy. The commonly taught tactic of frequently repeating the name of the person you're selling to, which dates at least as far back as Dale Carnegie's *How to Win Friends and Influence People,* is one example. A person's name, Carnegie advises, is "the sweetest, most important

sound in any language." Repeating it often, the idea goes, will ingratiate the seller to the customer.

Another supposedly ingratiating tactic that has gained way too
much popularity over the years is "mirroring" a prospect's body language, which is meant to subliminally appeal to people. There is a
basis in human psychology for believing that mirroring can lead to
connection, but the rapport it builds, if it builds any at all, is based
on mirroring being a *natural* inclination when we're authentically engaged in a conversation with someone and are relating to them. If
we're talking to someone and all we are thinking about is crossing our
legs when they do, or putting our hand under our chin like they are,
we're not paying genuine attention to what they're saying, which can
hinder the connection.

If you add in the classic I-can-squeeze-harder-than-you handshake, you've got the Holy Trinity of sales inauthenticity that Andy
Bernard, the salesman in *The Office* named one of the most annoying characters on TV, prides himself on: "I'll be the number two guy
here in Scranton in six weeks," he confidently asserted in one episode.
"How? Name repetition, personality mirroring, and never breaking
off a handshake. I'm always thinking one step ahead."

Maybe some people feel good about putting on the persona, but
our experience with thousands of sellers across a slew of industries
has taught us that most people despise putting on an act, if not at first,
then before long. David Ogilvy, one of the most influential advertising
creatives of all time, wrote, "The worst fault a salesman can commit
is to be a bore." Sure, selling shouldn't be boring, for customers or for
those doing the selling. But we'd argue that the worst fault in selling is
to be disingenuous. It's bad for our reputations, our relationships, and
our business, and research shows it's even bad for our health.

Why Inauthenticity Is Such a Turnoff

Hamet Watt, former founder of MoviePass and partner at the prestigious Upfront Ventures, now founder and CEO of Share Ventures, a human performance–focused venture lab and fund, told us "a founder can check all the boxes, but sometimes there's something deep down in my gut that says we should pass on a deal, there's a feeling they are being inauthentic about something. I can't explain it, but I pick up on it." It's human nature to despise phoniness, and we're exquisitely capable of perceiving it. Rather than convincing ourselves we can master manipulative tactics, or that they're just part of the business of selling, the equivalent of little white lies, we should be mindful of what business professor and researcher Peter Wright dubbed consumers' *schemer schema*. This is the awareness we develop of persuasion techniques sellers use on us and our ability to shield ourselves from the hoped-for influence, with what Wright calls our "persuasion coping knowledge." It's a fancy way of saying that buyers see what sellers are up to and they have their walls up.

Researchers call the reaction Hamet Watt described *inauthenticity aversion*. Studies of consumer responses to claims made by individuals and brands have revealed "the powerful outrage consumers display at perceived inauthenticity." Even once customers have come to believe in the reliability of an individual seller or brand, as Wharton School researcher Ike Silver and colleagues write, just one piece of inconsistent information can undermine those beliefs. In short, they say, "a drop of inauthenticity poisons the well."

It's like the previously mentioned tactic of repeating a person's name when you're selling to them. We've almost certainly noticed a salesperson doing this to us, and it's awkwardly unnatural every time.

Do you ever do it with your friends and family? Of course not. If a salesperson is doing it to us, not only are we likely to notice, but we get annoyed they think we're not sharp enough to pick up on it.

Or take another staple of sales advice: repeating what you've heard a customer say. This is often taught as part of the practice of "active listening." While it can be done in a way that shows someone you care about what they are saying and you want to hear them right, Colleen Stanley, an expert on emotional intelligence in sales, warns that, in selling interactions, it is likely to come across as fake empathy. *I totally understand, Kathy.* (Hey, why not throw their name in, too!) *It sounds like you need a solution. After all, you did say your team spends dozens of hours a week on this problem.* If the seller was mimicking Kathy's body language at this point, Kathy would probably be rolling her eyes. The slightest hint that our feelings are being used to sell to us makes us feel icky.

Even one of the most common ways that many of us put on a bit of an act can be easy to spot: fake smiling. Of course, we often do this for altruistic reasons, like making that annoying relative think we're more excited to see them at Thanksgiving than we are. But in selling, it's way too easy for customers to pick up on the ulterior sales motive. Psychologist Richard Wiseman conducted research in which he showed thousands of subjects photos of people who are genuinely smiling mixed in with ones putting on fake smiles, and he found that people can distinguish a bogus smile from a real one nearly two thirds of the time. And that's when the person isn't standing right in front of us.

The ultimate irony of resorting to inauthentic "persona selling," though, is that it's not only customers who are turned off; the ones doing the selling don't like being inauthentic either.

We Don't Like Fakes, Even When *We* Are Doing the Faking

Most of us hate being expected to act like someone we're not. The implication is insulting; we're not impressive enough as we are, not polished enough, not smart enough, not confident enough, not upbeat enough. Even more than that, we hate being glad-handed, pressured, and manipulated by sellers pretending to be someone *they're* not, morphing into some version of the stereotypical salesperson. Knowing buyers feel this way is why so many people in sales, and in what author Daniel Pink calls "non-sales selling" situations, feel *stereotype threat*. This is the fear, on the part of those in a stereotyped social group, that they will be perceived as behaving in ways that live up to the stereotype. This can show up in countless ways. For example, some might perceive a stereotype that successful tech executives are all young, single workaholics. Because of this, an older employee with a family might feel there is a ceiling on what they can achieve, and this belief might prevent them from living up to their maximum potential.

When it comes to selling, those who don't subscribe to the "get the sale by any means necessary" mentality often feel stereotype threat, because they know the clichés about selling are so deeply ingrained. Salespeople may feel the sting when they're asked what they do for a living, or whenever they pick up the phone to call a prospect. They might feel the threat even when they interact with colleagues from other departments in their company, thinking they're seen as a necessary evil. For many, it shows up when it's time to ask for the sale. Research shows the stereotype threat takes its toll on how people feel about their work *and* their actual performance.

One reason that's true is that it exacerbates what psychologists George Dudley and Shannon Goodson have dubbed *sales call reluctance,* a fear of making calls due to feelings of shame that stem from the image of salespeople as pushy, disreputable cousins of used car peddlers. It leads people to literally not pick up the phone or do the other things they need to do to sell. When we told a friend about this, she immediately recognized it in herself, responding, "That's what I felt when I was doing 'get out the vote' calling!" Even though she was serving a cause she deeply believed in and wasn't shilling for money, she felt stereotype threat that she'd been seen as pushy or annoying and hesitated picking up the phone because of it.

Ironically, when people suffer from stereotype threat they often end up adjusting their behavior to compensate, taking on a different persona that they perceive will counter the stereotype. They can end up selling the persona as much or more than whatever they're meant to be selling. And that can be stressful. We tell ourselves, *I'd better pull this off or they'll think I'm not fit for the job; the product isn't up to par; the proposal isn't legit.* For those who aren't in traditional sales jobs, they put the experience out of their minds and figure, *phew, got through that, and thank goodness I don't have to do it again for a while.* But before long, they're in another selling situation and feel the dread creeping back in. For those in traditional sales who are selling every day, the psychological impact can begin to undermine not only their career satisfaction and success, but how happy they are in general.

The Vicious Cycle of Inauthenticity

In our work we've observed a common destructive pattern. Many people, when they're first starting to sell, attempt to take on the persona of a successful salesperson they've internalized. They don't think they're good enough as themselves since they don't resemble what they think a successful salesperson looks like. Customers see right through the façade, though, and the salesperson is unsuccessful. The first twinge of shame sets in, both because of their poor results and because they're acting like someone they're not.

In response, they double down on pulling off the persona, submerging themselves in those traditional sales books, trainings, and podcasts, trying to learn how to act to get the persona to work. Now suddenly they are social selling, SPIN selling, value selling, complex selling, gap selling, challenger selling, or selling in whatever other style is popular that particular week. But they still get told *no* often and even more shame of rejection creeps in.

Since acting like their *idea* of a salesperson didn't work, they decide to mimic a standout performer they know instead. They pick their new role model's brain about how they approach selling, start reciting soundbites they've heard them use by listening in on their calls, sending the same emails, and telling the same jokes and stories. But they're *still* not seeing better results, which is especially frustrating since they're doing *exactly* what the great performer does. They start getting desperate, telling customers anything they can think of to keep them in conversations.

This is where many people hit a dangerous inflection point: They start blaming the customer because, since they're doing everything they've been told, plus all the things that work for other successful sellers, it can't possibly be their own fault. They start cursing after calls, slamming down the phone, venting to anyone who will listen about how their prospects are morons. Underlying that anger is growing shame, not only because they aren't succeeding, but because they've ended up behaving exactly like the pushy, desperate salesperson they never wanted to be.

If nothing changes, the cycle of inauthenticity ends with a crippling sense of insecurity, immobilizing the salesperson until they burn out and either quit or get fired. Much of the negativity could have been avoided by breaking the cycle, which requires ditching the act and learning to sell authentically. If you ask us, the reason only about 20 percent of salespeople hit their numbers is because the 80 percent are trying to be like the 20 percent, while the 20 percent aren't trying to be like anyone besides themselves.

Rejecting the Persona

Throughout his decades-long career in music, Snoop Dogg has been unapologetically authentic. When we spoke with him, he summed up the importance of being yourself beautifully. *"Master doing you,"* he told us. "Do that and everything else will be fine walking this Earth." Instead of looking for some silver bullet combination of persona and sales tactics, we should appreciate that the magic in selling is in simply being who we are. Colin accidentally discovered this *and* got firsthand experience of the toll inauthenticity can take both on performance and self-perception during those rocky first few months after college selling the fractional vacation ownership packages that were definitely not timeshares. The company he worked for trained him to be a certain kind of salesperson. He was expected to dress a particular way and had to trade in his newly purchased, Jay-Z-inspired "crisp pair of jeans" and "button ups" for a closet full of Tommy Bahama shirts and "island performance" pants. He was also trained to follow a rigid script that led customers down a path that ended in what most would call a "hard sell." Because of how expensive it was for the company to get leads in the door, the pressure to close was intense, to say the least. Colin didn't feel good about any of it, but he went through the motions because he didn't know he had a choice. He hated the work and wasn't selling anyone successfully, including himself. What he did get really good at was blame displacement! In his mind the customers sucked, he was too educated, too young, the product was horrible . . . the problem lay in everything and everyone but himself.

After two months without success, he was put on a "performance improvement plan," a sales manager's fancy way of saying he was about to be fired. Feeling he had nothing to lose, he decided to screw the establishment on his way out. He intentionally broke almost every "rule" he'd been taught, and in doing so unintentionally changed the course of his life. He showed up on the first day of what was presumably his last month on the job and did the exact opposite of what he had been trained to do. He acted exactly like his true self, which was the antithesis of a "good" salesperson. He hung up the Tommy Bahama silk for something that felt less like a costume to him. He only laughed when he thought something was funny, and he admitted "I don't know" when he didn't have an answer to a question. When he knew the answer was *no*, he said so instead of stalling and saying "let me look into that for you." He only asked questions he *actually* wanted to know the answers to instead of the ones in the script. Some of the questions he asked were about the customers themselves, and he was kind of, sort of, accidentally starting to enjoy the conversations he was having. Soon, he found himself looking forward to having more of them.

Next, he realized he was looking for the good in clients instead of obsessing about overcoming their next objection. He also started to see the good in the product he was selling. His view of the product changed because his view of the customer changed. As he started having authentic conversations, prospects became real people to him with real families and real priorities. He realized many of the people he was talking to weren't letting themselves spend the money to do the exact thing they said they cared about the most: creating memories with their families. They would tell him about their aspirations for dedicated family time with their young children on a beach or in a cabin, reminiscing about their favorite childhood vacations. Then in the next sentence they'd say they'd never actually take such a trip even if they could afford it because they didn't like spending that much money on something that wasn't tangible, that they could never use again.

It was these genuine, honest, vulnerable moments when prospects shared their goals and frustrations that turned Colin into an advocate for them, changing his approach to selling. He wasn't pretending to care, he *actually* cared; and he started seeing himself in these people he was talking to. Connecting the dots between a product he now believed in and what was best for the families he was speaking with became easy.

He accidentally figured it out: If you show up as the opposite of who people expect a salesperson to be, something profound happens. People start to treat you as a *person*, not just a *salesperson*, and you start to view those you're selling to as *real* humans, not just prospects. This results in a genuine curiosity about each other. Before long Colin was not only breaking the company's sales records, but at the ripe old age of twenty-two he was asked to teach his "approach" to the sales team, eventually becoming the company's youngest director of sales. How ironic, people needing to be *taught* to be authentic. That's how deeply ingrained the notion that sales requires a persona is. But we can choose to reject it.

Each of us has an authentic voice that we use perfectly all the time when we aren't selling, in our conversations with friends and family.

One sales leader we spoke to made this point to us vividly: "I can't tell you how many times I've listened in on a call, and then had to ask the salesperson, 'Who was that I was just listening to? That wasn't the same person I had a beer with last night.'" Sales is about connection through communication, and that connection shouldn't be any less genuine than when you're spending time with your friends at happy hour.

So many talented sellers have told us they discovered this and were so much happier and more successful afterward. Jon Dahan, CEO of the MindMedium creative agency, which represents decision-makers, influencers, and brands like Nike, Google, and Pepsi, told us, "When I started my career, I wasted three years trying to be someone I'm not." He eventually decided to be himself, and his success took off. The authenticity he fostered transcended his own persona, serving as a foundation for his team and the company culture as a whole. When we spent time with them, it was clear they act the same with customers courtside at a Lakers game as they do when they're just hanging out with each other at the office.

Proof Authenticity Works

The evidence for the power of authenticity in selling isn't only anecdotal; research has recently been done showing that it's great for customer relationships, as well as for employee satisfaction and retention. While a great deal of research has been done about the importance of authenticity in messaging by brands, attention has only started to be turned toward authenticity in individual interactions with those in selling roles.

One study was conducted with employees of a Wipro call center in India that was experiencing high employee turnover. The researchers thought the problem might be the messages given to employees in their orientation process. Employees were told exactly how to behave with customers, including that they should mimic a British or American English accent. Now don't get us wrong, we love trying to pull off a British accent as much as the next bloody Yank, but not as a way to ingratiate ourselves to people for inauthentic reasons.

The researchers created a new employee orientation process designed to convey to the workers that they were appreciated for who they were, asking them to share about themselves and "to reflect on their signature strengths and how they could actively put them to use as part of the new job." The results were striking. Retention increased by almost 50 percent. Customers surveyed later also reported higher satisfaction with these employees. The results were due, the researchers argue, to the workers "being encouraged to present themselves in a manner that's consistent with their authentic best selves." Our experience has shown this to be true for employees throughout *all* their time with a company, and their entire career. Similarly, research by Ernst & Young done with insurance company representatives and their customers has also shown that when reps are allowed to "be fully themselves" in interactions with policyholders, they score higher on customer satisfaction. As for employee satisfaction, the authors of one study summarized their results as "the more that work can allow for employees to show their real self, the more engaged they will be."

Being authentic is also good for our psyches, and our physical health. In fact, psychologist Abraham Maslow identified living according to "one's own intrinsic, authentic values" as vital to achieving the ultimate human aspiration of self-actualization. In more recent years, research in positive psychology has produced strong empirical evidence of the connection between living authentically and overall well-being. In his book *Authentic: How to Be Yourself and Why It Matters,* British psychologist Stephen Joseph writes that psychologists have realized that "Authenticity . . . is no soft option but the cornerstone of a good life." Specific benefits he points to are that "people who score high on tests for authenticity are more satisfied with life . . . have higher self-esteem . . . are less likely to be depressed and anxious, feel more alert and awake, and cope better with stress."

Authenticity is also associated with more willingness to learn about ourselves, both strengths and weaknesses, and stretch ourselves to grow, which, as we'll explore in more detail in chapter 3, is a leading contributor to career success. This link between authenticity and personal growth highlights that being authentic doesn't mean discovering at some point in life who we truly, deeply are and then sticking with that until our time here is done. We can and should keep evolving, and being authentic helps us to keep finding out more about what we're capable of so that we can cultivate the person we most want to be.

We found a great example of how authenticity can evolve when we spoke to world-renowned chef Roy Choi. He is best known for changing the restaurant landscape when he started selling Korean/ Mexican fusion tacos out of his Kogi food trucks in Los Angeles (more on this in chapter 7). He's since opened restaurants, created and starred in multiple TV shows, and even had a movie loosely based on his life, *Chef* with Jon Favreau. Chef Choi told us, "I lived through multiple authentic selves. As my experiences have grown, so have I . . . I wouldn't be the authentic version of myself today if I wasn't first the authentic version of myself ten years ago."

Sellers with an Unsold Mindset shared time and again with us that selling has been a great means of developing themselves. They don't change for customers, they change *because* of customers, constantly learning from their interactions with them.

A final reason authenticity is good for us, and for our selling success, is that high scorers for authenticity prioritize intrinsic motivations in their work, seeking experiences and skills that they are genuinely enthusiastic about, much like what Colin did in that first job when he became genuinely interested in who he was speaking with. And being intrinsically motivated is a strong contributor to happiness as well as to making us more tenacious in pursuit of goals. Given how often salespeople have to deal with rejection and failure, that's clearly a huge benefit.

Show Your Work

Remember when you were a kid in math class and teachers wouldn't just give you a good grade for getting the right answer, you also had to show them *how* you got to the answer? "Show your work," they'd say. They wanted to make sure you learned the correct thought process. Well, in "the real world" outside of school, the same premium is put on showing your thinking.

Google is famous for hard-to-answer interview questions like *How many gas stations are there in the United States?* or *How many golf balls can you fit into a school bus?* Hiring managers at Google don't care about the specific answers candidates give, they care about understanding candidates better by seeing how they think. Showing how you're thinking is also a great way to authentically give the people you're selling to that understanding and build stronger connections with them.

An example of showing your work that we've seen often among

sellers with an Unsold Mindset is that they unintentionally talk to themselves, *out loud*, in front of the person they are selling to. We didn't recognize how common this was until we realized one day how endearing we found it while conducting one of our interviews. It was very early in our interview process, and we were watching the recording of a conversation we'd had with a senior sales manager at a large software company, trying to pinpoint why we both liked him so much. He introduced himself to us at the beginning of the interview as a "sales leader," then stopped himself mid-sentence, stared off for a second and reprimanded himself aloud, "Dammit! I gotta stop doing that." Then he looked back at us and asked, "Can we try again?" He went on to say that he'd been questioning whether he'd let his career define who he is as a person, and that he'd been working on intentionally not defaulting to his "title" when introducing himself. We realized after watching it again that the moment he talked to himself in front of us was the instant we felt connected to him. For a few seconds we had an unmanufactured window into his raw, behind-the-scenes self. We've started to think of this behavior as the quintessential example of "showing your work," and as soon as we started to look for it, we found successful people doing it all the time.

In one sales demo we watched, which wasn't going well, the seller stopped and said to herself aloud, "I feel boring," then looked at the customer and asked, "Do I sound boring?" The customer laughed, and the seller lightened up and became more herself and a whole new chemistry coursed between them. Robert Simon, a one-time telemarketer who is now one of the top trial lawyers in California, told us about a time a judge asked him to repeat something, and as he stumbled into a pause while attempting to recollect, he sheepishly looked toward the courtroom ceiling and said to himself aloud, "What *did*

I say?," and then looked at the judge and continued, "Your honor, I honestly have no idea what I just said!" The entire courtroom, including the jury, erupted with laughter at the authentic moment. Simon suddenly became a *person* for the jurors and not merely a stereotypical lawyer trying to persuade, cajole, and convince.

The appeal of spontaneous self-conversations is not only that people are letting us into their thought process, they are also making us a partner in their thinking. And that often opens the door for input they might not have received otherwise. It's also appealing because it's evidence they're not perfectly on top of every little thing, acting like an all-knowing, totally polished, overconfident, stereotypical seller. In fact, another way we've seen people show their work is owning up to mistakes and wrong turns midstream, right in the middle of an interaction. For example, say you've made a joke that fell completely flat, which we've all done. (Just ask anyone who's seen us speak!) Owning up to the flub makes up for it. *Saturday Night Live* "Weekend Update" host Colin Jost is great at this. In almost every episode he'll tell at least one dud, but by immediately owning just how horribly flat it had fallen with a wry comment or an earnest shrug, he gets the laugh he was originally aiming for, and big applause, too. The failure ends up being stronger than the joke. Being fallible is endearing.

Acknowledging missteps also allows you to make up for them. One of our favorite stories of a course correction was told by Sara Blakely, founder of Spanx. Our class was invited to hear her speak when she came to USC, and we were blown away by how proud she was to be a self-proclaimed salesperson, especially with the title CEO. She said that very early on in launching her company, she was in the middle of a pitch with a buyer from Neiman Marcus and it just wasn't going well. Sara could see the buyer's attention shifting and knew she was a couple of minutes away from totally losing her. The ending of this story has become legend. Sara tells how she interrupted protocol and said, "You know what, Diane? Will you come with me to the bathroom? [Diane] goes, 'excuse me?' I go, I know, I know; it's a little weird. Will you just please come with me to the bathroom. I want to show you my own product before and after. And she . . . she said okay. I had on my cream pants—that were the reason I invented this—without Spanx on. And then I went in the stall and put Spanx on underneath and came out. And she looked at me, and she goes, 'Wow, I get it. It's brilliant.' And she said, 'I'm going to place an order, and I'm going to put it in seven stores and see how it goes.'" Fast forward a few years and Blakely landed herself on the cover of *Forbes* for being a self-made billionaire.

The key to all of this is self-awareness. One of our Golden Rules for selling is this: If you think you sound cheesy, you probably sound cheesy. If you think you sound boring, we'd almost guarantee you're right. The best way out of situations like those is to acknowledge them. One cardinal sin that typical sellers make all the time, is that when they make a mistake or feel like something's off, they try to ignore it. For example, if they realize they've mispronounced a word or a name, and the whole room hears it, for some reason they just keep talking instead of pausing to acknowledge the gaffe. Great sellers on the other hand, are very comfortable saying what they're thinking, calling out the elephant in the room when there is one. If they sense that a customer is losing interest during a demo, they'll mention it instead of powering through. If they don't understand something, they'll ask about it instead of pretending to know what they're talking about to look smart. If a joke they told falls flat, they'll call themselves out on it, playfully saying something like "That was pretty bad, huh?" Making mistakes makes you human. In order to course correct in real time, you must first acknowledge that you're off course. It would be selfish not to bring the customer on the journey with you.

As psychologist and Wharton professor Adam Grant writes, in addition to being true to oneself, "authenticity is about . . . expressing your inner thoughts and feelings on the outside. Instead of wearing a mask, you let people see what's really going on inside your head." Show your work.

Authenticity for Introverts, Assholes, and Everyone in Between

If a personality trait is authentic to you, it can be a selling strength. It doesn't matter if you're logical or emotional, disinterested or serious, a data person who loves doing research or a lover of endless conversation. If you're quick witted, let it show in your selling. If you're a data wonk, find ways to show people that. The Unsold Mindset doesn't discriminate, it comes in every flavor.

One of the questions we get most often about selling is whether you have to be an extrovert to be good at it. Short answer: Absolutely not. In fact, Hilary Headlee, former head of global sales enablement for Zoom, and one of the executives responsible for scaling Zoom's sales team to help drive the company's massive growth after Zoom became a household name during the COVID pandemic, told us that some of the best sellers she knows are introverts. In our work with sales teams we've occasionally used personality tests to help us understand them better, and we have found that most salespeople do tend to be extroverts. That's almost certainly due to self-selection bias. We suspect the stereotype of the "always on" salesperson dissuades many introverts from applying for jobs that involve selling. People hiring for those roles may also have a bias for extroverts because of the stereotype. But do extroverts really have an advantage in selling? Not necessarily. Yes, extroverts tend to relish meeting new people and are naturally more gregarious, but as Susan Cain emphasized in her book *Quiet*, introverts have conversational strengths of their own. They may well also enjoy talking to strangers. Cain showed that it's not that introverts generally don't enjoy talking to people, including strangers, but that they don't enjoy idle, meaningless chitchat or performative attention-seeking in conversation. They prefer meaty and more intimate conversation, one-on-one or in small groups. That's a real bonus for sales interactions. Introverts also tend to favor listening to others over dominating conversations. Listening carefully is vital to good selling. So are understanding complex ideas and relaying them in a digestible format, collecting data and crafting it into meaningful solutions, and putting someone else (the customer) at the center of every conversation. All of these skills are more natural for introverts.

Chef Choi also credits being an introvert with his business success. When we interviewed him, he told us that because of his introversion, he doesn't need to be the center of attention. "A great salesperson can take themselves out of the equation," he said, "and introverts do that well." That's a way of being more inclusive, he highlighted, allowing others to express themselves authentically, too. "We deprive each other by excluding each other," he commented. He says his introversion had led him to be highly intentional about listening more and speaking less, in the boardroom *and* the kitchen. He also considers his responses to questions or objections extremely carefully because, like most introverts, he needs to have a high degree of confidence in what he's saying before he says it. We've probably all known that generally quiet person that everyone listens to because we know that speaking up takes them out of their comfort zone, so we assume if they're talking, they have something important to say. Building his business, Choi says, "made me realize that my personality is a strength when I sell."

The features of being introverted that Choi highlights account for something we've observed about introverts working with customers. We've seen that often customers begin to try to endear themselves to the salesperson, flipping the usual dynamic, because they want to *earn* a connection with this person they respect. Introverts also tend to naturally follow many of the other practices we'll describe in later chapters.

Of course, this doesn't mean natural extroverts should behave like introverts when selling. It does mean that you have permission to re-evaluate *any* of your personality traits when it comes to who you think you're supposed to be as a salesperson. Use your authentic strengths to ensure you show up as the best version of yourself.

The Boundaries of Authenticity

Is it possible to be *too* authentic? As Adam Grant highlights, being authentic doesn't mean we should let people see *everything* going on in our heads, and hearts. Doing so could easily become self-indulgent, and in selling situations quickly become a real turn-off. He writes, "Authenticity without boundaries is careless." Choosing to keep certain thoughts to ourselves is just basic human kindness. Conforming to certain widely appreciated norms of behavior is often important to getting along with others. There's nothing necessarily wrong with putting on the proverbial blue suit if that's what decorum and custom calls for.

Another "non-sales seller" with an Unsold Mindset talked about this with us. Ari Melber is the chief legal correspondent for MSNBC and host of *The Beat with Ari Melber*. In addition to his stellar journalistic track record, he's become well-known for quoting lines from rappers and hip-hop artists in his news stories, which is authentic to his love of the music. But he still wears a suit and tie when he's on the air, even though jeans and a hoodie would be more his style.

As is always true with selling, of any kind, Melber's credibility is critical to his success. "There are styles and habits we associate with objectivity even though they don't prove it. Looking like your grandpa's anchorman connotes objectivity. That doesn't mean it's true. Someone can deliver the news in a leather jacket or tatted up and still be objective. But in a visual or social medium they might be taking on additional complexity because they have to prove themselves that much more to the people they are speaking to." Ari has judiciously walked a line between distinctively expressing himself and conforming to valid expectations.

To Ari's point, being our authentic selves isn't about always behaving in some absurdly distinctive way. No doubt each of us is a unique individual, but we also share a whole lot with one another, starting with 99.9 percent of our DNA. We've also learned lots of thoughtful behavior that society expects of us. Some conformity in life is key. The training we get growing up about social graces and proper ways of handling any manner of situations involves norms of behavior that are critical to functioning in society. If our natural inclination would be to act like an asshole, to never express appreciation, to laugh freely at others' expense, and to constantly judge everyone, we'd be far better off to evolve and grow out of those aspects of our authentic selves. Tailoring our behavior to positive social norms isn't disingenuous persona adoption; it's a crucial part of personal growth. Hopefully, we come to accept those positive behaviors as part of who we are. Smiling at people we're meeting for the first time is not a bad thing. Offering sympathy for someone's misfortune, even if we can't quite imagine just how they're feeling, is a basic kindness. The question is *why* we're acting in these ways—to ingratiate ourselves to make a sale, or to be good humans.

Any of the elements of good selling we cover in this book can be weaponized, used disingenuously for the sake of manipulating or influencing someone. That might fool some people occasionally. But the key is, it won't fool you, and not fooling ourselves is at the very core of being authentic. Focusing on what *we* are thinking is way more indicative of success than focusing on what the person on the other side of the table thinks.

• • •

A great irony about being authentic is that, given the cultural messaging we're exposed to about putting on personas, it can be challenging to start truly being ourselves. For one thing, what will our colleagues think if we suddenly start showing up as someone different? Won't we be vulnerable? Won't rejections be even harder to take if we've shown our true selves in the selling process? What if we're boring? Colin tore off the phoniness Band-Aid with one rip in his first sales job because he had hit his limit and figured he had nothing to lose. But if you're not in a situation that affords you such confidence, taking a phased approach also works. And some lapsing back into persona is almost inevitable at the beginning. It sounds a little crazy, but showing up as the most authentic version of yourself will probably at first be somewhat like learning how to meditate. Not dwelling on thoughts sounds easy, until you sit still for fifteen minutes and try not to dwell on any thoughts. It's like saying "don't think about giraffes" to someone. Once you tell them that, they can't think of anything but.

As you work to put away the persona for good, give yourself permission to try some things that seem out of your comfort zone. When you mess up or sound awkward in front of a customer, acknowledge it. And when something feels right, like it's authentically you, lean into it. If you change how you think about what it means to sell, give yourself permission to do it your way, and keep at it, you'll find it becomes genuinely liberating.

We chose authenticity as the topic of the first chapter because it's the thread that ties all the characteristics of the Unsold Mindset together. It's the key to getting the most out of everything else we'll introduce from this point on. The reason any of the practices we share work is because they're done authentically. The book is emphatically not about recommending another set of ways to *act like* a salesperson; it's about showing you that being the truest, sometimes rawest person in the room, the one who's not afraid to be seen as imperfect, might just make you the best seller in that room.

CHAPTER TWO

Intentional Ignorance

Selling isn't usually a life-or-death proposition, but during most of General Stanley McChrystal's career, it was. Over the course of nearly thirty-five years in the US military, General McChrystal served as a member of the 75th Ranger Regiment, a counterterrorism specialist, leader of the Joint Special Operations Command (JSOC), and, ultimately, commander of US Forces Afghanistan and NATO International Security Assistance Force, leading 150,000 troops from forty-six coalition nations. As a military leader, it was his job to "sell" those under his command on missions large and small, many incredibly complex, and often with the highest stakes imaginable.

We had the honor of sitting down for a long conversation with the general to ask him about his experience and his thoughts on selling. In the military, the selling generals must do is referred to as leadership, and General McChrystal explained it's not always done the way you'd expect. "There's a certain caricature of military guys, particularly generals," he told us. "People expect generals to be a certain way and if you're trying to motivate and inspire groups, there are times when it's helpful to act like that image of a general, to look the part and puff your chest up and give a big speech. But there are other times when it's better to be the opposite; to be nonthreatening and relatable, different from the stereotype."

When he said this, our ears perked up. It's one thing to do the unexpected and buck a stereotype in a business setting, but we assumed in the military it's always important to do *exactly* what's expected. Even more surprising, he told us military leaders must *choose not to know* certain details of operations they're overseeing, even though the stakes can be as high as they come.

"There is a temptation when you reach a certain level in the military to think you have to act a part and to be all-knowing, to be omniscient, to have an answer to every question because you think if you're not doing that, you're not living up to the role that's expected of you," he said. "What the better commanders understand is that it's much more nuanced. The nuance is you don't know everything. That's not your role. Your role is to make the organization work. You don't have to have the right answer to the question, the organization has to have it, and you've just got to find it."

He said it's important for leaders to intentionally not become specialists in every detail of operations. Reflecting on his time in counter-terrorism, he recounted, "There were all kinds of technological things that we literally invented, and I had a working knowledge of what they did, but I wasn't about to learn the details of how they worked." For one thing, he told us, it would have taken too much time, time away from other important work he needed to be doing for which he was primarily responsible. But he also chose not to know because people want to know you respect them and their knowledge. "[Other people] want me to respect their world enough to get a working understanding, but they want me to look at them and say, 'You're the expert on this. Tell me how it works and what we ought to do.' That's a sign of respect to them and it's powerful."

As it is with generals, the traditional notion of the "perfect" salesperson is that they have all the answers. They know everything there is to know about the product they're selling. They know which objections will be thrown their way and how to handle them like softballs. They know everything there is to know about the competition so they can make a strong case for how much better their product or service is. They know minute details about the people and companies they sell to, things like how well the company has performed over the past few quarters, how long the prospect has been in their current position, and even that their last personal Instagram post was a gym mirror selfie (#cardio). "Knowing it all" is thought to be essential to mastering the sales craft. But having an Unsold Mindset like General McChrystal has means they *don't* believe they have to know all these things; in fact, in many instances they *choose* not to know them.

They practice *intentional ignorance.*

Intentional Ignorance Is Bliss

Of course, there are certain things you *must* know when you're selling something. What these are varies between offerings. Some sales will require you to know every detail about the product you're selling, others may require only a general understanding of the basics. Many of the great sellers we've met not only identified things they don't need to know, but things that make them better at selling *because* they don't know them.

Danny Jacobs is a top performer at HubSpot, the massive marketing, sales, and customer service software company. HubSpot's is a fiercely competitive industry, with rivals including Microsoft, Oracle, SAP, and the industry leader, Salesforce.com, constantly tweaking their offerings, trying to get an edge over the others. Conventional sales advice would recommend that Danny learn all he can about the other companies and their products. And plenty of salespeople spend long hours putting together "competitive matrixes" and reading the latest reports from whatever sources they can dig up on what each competitor has to offer. Their companies provide them with giant lists of feature-to-feature comparisons so they can formulate a response to every possible comparison question a customer might ask.

Danny is different. He told us, "That is something I've refused to do. I have never looked at any competitors *ever.*" Instead, he prefers to be singularly focused on what is great about his own product. He wants to be all in on what he's selling, and he believes in the product he sells. It's sort of like being in a committed relationship and choosing not to download Tinder. He's intentionally avoiding any information that might have a negative impact on the enthusiasm he gets from his genuine belief in his product.

But isn't it irresponsible to not know everything about your competitors when you're selling against them? Won't prospects be turned off when you say you don't know something? Actually, they'll likely feel the opposite. As we'll show, not having all the answers at the tip of your tongue has many advantages. For one, in Danny's instance, his intentional ignorance gives him permission to honestly say, "I'm obviously biased, so I don't think I can give you an educated and objective answer about the competition. I could introduce you to some of our customers, they've spent a lot more time evaluating the competition than I have." He shows he values accurate information and won't just say what's self-serving. That's not what most people expect when they're dealing with a salesperson.

Now, maybe, unlike Danny, you're someone who *loves* to learn all about your competitors' products. Maybe you feel it gives you an advantage to be a "one-stop shop" for your customers when they have questions about their options. Then by all means, spend time on that. Digging in that way is you being authentically you. We're not recommending intentional ignorance as a manipulative tactic, that you put on a persona of someone less knowledgeable than you are. We are saying give yourself the latitude to choose some things *not* to know, often according to what you'd really rather not know, in order to maintain a mindset that allows you to show up authentically excited about what you *do* know. Different people will practice intentional ignorance in different ways, and that's how it should be.

We get that choosing not to have as much information as possible to use when selling might make some people uncomfortable. After all, the cultural imprinting that a barrage of data will impress and persuade those we're selling to runs deep. But research conducted by the former consultancy CEB, Inc. (acquired by Gartner) evaluated the effects of providing B2B customers with "all the data, cases, and testimonials they might need to guide their decision making." Doing so drove an 18 percent decrease in "purchase ease" versus a simpler, more tailored amount of information. The sellers who provided *less* information were 62 percent more likely to close a sale!

An advertising technology salesperson told us that in a meeting early in her career, a prospect had asked her several questions she couldn't answer, and she'd been horribly embarrassed. The meeting became awkward, and she left without a deal. Her reaction was to throw herself into learning as much about her product and her customers as possible so she never had to feel that embarrassment again. She spent endless hours reading and researching, learning everything she could about her industry. Her social life suffered because her free time was dedicated to becoming a one-woman industry encyclopedia. And yet, all that work led to *fewer* sales.

If she could go back in time, she says, she would have turned her inability to answer all the questions in that early meeting into an asset. She would have gone into that meeting as she does now, with the *intention* of not having all the answers. What she eventually discovered was that in her industry, displaying resourcefulness in finding answers is more valued than already having them. In truth, the marketing automation tools and analytics she sells aren't much different from her competition's. But what she *can* make different, she realized, is the quality of the relationship she builds with prospects; her willingness to go find answers for them is a great way of showing her dedication to them. It also allows her to demonstrate that their needs and desires are unique, and she doesn't assume she knows everything they need to know from her. She learned an important lesson of the Unsold Mindset: Saying "I don't know, but I'll find out for you" is a powerful way to connect.

Another seller we met uses intentional ignorance in a different way to influence his mindset. Ryan Ferguson has been one of the highest-ranking sellers on every sales team he's ever worked for from Adobe to Cisco, and now, for ServiceTitan, a "unicorn" software company that sells to small- and medium-sized businesses. For every potential customer he's assigned, he has access to a significant amount of data—demographics; online behavior; whether the lead is from a high-performing source, like a tradeshow, or a low-performing source, like a social media advertisement; and so on. He refuses to look at any of it, he says, because he doesn't want to prejudge the person he's about to speak with. He wants every call to be an improvisation. "I get excited each time *any* lead comes my way," he told us. "Why would I want to look at that information and risk being not *that* excited for every call?"

For example, the data might show that a lead from a certain geographic region is 40 percent less likely to purchase. Ryan worries that focusing on that might make him quicker to seize on reasons the person isn't interested and miss opportunities by not exploring enough with prospects. He told us he would rather have the conversation and let his *actual* experience on the call guide how he conducts it. Intentional ignorance allows him to stay passionate and engaged on every call, and more often than not, he's able to outperform the expectations based on the data.

The irony of believing we must know everything as a salesperson—or at least give the impression we do—is that it can lead us into traps that undermine the impressions we make, and the quality of our relationships with those we're selling to.

Nobody Likes a Know-It-All

We've all had the excruciating experience of interacting with someone, personally or professionally, who can't resist trying to prove how smart they are. They're far from impressive; they're infuriating. *Please stop,* we think to ourselves, *I get it, you know sooo much!* Psychologists explain that this negative reaction may be due, in part, to an instinctive sense that we should be wary of people who use "knowledge" to elevate their own status. Some who act this way do so out of a mistaken belief that they know more than they do. This is a bias called *belief-superiority*. They think their beliefs are based on higher quality knowledge than those of other people. A recent study found that even when people with this bias were provided with clear facts that contradicted their beliefs, they still argued that their beliefs were correct. We likely evolved to develop an aversion to their show-off behavior because we learned these people were untrustworthy. Sellers who have an immediate answer for every objection because of their "superior knowledge" risk turning off customers instead of coming across like the expert they think they are.

One reason psychologists cite for peoples' tendency to want to display their vast knowledge even though it doesn't get the expected results is insecurity. People believe their display will mask their self-doubts. Of course, being leery of information provided by people who doubt themselves also makes a ton of sense. On the other hand, as General McChrystal emphasized, people who are self-secure tend to be more comfortable admitting what they don't know. And that earns them respect. It's precisely why people respond poorly to salespeople who know it all and gravitate toward the ones who genuinely don't. Buyers want to make their own decisions.

Nobody Wants to Feel Sold

A *sense of agency* is among the most important gifts a seller can give to a buyer. When someone has agency, they feel in control of their own circumstances and decisions. Take that away and they feel manipulated, as if their hand has been forced. Great sellers consciously work to drive the opposite behavior. They genuinely want their customers to make their own decisions based on what's best for them.

General McChrystal stressed to us that it's sometimes important for high-level military leaders to beware of coming across as someone who has all the answers for that very reason. "They may be the smartest person in the room, and they may know exactly what to do," he said, "but they know if they can get the organization to come up with the answer, it's a different sell, because the organization has sold themselves. They're not executing an order; they're executing a decision they made."

Everyone wants agency over what they do, and that includes their buying decisions. The "I've got all the answers for you" approach to selling makes people feel the salesperson isn't affording them any latitude of choice or respecting their judgment and right to have their own preferences.

We can't tell you the number of times we've listened to salespeople vent about doing everything *right*, only to still yield the *wrong* result. They've given the customer all the available information, satisfied all the buying requirements, so the buyer *should* buy, but they don't. The story is always similar: "I don't understand what happened. They are an *ideal* fit, we have buy-in from the decision makers, the budget is available, and they love us! I handled their objections, and none of them were deal-breakers. Yet when I asked them to buy, I heard it again: 'You're a good salesperson, BUT . . . I'm not buying.'"

The assertion customers are making, implicitly, is that since everything the salesperson has said is true, there can be no choice; there's only one possible "right" decision. But people don't want to feel like their hand is being forced; they want agency over their choices. When we feel that people selling to us presume they know better than we do about what we should want, we don't feel like we're buying, we feel like we're being sold. And *no one* wants to feel sold. The aversion to that feeling is so strong that often people will say *no* even when what you're selling really *is* the best decision for them.

When you intentionally avoid know-it-all-ism, your customers are empowered to make their own decisions, with you serving as a leader and a partner, not a dictator.

The Curse of Knowledge

One last way we've seen knowing be an impediment to selling is that it can cause people to assume their prospects know more than they do. This problem, called the "curse of knowledge," can lead to a lack of understanding about what potential customers comprehend and what they have questions about, making it difficult to communicate with them in language they understand. It's a cognitive bias where, because you've armed yourself with so much information, often with industry-specific lingo, you fail to appreciate that others may not have that same knowledge. As a result, you can't adjust your conversation to communicate on the same level.

Chip and Dan Heath, authors of *Made to Stick*, a book about persuasive communication, explain the essence of the curse of knowledge: "The problem is that once we know something—say, the melody of a song—we find it hard to imagine not knowing it. Our knowledge has 'cursed' us. We have difficulty sharing it with others, because we can't readily re-create their state of mind." We can't appreciate what they don't know.

We see it all the time, especially in industries with lots of jargon and acronyms. When it comes to selling, the curse of knowledge often manifests in the salesperson spewing statistics and buzzwords without hearing how annoyingly they're coming off to the person they're talking to. They come across as oblivious, at best, but too often arrogant and condescending. What's more, prospects often won't ask for explanation for fear of being seen as stupid, which prevents the seller from doing their job.

The curse can also lead to miscalculation of what prospects *should* want to know, and what they *should* find impressive about a product, service, idea, or person. Economist George Loewenstein and colleagues, who coined the term "curse of knowledge," showed that highly knowledgeable people selling products, such as investment specialists selling securities and wine experts selling wine, often run into difficulty hitting quotas because they overestimate the price that customers should be willing to pay for their goods. They do this because they have so much refined knowledge about which are the higher quality products. This, in part, explains the breakaway success of Yellow Tail wine. As profiled in the book *Blue Ocean Strategy* by W. Chan Kim and Renée Mauborgne, the Yellow Tail producers sold boatloads of wine by specifically designing wines that aren't meant to compete with higher-end brands on quality, complexity, or prestige. "Instead of offering wine as wine," the book's authors write, Yellow Tail offered wine as "a social drink accessible to everyone," appealing to people who usually drank beer or cocktails. By aiming for mass volume sales, with an intentionally lower-quality product, Yellow Tail disrupted the whole wine industry. In short, Yellow Tail garnered runaway sales by appreciating what their customers *didn't* know.

We keep this in mind when we prepare for a class or a speaking event. Everyone in an audience has a different baseline of knowledge and their own unique experiences. Our goal is always to facilitate a learning experience for everyone involved. We try to learn as much interacting with the audience as we hope they learn hearing from us. We ask them to share since they're the only ones who have *their* perspective, and when they share, they feel empowered *and* inspire their peers to speak up and get the same feeling. When we're in this flow our audience is receptive to everything we're "selling," and we as teachers selling a message enjoy the process more, too. We've seen the same dynamic watching sellers with an Unsold Mindset. They value their customer's perspective.

Never underestimate how much appreciation, and respect, you can earn from those you're selling to when you bring them into the fold and make *them* a key part of the process. Tell them what you don't know and ask them to contribute. Make the process a give and take.

Focus on the Parts You Love

Another highly successful salesperson we talked with has maintained his love of the work by staying intentionally ignorant of the parts he has no interest in. Jason Oppenheim, owner of the Oppenheim Group and star of the Netflix show *Selling Sunset,* told our class he didn't think he was particularly good at real estate sales when he was starting out, so he asked himself how he might differentiate himself from all the other agents targeting the high-end market. He looked at his strengths, specifically the skills he acquired during his prior career as a lawyer, and realized that his work ethic and interest in details that others don't pay attention to would be a great place to start. For him, the details he was most interested in had to do with architecture and construction, and he excitedly became an expert in them. He can answer questions on the spot about renovations that may need to be made or how much a renovation might cost. Yet if a prospect asks him about commercial real estate, he immediately refers them to someone more knowledgeable. He could have learned everything there is to know about it, and you might expect that such a top-rated realtor would want to be perceived to know it all. But Oppenheim says commercial real estate bores him. Rather than learn all about it himself, he has built a team around him with others who are experts in it.

We tend to think that to be great at our work, we must be passionate about most, if not all, parts of our job. We've all heard the mantra "follow your passion," and it makes a great point, but it misses a vital nuance. We most likely aren't going to find any job that we love *all* aspects of, but it is possible to craft our work to suit our passions more optimally. A common notion is that if we're going to love our work, we've got to enjoy learning all the information we need to do it well. If we're a financial advisor, we should probably love studying the markets and meeting with clients. If we're a trial lawyer, we'd better like taking depositions and writing briefs. But what we've seen with selling is that it's entirely possible to be great, and to love doing the work, while completely lacking passion for some of the information it would seem we should have to know. How? By focusing on the parts of selling your product you love and staying intentionally ignorant of aspects you don't.

We are all inspired by different things, and that's true of our work in sales, too. Some of us love everything about a product and want to dig into every little technicality, while others find the technical details painfully boring, or perhaps don't have the aptitude for absorbing them. Some can't wait to get into the ins and outs of financing, while others would rather talk about literally anything else. We can feel free to tailor our approach to our work in a way that emphasizes our interests. As we've said before, there is no one "right" kind of salesperson for any product. People with very different passions can be great at selling the same things. Staying intentionally ignorant is yet another way we can be authentically ourselves.

In an interview, Hall of Fame NFL linebacker Ray Lewis once said, "You pay me for Monday through Saturday. Sundays are my pleasure. I do Sunday for free." In other words, his mindset was that his paycheck was for practicing, studying film, treating injuries, weight training, travel, and the million other things a professional athlete has to do to stay at the top. But Sundays, under the lights, competing in front of thousands of fans (and millions more on TV)? He'd still do that if he wasn't getting paid at all. Optimizing the amount of time doing what you'd do for free is a common trait of those with an Unsold Mindset, so while we agree with the advice to follow your passion, the point we want to add is that to do so optimally, we should look for ways to avoid spending time on the inevitable aspects of work that drag our enthusiasm down. This is a form of "job crafting," a concept introduced by Yale School of Management professor Amy Wrzesniewski and her colleagues. Job crafting is when people "redesign their own jobs in ways that can foster job satisfaction, as well as engagement, resilience and thriving at work." Research shows it also significantly increases productivity.

Crafting our jobs in accordance with our interests is great for selling because it allows us to stay energized. Think about something you're passionate about. When you get to talk to someone about that subject, you light up. You are animated and engaging. Colin gets so worked up talking about sneakers that he even got Garrett to buy a pair of Nikes on the after-market, sneakers Garrett *never* would have purchased otherwise, let alone looked at. Garrett still doesn't know why the shoes are cool, or if they'll still be cool by the time you're reading this, but because of Colin's excitement, he bought them. Since we are more compelling when we talk about something we love, focusing discussions with customers on the things you care about will lead to better relationships—and better results.

Listen to the Experts

Of course, your ability to indulge in intentional ignorance is constrained by the resources available to you for getting information to prospects. You may have a wealth of resources to draw on, even if they're not officially provided by your company, as was true for our sales team at Bitium. We had sales engineers and product experts readily available to provide answers. Plenty of companies provide this kind of support, but we've often heard from salespeople that leaning on such others for expertise to do their selling is seen as a sign of weakness. They prefer to try to learn everything themselves so they can answer any question on the spot, thinking they'll look uninformed if they have to hit pause on a conversation and turn to someone else. This simply isn't the case; using your team and other resources available to you is a gift to your prospects, and to yourself.

Chuck Ueno, sales manager of one of Audi's most successful dealerships in California, told us the company doesn't think it's the best use of a salesperson's time to *act* like they have a master's degree in engineering. Instead, Audi has support personnel who do have that expertise, and salespeople refer customers to them when customers have detailed technical questions about their cars. "We also don't require our sales reps to become experts on our financing process," he explained, instead, making financing experts available to handle that part of transactions with customers. "Doing this allows our salespeople to specialize in getting to know their customers," he said, "understanding them, teaching them about the things they know the most about, and guiding them through the buying process, by getting them to the best possible resources available." When salespeople don't feel pressure to put on an act, pretending to have all the answers, they don't slip into stereotypical "car salesman" mode.

If you don't have experts specially charged with advising you or speaking directly with prospects, you may be able to get great answers from people not specifically appointed to provide them, like coworkers, mentors, people in your extended network, or even existing customers. Tapping into these resources requires building authentic relationships, and turning to these allies may not be something you can do often, so you'll need to factor that into where you choose to be intentionally ignorant. If asking an existing customer to help with something is going to be a strain on their time and your relationship, don't do it. But we've generally found people are willing to help, especially when the request comes from someone who's treated them right.

If you don't have colleagues or customers you can turn to, try leaving research into the topics you'd rather not dig into until customers have asked you about them. Knowing they want to know will make the research more engaging, because you're doing it for a specific person, and you know they'll be grateful for it.

Staying Fresh

Another benefit of practicing intentional ignorance is giving yourself space to improvise and be spontaneous. There's no escaping that the sales profession often involves having similar conversations over and over. Many prospects are going to ask about the same things. If a product demo is part of your sale, you can start to feel coin-operated after your twelfth demo of the week. This is another reason burnout is such a huge problem; selling can be painfully repetitive. A simple antidote is to stay intentionally ignorant of scripts, soundbites, or talk tracks. Lots of sales trainings recommend dispensing with scripts, and they typically focus on the perceived authenticity and human connection that arises from doing so. That's all true, but going off script is also just a lot more fun. Remaining ignorant of at least a portion of the information you're supposed to make use of and ditching some or all of your script allows every conversation to feel fresh.

Kevin Williams, a medical device sales professional, told us that at two different companies, one publicly traded and the other an international brand, he was sent out into the field with almost zero product knowledge or intel about the doctors he was selling to. This tactic is not incompetent; the companies knew what they were doing would benefit their sales teams. Kevin was encouraged to use his communication skills, ask questions, seek advice, and be vulnerable by telling people he was new. He would learn through experience, but more importantly, he'd build relationships by actively engaging with his prospects instead of trying to impress them with knowledge from a training course or manual. The companies understood that it was important for him to learn about their products from the *customer's* perspective and get him used to asking questions about their unique needs.

Attesting to the bonding with prospects that can come from a lack of knowledge, Kevin remembers saying to one of his customers, "Dr. Kim, I'm new and I've only seen this procedure once. Would you mind running me through why approaching the surgery laparoscopically adds more risk in this case?" He was asking a busy doctor to give him advice, to teach him, and he was delighted, and surprised, when Dr. Kim responded with a resounding "Yes!" Kevin and Dr. Kim have a strong relationship to this day, and Kevin is still able to go to him and ask questions or seek advice.

There's a saying in the medical device industry, Kevin says. "You're only new once, take advantage of it while you can." He also says rookies usually do well in the industry, but many suffer a drastic dip in sales their second year, which he attributes to their asking fewer questions because they think they know all they need to. "When you ask a doctor or nurse for advice and they give it to you even though they don't have to, it means they respected that you asked," Kevin explained. "I'm always so grateful for their feedback, and I make sure they know it. I think a big part of why I'm a high performer to this day is because I spend most of my time asking for advice." We've come to call this adherence to a beginner's mind "staying fresh."

Kevin's willingness to admit to himself and to his prospects that there are plenty of things he doesn't know is particularly impressive because he sells to doctors. As we've all probably experienced, doctors can be incredibly intimidating. It's human nature to be cautious, embarrassed, even resentful, when we perceive we're talking with people who know more than we do. We can become defensive, and that can lead to missteps, like pretending to know more than we do, providing bad (or made up) information, or hauling out the proverbial firehose and spouting off as much data as we possibly can.

We saw the effects of staying fresh ourselves in a stark contrast between the experiences of two early members of Bitium's sales team. The two were close friends and started working for us on the same day, but they could not have been more different in their approaches. One of them was a machine who did the same thing over and over.

He was a good performer and got results by plowing forward reading the script word for word day after day. If he made seventy-five calls a day, he had virtually the same conversation on every call.

The other colleague spent weeks memorizing the parts of the script he needed to know to confidently engage with prospects, and then never used them again. Over time we watched him improvise, becoming more comfortable ad-libbing, iterating, laughing, surprising customers, and being surprised by them. His conversations flowed naturally and led to unexpected, interesting turns, often leading to discoveries about personal and professional details that would never have been uncovered if he had stuck to what he'd been taught to say. When he was asked about the two-year product roadmap, he'd call a sales engineer to come over to give the answer *and* while they waited for the engineer to arrive, he'd get a better sense of where the prospect saw their own company in two years. When a prospect asked about cancellation language in a sales contract because they'd been burned in the past, he'd say he'd find the language *and* dive into a conversation about what the prospect had learned from that experience. He was genuinely intrigued, and he was having fun.

The two got similar results for a while. But over time, the first one started to fall behind. For him, the job got tedious and he began to burn out, which showed up in the form of growing irritation with customers. He became less interested in his prospects, his responses grew short, his calls started to sound robotic, and he was so scripted that he'd sometimes cut off a customer and start "overcoming" their objection before they'd even finished articulating it. He blamed prospects for not buying, ranting about them to anyone who would listen, and before long, he left the company. The other guy not only continued to build on his strong sales numbers, but ended up learning more about how the company worked than if he had just memorized the script, since he was forced to engage with different departments frequently to gather answers he intentionally didn't have. He stayed fresh and eventually got promoted.

Sure, when a salesperson is first learning a new process it's helpful to have a guide for what to say, but once you've got your footing, it's time to start freestyling. Many of your conversations will still be similar; the questions customers have and the needs you're addressing will often be the same. But people themselves contain multitudes, and there's always opportunity to invest in a conversation that draws out a note you haven't yet heard, like a jazz musician finding a new riff to play in a song they've played hundreds of times before.

When we first started speaking, we fell into the trap of trying to map every word, sticking to a script guided by a series of PowerPoint slides. But every time we did, we never felt as good about the results as we did when we took a less rigid approach. At one point we decided to go off-script for all our engagements—no exceptions—and now there are few things we love doing more. We have a broad outline of the key points we want to make, and how we get there depends on what the room is responding to. Every audience we speak to is different, and that means when we improvise, every event is different.

Our editor once told us there's a saying taught to aspiring writers: "No fun for the writer, no fun for the reader." This is just as true for sales. If you're having fun while you're selling, the people you're selling to are more likely to be enjoying themselves, too.

Intentional Ignorance Without Intention Is Ignorant

To practice intentional ignorance, you have to identify what you can responsibly choose to ignore. Ask yourself what you absolutely need to know, and then challenge yourself about why you think that's so. Then take some time to reflect on the aspects of what you're selling, what you're most enthusiastic about and how you might focus more on those. When, and why, in other words, will ignorance be bliss?

Here are questions to consider when deciding what you can be intentionally ignorant about:

- What do you love about what you're selling and what areas don't excite you?
- In which parts of the job do you really excel? Are they also the parts you love doing?
- Does it matter if you can speak to a subject immediately, or is it okay to say you'll get back to a prospect?
- How might your conversation unfold if you don't know the answer to a question? What's the upside to admitting you don't know?
- If you don't know something, is there another resource you can use that will be as (or more) effective in giving the information to your customers?
- Who might you ask for information both inside the company and outside?
- Are you making the best use of these resources you can? If not, why?
- How might you cultivate relationships inside and out of the company to provide you with expertise?

If the thought of abandoning some of the scripts, facts, and figures you have at your disposal makes you uncomfortable, take a gradual approach. Start small and see how prospects respond. When the sky doesn't fall the first time you tell them "I don't know," you'll feel the nagging need to know dissipate. Try reaching out to stakeholders in other departments to see if they'll give you advice. Then try it with another. See how your customer responds to that request. Cultivate relationships with various experts of your product and regularly bring them into the fold. Can you hire someone for that purpose? Contract with them? If you've been following a script—even if it's one you've written yourself—put it aside and try having a real conversation without it.

Each person has to work out what comfort level they can come to when it comes to not knowing it all. No one else can do it for you. But push your boundaries of comfort and see what happens. And keep in mind that living outside our comfort zones and focusing our time and energy on the things we're most passionate about is good for us, and also for others. This notion has been around for a long time in the form of the ancient Indian spiritual concept of *dharma*. Dharma has been described as "the path of right action, the path that is of maximum benefit to ourselves and the planet." In other words, your dharma is the thing that you are passionate about that also happens to contribute to the greater good. Some teachers have incorporated skill into the definition, saying that a key component of well-being is finding the intersection between what you love, what you're *good at*, and what the world needs. People with an Unsold Mindset use intentional ignorance to spend as much time as possible where those things converge.

• • •

Paul McCartney is considered by many to be the greatest songwriter of all time. He's written a mind-blowing number of iconic songs, including "Yesterday," "Hey Jude," and "Let It Be." He's also played an incredible range of instruments on recordings over the years, including bass, acoustic and electric guitar, drums, piano, and keyboards. While it might seem like he can do it all musically, there is something he can't do: Paul McCartney, legendary member of the Beatles and Wings, platinum-selling solo artist, collaborator, and all-around musical genius *can't formally read or write music.* "You can know too much," he said in an interview. "None of [the Beatles] could handle music lessons because it was boring."

From his earliest days, McCartney was unsold on what he needed to know to be a great musician. He took the stereotype of a technically perfect music prodigy and flipped it on its head to become a legend on his own terms. He focused on what he loved, learning by listening to blues greats and rock and roll pioneers and collaborating with John Lennon, and the world loved him (and his music) for it. His intentional ignorance of traditional music composition was a feature, not a bug.

Staying intentionally ignorant in any aspect of our lives, including selling, doesn't mean we aren't doing the hard work. Giving ourselves permission to let go of the pressure of having to know everything ensures we have the bandwidth to work our asses off on the things that allow us to have the most impact and make us the happiest. It makes us better because we aren't burdened with the things that don't allow us to show up as the best version of ourselves for the people we're interacting with. It also frees us up to be open to *new* information, ideas, and opportunities that are aligned with our dharma when they come our way.

CHAPTER THREE

Growing into an Unsold Mindset

J ay-Z is one of the most successful musicians of all time. He has sold over 50 million albums and is the first living solo rapper to be inducted into the Rock & Roll Hall of Fame. He's also a massively successful entrepreneur. He's founded a clothing company (Rocawear), an entertainment company (Roc Nation), a chain of luxury sports bars (40/40 Club), and two spirits companies (D'Ussé and Armand de Brignac). He has owned a stake in an NBA team (the Nets), was an early investor in Uber, and purchased music streaming service Tidal, which he later sold to behemoth payment processing company Square, where he now sits on the board of directors. All of this has made Jay-Z a billionaire.

Jay-Z's success *wasn't* inevitable. When he was first starting out, he couldn't land a record deal to save his life. Over and over again, he got rejected. No one was buying what he was selling. "I went to every single record label," he recalled in an interview, "and they was like, 'This guy is terrible. He's nothing.'"

Many of us would give up after this much rejection. Or change ourselves or our music to be more like what the record label wanted us to be. Jay-Z had a different mindset. "[The rejection] made me appreciate it so much more," he said about his eventual success. "No one gave me anything. They didn't give me a record deal. I really just took my time and grew it step by step by step by step. I could have easily been like, 'Maybe what I'm talking about ain't right! Nobody wants to sign me!' That would have stopped the suffering. But I didn't."

Jay-Z, like others we've encountered with an Unsold Mindset, didn't view his struggles and setbacks as reasons to compromise on his vision, blame others, or quit. He saw them as opportunities to grow, which is exactly what he did. He made a decision to learn everything he could about the music business, including how to press singles, sell records to stores, negotiate distribution deals, and anything else he needed to know to start and run a record company. He took this knowledge, founded his *own* label, Roc-a-Fella Records, and released his first album himself. That album eventually went platinum and ultimately served as a platform for everything that followed.

Unfortunately, for so many of us, finding opportunity in the face of rejection isn't easy. Getting told *no* can often feel like a judgment on us as a person, rather than on whatever we're selling. When success is only measured by wins, inevitable rejections can take their toll, causing us to get frustrated, burn out, or give up. It's another huge reason so many people are so averse to selling.

People with an Unsold Mindset view setbacks differently. They don't like getting told *no*, of course, but unlike most people, they don't dwell on or internalize it when it happens. Instead, they see rejection as an integral part of selling, one that allows them to strategize, learn, and, ultimately, to grow. Hurdles become billboards telling them where they are, where they need to go, *and* how to get there.

This counterintuitive approach to challenges, combined with an obsession with learning, even when the lessons are painful, is a major reason those with an Unsold Mindset seem to be more successful than not. It's also a big reason they love to sell.

Growers Not Showers

In our interviews, we kept hearing similar takes: *How else am I going to know where I need to get better?* or *I'm just as successful because of the deals I didn't close as the ones I did.* Having an Unsold Mindset broadens their definition of success in selling. And among the things sellers enjoy most is that there's always something new to learn.

Stanford psychological researcher Carol Dweck writes about this way of thinking in her influential bestseller *Mindset*. Dweck studied how people in a wide range of professions, from athletes to business executives to scientists, thought about their talents and went about meeting challenges. In the process, she identified two dramatically different ways of thinking: the fixed mindset and the growth mindset. Which one dominates people's approach to challenges has a powerful influence on their success in life, from work, to education, to athletics, to relationships.

People with a fixed mindset think their intelligence and other skills stem mostly from natural ability and can only be developed moderately, if at all. Because they believe *this is as good it gets*, they act accordingly. They may focus more on trying to *look* smart rather than working to *become* smarter; they might avoid challenges because they think if they don't perform well others will think they lack ability. They tend to give up more easily when they are struggling with a task, thinking, *What's the point? I'm just not good at this*, and they tend to view feedback as criticism. Another unfortunate feature of a fixed mindset is that other people's success can be threatening since fixed mindsetters often compare their own talents and success to those of others. They are hard on themselves for just not being talented enough in their minds. On top of all this, a fixed mindset is self-reinforcing; by causing people to try less hard and miss opportunities to develop their talents, disappointing outcomes become that much more likely. They see those outcomes, in turn, as confirmation that they simply don't have the ability to do better. Dweck found that, as a result, fixed mindset individuals often plateau in career success early and achieve less than their full potential.

We see signs of a fixed mindset in sellers all the time, often coupled with frustration and self-doubt about why things aren't going better. We might suggest someone take a different approach in the discovery process, and they'll either tell us they already tried it and it didn't work or come up with a reason that it won't. We might advise they take a new approach when prospecting, and they'll have plenty of explanations for why their approach is not the problem. To most of them the economy is the problem, or the buyer, or their circumstances—they're just not naturally good at selling, they just don't have the patience, or it's just not a good fit. They're not seeing opportunity to better the situation by bettering themselves.

Conversely, people with a growth mindset believe intelligence and talents of all kinds can be developed. They embrace challenges, persist in the face of setbacks, see effort as a path to mastery, learn from criticism, and find lessons and inspiration in others' successes, and even in their own failures. They're intent to keep learning and challenging themselves so they can keep getting better, and they see mistakes they've made as steps to getting where they want to go. This mindset helps people cope with disappointments and allows them to feel more empowered to achieve goals they aspire to, and Dweck's research shows that they do more often fulfill their potential. A growth mindset also inspires people to love their work, even when things aren't going as planned. "The growth-minded athletes, CEOs, musicians or scientists all loved what they did," she writes, "whereas many of the fixed-mindset ones did not."

As we spoke with more and more people with an Unsold perspective, we heard them echoing the tenets of Dweck's growth mindset to a tee. It shouldn't have surprised us, especially since Dweck specifically discusses a link between growth mindset and authenticity. She writes that some with a fixed mindset worry "you won't be yourself anymore" if you're growing and changing. This brand of fixed thinkers believes merely being born with their talent makes them who they are. They worry that if success comes more from growth than from innate talent, then maybe that means there's nothing special about them after all. They fear, she writes, that they will "become a bland cog in the wheel just like everyone else." But she found the opposite was true. "Opening yourself up to growth makes you *more* yourself, not less."

We tell our students all the time that the hard part about having a growth mindset isn't the work you put into the growth, it's having the self-awareness to acknowledge that growth is needed. That self-awareness and honesty about who we are *today*, warts and all, is key to understanding who we will be in the *future*. If someone tells you it seems like you're not listening and instead just waiting to speak, growing out of that habit will only happen after you stare at yourself in the proverbial mirror and admit you could be a better listener. With a true growth mindset, that honesty with oneself isn't damning; it's forgiving and inspiring.

A growth mindset is not everyone's default way of thinking. The good news from Dweck's research is that if we work on adopting a growth mindset with intention, we can develop one. We all have incredible capacity for growth, whether or not we believe we do.

Moreover, most people don't exclusively have a growth or a fixed mindset. We're not born only thinking a certain way. We're conditioned to lean in one direction or the other by the lessons we learn from our parents, our friends, in school, from coaches, and in our careers, but we all have growth mindset moments, just as we all have fixed mindset moments. After all, some challenges we're faced with are hard—really hard—to see as opportunities for growth.

If we're intentional about it, we can change the balance of the fixed and growth thinking we do. We can build up our growth mindset capacity like a muscle. That begins, as Dweck writes, with "what psychologists call an Aha! Experience" about the two mindsets, after which people "feel their mindsets reorienting."

We saw how quickly adopting a growth-minded approach to selling can lead to change when we worked with a sales manager who had hit a plateau. He'd been a successful sales rep but wasn't cutting it as the leader of a sales team for one of our clients. His team's results were lackluster, and our client hired us to work with him to figure out how he could become more effective. When we met him, he made it immediately clear that he wasn't in favor of our coming on board; he told us he already knew what the problem was, and "no offense" but they didn't need to hire outside experts to figure it out. It was textbook fixed mindset. In his mind, the problem had nothing to do with his lack of openness to change; his team was the problem. If he only had approval to hire more high-quality people, he'd hit his numbers. To change his thinking, we put him through an exercise. He could hire the five new sales reps he'd been asking for, as long as he could tell us how each was better than he was at sales before he made them an offer. The process was designed to make him acknowledge he was part of the problem, and that there were things he didn't know that others, even those working under him, could teach him. That simple exercise helped him realize his role was not to be the smartest person in the room, but to build up the collective ability of his team. That, he came to appreciate, would require him to clearly see shortfalls in his own approach to selling, intentionally looking for his own blind spots and not just everyone else's. He realized the benefit of hiring people who don't think like him and acknowledged "my way" is not the baseline for a perfect seller, because there is no one way to be great at selling.

He ended up hiring a rep from Salesforce.com who showed the team new insights on data reporting. Another hire had over thirty thousand connections on LinkedIn and was masterful at building out social media communities for lead generation. A third came from a startup backed by leading business accelerator Y-Combinator and brought access to a huge network of local talent. Within six months the manager was leading the fastest-growing team in his company. The team grew collectively, and he grew with them.

A fixed mindset can lead people to act like knowers. Someone who thinks their intelligence and skills are relatively static also thinks others are thinking the same thing about them. This leads to them having to constantly project the image to the world that they're in the capable category. They'd better look like they know everything they need to know to be respected and secure in their jobs, whether that's in the view of their boss, colleagues, or customers. This view is reinforced by the powerful cultural messaging that to become a professional means becoming a master of our work. And if we want to be *seen* as professional, we think, we'd better *be* a master. Soon enough, we've convinced ourselves we are. At this point, we're no longer acting like we have all the answers, we're believing we really do. But ironically, convincing ourselves we've mastered something often causes us to stall out and fall behind.

To have an Unsold Mindset, you have to be a learner. In almost every one of our interviews, the people we spoke with expressed in one way or another that they still have tons to learn about their work and the world around them, and they believe the lessons can come from anywhere. Manny Martinez, founder of American Branding Agency, who represents Champion clothing and is credited for the brand's massive resurgence into pop culture and mainstream fashion, told us one of his core beliefs is that you can learn and grow from everyone you meet. "You can't treat people like they are dispensable," he said. "Everyone has ideas you can learn from." He talked about the lessons he's received from the maintenance team to interns to top brass. His comments reminded us of something Jay-Z once said: "Everyone is born with genius-level talent." Imagine if we all thought that way; how could we choose *not* to learn from everyone we meet?

Be a Creator, Not a Victim

Another welcome side effect of a growth mindset is that it combats a *victim mentality.* When someone with a fixed mindset doesn't get the desired outcome in any selling effort, whether it's a pitch to a customer, an interview for a job, or a presentation to the marketing team, they'll often blame the failure on something over which they had no control and see themselves as the victim. This leads to feelings of powerlessness or lack of control, and sometimes to "catastrophizing," viewing problems as disproportionately larger than they really are. It can even lead to the mistaken belief that people are intentionally targeting them for failure.

The victim mentality is usually easy to spot, via the language people use to explain why they haven't been more successful. *My leads were trash. The customer was dumb. The competition lied about us. The group I was presenting to didn't stop looking at their phones the entire presentation.* We can easily become caught up in justifying failure with victimhood instead of focusing on how to improve results. Even if some of the justifications we come up with are valid, at least in part, do we really want to be victims of our circumstances? Psychologist Rahav Gabay writes that this victimhood perspective stems from having "an external locus of control," meaning that one believes circumstances in life are mostly due to "forces outside one's self."

People with the Unsold Mindset, by contrast, believe in their power over circumstances; they have an internal locus of control. In our research into the liabilities of the victimhood trap, we found the insights of executive coach David Emerald particularly compelling. In his book *The Power of TED (The Empowerment Dynamic)*, he writes about the counterpart to the fixed victimhood mentality, which he calls the "creator orientation." It perfectly describes the great sellers we've observed and interviewed. Instead of succumbing to "what am I supposed to do?" thinking when setbacks arise, a creator feels empowered to focus on what they *want* to see happen, and how to manufacture the conditions to make it so. They *own* the situation and the way they handle it. They believe they have a large degree of control over situations, and that leads them to look to create their own solutions. Instead of telling themselves, *the customer was incompetent and didn't understand,* they hold themselves accountable. *I fell into the "curse of knowledge" trap and treated them as if they knew as much about the company as I did. I won't make that mistake again.* In the face of adversity, they ask a key question: "What can *I* do to create the outcome I want?"

We worked with a founder and CEO who went through a powerful transformation from a victim mindset to a creator mindset. She was having a hard time fundraising, even though she had a great product and promising customer adoption and revenue. Again and again, she was respectfully (and sometimes disrespectfully) declined during her fundraising roadshow, and she came to us for counsel because she couldn't figure out what was going wrong. Listening to her describe her experiences, it didn't take us long to realize she was viewing herself as a victim. "They don't understand the opportunity," she told us. "They are closed-minded and they're not looking at the big picture. They want a specific type of founder, and it's not me." So we asked her a question we could see she'd never thought about before. "Outside of a term sheet, what do you *want* to happen in these meetings?"

She looked perplexed, but after a brief pause she said, "I don't want them to be narrow-minded, I don't want them making assumptions they don't even know are true, and I don't want them to treat me differently because I'm a female CEO and founder." As is often the case when we ask a similar question, she answered with what she *didn't* want to happen. But we were trying to learn the behavior and outcomes she *did* want. When we pointed this out, her eyes widened and we could see her shifting her perspective. "I want them to be open-minded," she said. "I want them to see what's great about the company. I want them to see how big an opportunity this is and not just what could go wrong . . . and I want them to see a female CEO as an asset."

Now she was articulating things she could take actionable steps on. We could sense her excitement. She was opening to the realization that she didn't have to see the meetings as one-way pitches that were either successful or not, depending on how a particular venture capitalist (VC) reacted. She could *create* the meetings she wanted, not only accepting their responses, but probing into the VCs, asking for more insight and challenging and *learning* from them.

In her next meeting with the partners of a VC firm, five middle-aged men once again told her all the reasons they weren't going to invest. But this time, she listened carefully to their comments, absorbed them, and responded, "This is all really valuable feedback. I think I'm clear on all the areas you see a need for rethinking. Can I ask you, what do you *like* about the company?" Instead of the meeting ending, the partners took time to break down what they liked about her business and give her meaningful advice for growing the company. We wish we could say she changed their minds and they invested in her company right there on the spot; they didn't. What they did do, though, was introduce her to another firm that was a better fit for her company's stage and size, and *that* firm eventually invested in her funding round. She transformed her perspective from that of a victim to that of a creator, taking control of the situation to drive toward her goal. She didn't just raise a successful round, she *created* one.

Abbondanza (Abundance)

The growth mindset combats another disempowering belief common in selling: that there are only so many opportunities to go around.

This fear is a corollary to a fixed mindset; opportunities are seen as limited instead of plentiful. When you think this way, selling becomes a zero-sum game. Any sale you make is taking that sale away from someone else, and vice versa.

This way of thinking can also lead to stereotypical pushy selling. If you view deals as limited, each one becomes that much more precious and people will say or do whatever to avoid losing one, from unconsciously upping the pressure tactics, to making promises their product can never live up to, to just plain making things up.

More than thirty years ago, Stephen Covey wrote about this problematic perspective in *The 7 Habits of Highly Effective People*. "Most people," he wrote, "are deeply scripted in what I call the Scarcity Mentality. They see life as having only so much." By contrast, he described the Abundance Mentality, "the paradigm that there is plenty out there and enough to spare for everybody." A key point he makes about believing in abundance, which ties directly to a growth mindset, is that the abundance mentality "recognizes the unlimited possibilities for positive interactive growth and development." The equation works the other way, too; just as people who see abundance recognize opportunities for growth, a growth mindset fosters belief in abundance.

No one can be blamed for seeing through the scarcity prism. We're indoctrinated to some extent by our schooling, taught that there are only so many A's to be awarded, only so many slots for starters on sports teams, only so many kids who can be popular. As adults, it's reinforced in our work lives as we learn that budgets and opportunities for promotion are limited, and we wrestle with conflicting demands on our time. The fear that stems from this feeling that opportunities are limited drives so many stereotypical sales behaviors.

People selling with a genuine belief in the abundance of opportunity are largely spared the fear; they are confident they can learn something from a setback and make good use of it. When you hear someone drop the old cliché "everything happens for a reason," that person, knowingly or not, is speaking from a place of abundance.

The abundance mentality gives people more confidence in their ability to sell and empowers them to be adventurous, inventive, and resilient in their efforts. When things slow down, they believe they can find ways to *make* opportunities. Colin, for example, was once meeting one-on-one with Matt, the newest person on our team at Bitium. Matt walked into the room where Colin was waiting for him and sat down on the couch. Before Colin said a word, Matt started bouncing a little bit on the cushions, fondling the leather like he was inspecting a peach for freshness at the supermarket, and said aloud to himself, "This is a nice couch." Colin was confused. Why was this guy so obsessed with the couch? Was he nervous? His behavior was borderline creepy. But Colin was also intrigued, and he let Matt continue to inspect the couch as he slid back and forth on it from cushion to cushion. He asked Colin if he knew who made the couch, and Colin said he had no idea, barely disguising the fact he thought the question was bizarre. Matt jumped up, flipped over the cushion, saw on the tag that the company that made the couch was on the East Coast, and said, "Do you mind if I look up this company before we start?" He googled the company, realized it had thousands of employees and seemed to be in Bitium's target demographic. Then he identified a potential contact on LinkedIn and put a reminder in his phone to call the company after his meeting. While other team members had sat on that couch hundreds of times (some had ironically complained about the scarcity of opportunities while sitting on it), our newest salesperson came in with an abundance mindset and literally found deals in between the couch cushions!

People with an abundance perspective are often deemed unrealistic, sometimes even crazy (that's definitely how Colin felt watching Matt fawn over the couch!). When you see opportunity where others see none, they often assume you're the one who has blurred vision. Yet those who see opportunity where others don't also tend to *find* more opportunities. It's no coincidence they're more successful than their scarcity-minded counterparts.

Building Adaptive Resilience

A growth mindset is helpful in building one of the most important qualities of great sellers: resilience. But not all resilience is created equal. We want to cultivate *adaptive* resilience, which is "the capacity to remain productive and true to [one's] core . . . identity whilst absorbing disturbance and adapting with integrity in response to changing circumstances." It's not the proverbial "knock me down nine times and I'll get up ten" of enduring the same punishment over and over. It's the ability to try different things to get the result you want, even if you fail a bunch of times in the process.

In her book *Bouncing Back: Rewiring Your Brain for Maximum Resilience and Well-Being,* psychologist Linda Graham stresses this, writing, "Being able to adapt our coping to a specific challenge is the skill that allows us to find our footing when we're thrown off balance." To drive home the point she quotes Charles Darwin, who wrote, "It is not the strongest of the species that survives, nor the most intelligent, it is the most adaptive." This is a key way that growth thinking supports resilience; it encourages us to try new approaches all the time. For those with an Unsold Mindset, trying these new approaches and adapting as they go is a key element of selling.

Graham writes, "we all have an innate capacity for becoming more resilient," and we can "choose specific experiences to deliberately re-wire our brains" to enhance our resilience. We would add that we can *choose* to make our selling experiences growth opportunities and resilience-builders. We've discovered several ways to do this.

The Gift of a *Good No*

Because of their growth mindset, the Unsold change their relationship with the word "no." Instead of feeling dejected or defeated with every "no" they hear, they see the value of a Good No. What's a Good No? One that you learn from, that makes you better than you were before you heard it. Good No's are made by searching for the lessons. It's the difference between *They said* no *because they tuned me out when I was reading the PowerPoint presentation* (a *bad no* that doesn't change anything) and *They said* no *because I didn't communicate how we improve their business well enough* (a Good No with an actionable way to do it better the next time).

Any no can be a Good No if you consider it with intention. After a rejection, or any other undesired outcome, take a few minutes to reflect on the experience and ask yourself the six most powerful words in sales: *What could I have done differently?* The best sellers we've worked with ask this question constantly, and they don't stop there. They ask many probing questions to identify blind spots and deepen insights. Here are some of our favorite examples:

- Did you ask questions for your own benefit, or did the prospect also benefit from hearing their own answers?
- Were you listening or waiting to speak?

- Were you trying to win and treating them like an opponent on another team?
- Could you have done a better job setting expectations as a two-way street, instead of just focusing on what the prospect can expect from you?
- Could they tell you didn't really enjoy speaking to them?
- Were you qualifying the prospect based on too much emotion and not enough logic, or vice versa?
- Did your gut sense an objection early on, but you decided to ignore it in hopes it wouldn't come back up?
- Did you react unnaturally to an objection and the customer sensed your frustration?
- Did putting down the competition backfire?
- Did the prospect feel like the center of the universe, or did the universe revolve around you during the exchange?
- Did you treat the prospect differently because you wrongly assumed they were, or weren't, qualified?

Exploring what you might have done differently is especially productive when you also seek input from non-salespeople, or others who can provide additional context, like members of an audience for a presentation you gave, co-workers who engineered the product, or customers who have said *yes* or *no* to you in the past.

Set a high standard for learning from this exercise. Take a step back, put your big-ass ego aside (we all have one), and ask someone—or several people—what you could have done differently to get the result you wanted. Then act on that information.

Getting a *no* is one of the best things that can happen to you; getting the same *no* twice means you're not doing your job.

Reframing Rejection

Growing from *no's* is not easy. Many of us believe the *no's* are directed at us personally instead of at the products, services, or ideas we're selling. Sellers who are best at weathering the storm of rejection don't take *no's* personally; they're completely unsold on what *no* is supposed to mean.

It's not anyone's fault for taking *no's* to heart. Our evolutionary training has taught us to. As social creatures, we are hardwired to seek acceptance from others. For thousands of years, being accepted as part of the group was critical for survival. If you were rejected, you starved to death or got eaten by a sabretooth tiger or pack of hyenas. Those same instincts to please other people can make hearing *no* hard. Even though we know what we're selling isn't right for everyone, it still hurts when they tell us they don't want it. We feel like we've been shunned from the group. But with a growth mindset, we can reframe the experience of rejection and know that each one is a catalyst for learning something new and getting our next *yes*, so we're able to reframe the experience of rejection altogether. Before long, we build up the strength of our reframing muscles and instead of wearing us down, the *no's* are seen as an important part of the process.

One semester, to help our students get comfortable not taking rejections personally, we assigned a group project. The task was simple: They were to use everything they'd learned in class to sell a well-known person they admired on giving a virtual guest lecture to the class. Students selected an amazing cross-section of successful people, from CEOs to actors to musicians to political figures. While the students thought this was a lesson in closing, it was devised as an exercise in confronting what it feels like to come face-to-face with unreturned calls, ignored emails, and insulting comments from the assistants and gatekeepers VIPs use to field attempts to contact them. We also wanted the students to see how easy it is to slip into "stereotypical salesperson mode," pestering their targets with messages or trying to use "tricks" to get a response. We hoped they would be able to see that negative responses weren't about them personally, because all of them were likely to get the same treatment.

In each class we asked how things were progressing with their guest lecturer "sales process," and every week we'd hear how they were rejected by the publicist, the secretary, the agent, or sometimes the person themselves. After many stories of rejection, one student, Chelsea, said she had good news; she was able to get a direct response from her potential guest lecturer's assistant because of something another student, Jemma, had said in class the week before. Jemma had received a rejection and said, "In hindsight I should've thought more about why a successful person like that would even care to be a guest lecturer." After hearing that, Chelsea sent an email to her prospect with the subject line "Want to change some kids' lives for 20 min?" Focusing on what was in it for the recipient worked, and our class was treated to an inspiring Q&A session by David Rogier, CEO of Silicon Valley unicorn, MasterClass. We couldn't have paid him to hammer home our lesson on growth better. "When you stop learning, you're dead," he told the class. No wonder he built a company dedicated to helping others learn.

That semester, we ultimately heard from several great speakers, including executives, a religious leader, and Jason Oppenheim, the star of *Selling Sunset* on Netflix we introduced in chapter 2. And even students who couldn't successfully land a guest speaker learned lessons. Students traded messages with the late Virgil Abloh, renowned fashion designer and former artistic director of Louis Vuitton, and texted with Scooter Braun, the record executive and manager behind Justin Bieber and Ariana Grande, gleaning insights they were able to share with the class. One student was trying to land Grammy winner Alicia Keyes, and while she wasn't able to get Alicia to show up, she did end up meeting her business partner, Erika Rose Santoro, who absolutely captivated our class for an hour with her incredible story.

This exercise opened students' minds to the realization that poor responses weren't personal. Even their most seemingly confident, outgoing classmates ran into slammed doors, but all of them learned to grow from mistakes and shift their views of rejection.

Reappraise the Situation

Reappraisal is the well-established practice in cognitive psychology of looking at a situation with a less-than-desired outcome and identifying alternate ways of thinking about it and behaving in ways that allow you to see it more positively. It's not pretending everything is rainbows and unicorns, it's casting off baggage and negativity in our minds and coaching ourselves to look for the good we can make of experiences.

Using reappraisal, we can find good in situations we've previously seen as adverse. Psychologist Tchiki Davis, founder of the Berkeley Well-Being Institute, recounts in an article how she was inspired to feel gratitude in an otherwise crappy situation when her car's transmission blew out on her way to work one day. Instead of dwelling on the stresses of being late and having to fix the car with money she didn't have, she instead reappraised and felt lucky that she hadn't been on the highway when it happened, which would have been so much more dangerous. She also told herself to be grateful that the car could still run, albeit slowly and in third gear, so she was able to drive it to a repair shop. To practice reappraisal with her students, she uses an experience that *way* too many salespeople are familiar with: having your boss yell at you. She had people submit ways they could see that situation as positive. Answers included "Now I know what my boss is thinking," "My boss had the chance to blow off steam and will be less stressed now," "I learned how not to treat others," and "I have the opportunity to self-reflect."

Getting started reappraising is as simple as asking yourself the right questions in the moment. When a deal that was supposed to make your quarter implodes, looking for the growth opportunity clearly isn't the easiest thing to do. But asking one or more of Davis's questions might help you find what you're looking for:

- Were there, or will there be, any positive outcomes that result from this situation?
- Are you grateful for any part of this situation?
- In what ways are you better off than when you started?
- What did you learn?
- How did you (or might you) grow and develop as a result of this situation?

Linda Graham's "Finding the Gift in the Mistake" exercise asks a related but interestingly different set of questions regarding difficult, even traumatic experiences, advising that you write a new narrative to see what you can learn. You first think about, or write down, a description of what happened, and then detail:

- This is what I did to survive.
- This has been the cost.
- This is what I have learned.
- This is how I can respond to life now.

We can translate those for selling experiences into:

- This is how I responded to the negative reaction.
- This is the cost of the negative outcome.
- This is what I have learned from the rejection.
- This is how I can respond differently in the future.

If these exercises strike you as pollyannish, we get it. Tough experiences are painful even if we can find lessons in them. Anyone who tells you they don't mind rejection at all is lying to you, or they aren't truly invested. David Rogier told our class, "The *no's* hurt because it means you care." We could see our students feeling the truth of that. The key with reappraisal isn't to blind yourself to the negatives but to use them to course correct.

If reappraising still feels too woo-woo to you, we also love the advice of Trevor Moawad, the late author and mental conditioning expert to top global athletes. He always recommended aiming for *neutral thinking,* which he defined as "accepting the idea that when something good or bad happens, it happens. Instead of getting caught up in the negativity of a bad past or a mental or physical mistake, you just accept that it happened and move on." That might be the best that can be said for the value of, say, an abrupt and angry hang-up by someone you've tried cold calling.

One type of reappraisal we recommend helps neutralize the

emotional impact of *no's*, allowing you to see that the response is not necessarily about you. Remind yourself that it's the customer's job to scrutinize, poke holes, and get the best deal possible for themselves or their company. The predisposition of many prospects is going to be "thanks but no thanks" regardless of how thoughtful, informative, or well-targeted your pitch is. *No's* can be seen, therefore, as prospects fulfilling their mandate rather than you failing at yours.

Think about yourself as a buyer. Don't you understand their position? Are they really acting that differently than you would in the same situation?

Celebrate the Process

Most of us love to celebrate when we succeed, and we eagerly await those moments. This is another way the scarcity mindset is instilled; there are only so many things worthy of celebrating. One of the most powerful ways we've seen sellers nurture a growth mindset is by celebrating not only successes but the entire process of selling itself.

Say your job requires you to prospect your own leads and then do your own outreach. Maybe you find out that when you leave a voicemail and follow with an email, a significant number of prospects open your email, even if they don't return your call. Now you have a data point for just how effective that email is when you leave a voicemail. *Celebrate* that discovery. What if prospects neither call back nor open the email? That's equally important data you can celebrate.

What if you try a new pitch and get aggressively shut down more than once? Celebrate that the prospects have given you such definitive feedback that you need to iterate on that pitch. Say you're told in a job interview that the interviewer isn't convinced you really want the job. Celebrate that someone was honest enough to say you weren't convincing so you can better prepare for the next interview. Now you can work on being more vulnerable, or forthcoming, or direct for interviews in the future. Or you might celebrate that she was right, you didn't want that job and were subconsciously signaling that you didn't want to settle for something you weren't genuinely excited about.

The more you look for reasons to celebrate, the more you find them. Celebrating isn't a matter of the situation you're in, it's a matter of choice. If you can't find a reason to celebrate the process, it's because you're not looking hard enough for reasons. For a while, Garrett got into buying really great wine. This wasn't the stuff you pour out of a box; these were once-in-a-lifetime bottles you break out for the most memorable life events. The problem for Garrett was he would never drink them. The bottles were so nice there never seemed to be an occasion worthy of them. Garrett shared this problem with a friend who gave him a brilliant piece of advice. "Sometimes, the bottle *is* the occasion." It was such a simple shift in mindset, but it summed up the importance—and simplicity—of changing the meaning of what's worthy of celebration.

We've found that if people remind themselves to celebrate the process every day, they start seeing all sorts of things to be grateful for. If they get an objection they've never heard before and don't know how to respond, they celebrate because the next time they hear that objection they'll be prepared. Or maybe they'll never hear that objection again because they figured out the reason they got it is because they were targeting the wrong type of prospect. If an entrepreneur gets negative feedback about a product prototype, she can celebrate that she was smart enough to ask people about it so early, before pushing ahead as planned and wasting time and money.

By actively looking for things to celebrate, your days become a lot more fun. (And depending on your version of celebrating, so do your nights!) You're not as vulnerable to the emotional highs and lows of selling. You can even turn the celebration into an actual party. Teams celebrate the process differently, but the goal has always been the same: celebrate often enough that the wins become a by-product of the process, not the only focus. One team we worked with started a weekly happy hour they called a "Hang-Up Hangout." The team gathered to discuss their biggest failures of the week, setting three rules:

1. Celebrate the reason you failed
2. Figure out what you could've done differently
3. Never fail for the same reason twice

These hangouts nurtured a growth mindset and systematized celebrating the process.

By celebrating the process, sellers with an Unsold Mindset don't *wait* for something to make them happy; they *look* for things that will *keep* them happy along the way. What does that mean? It means that happiness can't be just about the win, because no matter how often you win, it will never happen often enough to sustain the level of happiness needed to endure the constant ups and downs of a sales career. No matter what you're selling, sales is not an instant gratification sport. Great salespeople don't look for instant gratification, and they're not patiently sitting around waiting for delayed gratification either. For them, the entire sales process is about *prolonged gratification*.

Change Your Vocabulary

Many of the great sellers we interviewed told us that they have engaged in another type of reappraisal; the way they talk to themselves about what they do. As cognitive psychologists have shown in research, just changing the words we use when we're talking to ourselves about difficult experiences can work wonders for our mindset. A popular example is *Would I rather deal with a problem or a challenge?* Instead of being "mad" about losing a sale, would you feel different if you were "frustrated" instead? Challenges and frustrations lead to more productive emotions, encouraging you to move on sooner to different opportunities. Legendary music producer Quincy Jones took it a step further, saying, "I don't have problems, I have puzzles." There's power in reframing your thinking by changing your vocabulary. One sales rep we know told us he used to tell himself, "I *have* to make eighty calls every day." Now he says, "I *get* to meet eighty strangers today." He has no idea how those conversations will turn out, but when we asked him why the word change made a difference, he said, "It reminds me that out of eighty calls, there are always a handful that are really interesting, and some are hilarious, too. I don't have to have entertaining conversations, I *get* to."

We sometimes lose sight of how negative the language we're using with ourselves, and with others, can be. One salesperson we worked with seemed to always be angry, and he was constantly saying as much. He complained to whomever would listen. In the snack room, elevator, or at any other watercooler opportunity he would moan, "I *can't stand* making all these damn calls . . . They load us up so much I don't even have time for prospecting anymore, but they still expect us to do it . . . Customers *never* understand our value prop." Then one day during a monthly meeting, another member of the team asked him, "If you hate what you do so much, why don't you just get another job?" His answer shocked the team. "Why would you say that? I don't hate my job!" He'd been proclaiming negativity for so long he didn't even realize what he sounded like. We suggested he become more aware of how he described his emotions both to himself and to others, and knowing that the eyes and ears of the whole team were on him, he stuck to his word. A month later, he was surprised to see he had generated more volume than he had the previous three months combined. Coincidence? Maybe, but we doubt it.

Seeing how effective this simple practice was, we made a game to help people reappraise negative patterns: take your ten most-used destructive words and stop using them. Substitute each negative word with a new word or phrase that describes the same feeling but triggers a more productive emotion. The practice is not only effective but often amusing. A sales engineer who was always "nervous" before demos with big clients decided he would tell himself he was "antsy-pantsy" instead, which had the fortunate side effect of causing him to head into those demos with a smile on his face because his new label was so ridiculous when he thought about it. A guy who was infamous in his office for shouting "SHIT!" after he got off a frustrating call decided he would say "poop" instead, which was so ludicrous it helped him see that he really should stop referencing doody altogether.

Words are powerful, and they can either give you power or take it away from you. Take the time to reflect on the language you use, both externally and when talking to yourself; you will then be better able to stay focused on the positives to be gained from whatever ~~problems~~ challenges selling throws at you.

• • •

The Unsold Mindset naturally fosters opportunities to be more growth-minded, to see abundance instead of scarcity, and to be a creator instead of a victim. For elite sellers, adopting that mindset isn't just about selling more. It's about growing into the person and seller you want to be, not the one you're "supposed" to be. Approaching sales as a tool for learning allows you to thrive both professionally and personally and empowers you to become deeply engaged in and satisfied by your work, feel a strong sense of purpose, and relish in the real growth you have the chance to experience every day.

Since a book like ours wouldn't be complete without at least one Rumi quote, here goes: Fear is "non-acceptance of uncertainty; if we accept the uncertainty, it becomes adventure." Sellers with an Unsold Mindset cherish growth. Instead of fearing challenges, rejections, and uncertainty, they know they are part of the journey. The world's greatest sellers view life the way they view sales. They see almost any moment as an important moment, good or bad. They don't predicate their celebrations on success, they celebrate based on impact. And any important moment can have an impact. This outlook helps them find meaning in their careers *and* their lives.

CHAPTER FOUR

Pathological Optimism

One day, flying out of Los Angeles International Airport with their two young boys, things weren't going according to plan for Colin and his wife, Margot. Anyone who's traveled with young kids knows some version of their story: One son urgently needed to use the bathroom, but they were already cutting it close to missing the flight because of a late, hectic start earlier that morning involving an Uber, a taxicab, *and* an airport shuttle. The other was crying because instead of naptime, he was being rushed through metal detectors and security lines. In the middle of all this chaos, Colin smiled at Margot and said, "At least we know we'll never forget our first flight as a family of four!"

"You're such a *pathological optimist!*" she responded in exasperation. She didn't mean it as a compliment, but Colin took it as one. Rather than focusing on the stress of dealing with a kid on the verge of a bathroom "pee-mergency" and the prospect of missing a flight, he was thinking about how this was going to be one of those special memories on the family timeline they would look back on and laugh about, because they'd gotten through it just like so many other typical traumatic family experiences and had been all the stronger for it. The good of spending uninterrupted time together with the most important people in his life far outweighed Colin's headaches of the moment. After all, the memories come from the chaos. The moments we look back on most fondly come from the times we've gone through things we didn't expect.

As we reviewed our interviews, we saw another pattern emerging, which prompted Colin to remember what Margot had called him in the airport that day. Whether it comes naturally to them or not, those with an Unsold Mindset all cultivate a mindset of obsessive, intentional, and habitual (in other words, *pathological*) optimism.

They understand that if they condition themselves to look for the good, they'll find it. Even when they find themselves in circumstances where looking for the good is insanely challenging, those with an Unsold Mindset find ways to prime themselves to see opportunity. At the very least, their optimism leads them to expect that things will eventually work out in some way, which keeps them doing the work that needs to be done when others shut down, burn out, or move on.

The power of optimism has been key to the success of healthcare startup Preveta. In late 2017, Preveta co-founder Shirley Lee's lifelong friend Becky Ramos started exhibiting symptoms of illness. Shirley, who was trained as a nurse practitioner and worked as a director of a cancer center, feared Becky might have cancer, and helped Becky's family contend with many challenges they faced in getting Becky the care she needed, like difficulty obtaining records, finding an appropriate specialist, and the unreasonably slow authorization of coverage by her insurer. All of those hurdles delayed diagnosis by three months, and by the time Becky finally received the tragic news that she had stage 4 ovarian cancer, it was too late for her to have surgery that might have saved her life. Preveta was born out of Shirley's optimism and the belief she could find a way to provide an exponentially better experience for patients and their families.

While virtually every founder is optimistic about their company's prospects when they start out, we were especially impressed by Shirley's belief in her mission because she was well aware that the behemoth healthcare industry has historically resisted change. But she felt confident that she and her data scientist husband, Victor, Preveta's cofounder, had a plan that could beat daunting odds. By using artificial intelligence algorithms, trained on large volumes of clinical data, they could provide software to physicians that would speed up diagnosis and treatment. Every investor Shirley spoke to told her their idea was great, but that it would be extremely difficult to infiltrate the notoriously complex system. Shirley's response to the naysayers? "Exactly!" The pessimism and doubt they were expressing further fueled her optimism; she and her team had a huge opportunity precisely because so many believed in the idea, but didn't believe the system could be changed, which is why few had ever tried prior to this point.

Fast forward a few years, and despite all the challenges, which the naysayers were absolutely on target about, Preveta graduated from the prestigious Techstars startup accelerator as one of their standout alumni. The company received multiple investments from venture funds, oversubscribing their first funding round, and immediately began chipping away at the archaic infrastructure of the healthcare system. The software is now used by several large healthcare providers, and best of all, a study of early results showed a significant increase in earlier detection of cancer progression among patients, allowing for more effective treatment.

Preveta's success reminds us of the classic allegory about a British shoemaker who was thinking of expanding into rural markets in Africa. The company sent two salespeople to different countries to see how they would fare opening the territory and driving sales within it. Not long after their arrival the salesmen reported back. One salesperson sadly announced, "Everyone here goes barefoot. If we enter this market we're not going to sell a single pair of shoes." The second excitedly exclaimed, "This place is perfect for us! Nobody here has shoes, and no one sells shoes either. We're going to make a fortune!"

Optimists as Realists

In our conversations with people who love selling, we discovered that they have an almost supernatural ability to look for the good in even the most challenging situations. We get that this might seem like we're simply putting our own spin on the all too familiar and sometimes condescending clichés "look on the bright side" or "turn lemons into lemonade." There's been pushback against such simplistic takes on optimism, with good reason. Toxic positivity, or the belief that you should put a positive spin on *any* situation, no matter how horrible or tragic, can have devastating effects. Barbara Ehrenreich, author of *Bright-Sided: How the Relentless Promotion of Positive Thinking Has Undermined America*, says optimism "was one of the reasons for the 2008 economic collapse. No one could see that anything bad was coming."

We're not suggesting that people with an Unsold Mindset suppress valid concerns about the reality of a situation or ignore facts. Yes, as Margot's exasperated reaction to Colin's positivity in the airport that day exemplified, maintaining an optimistic perspective even during times of adversity can seem like a form of delusion. But being optimistic is not the opposite of being realistic. Having an Unsold Mindset doesn't mean people bury their heads in the sand and pretend everything is great when the proverbial shit hits the fan (as it inevitably will from time to time). As we saw in the last chapter, they are generally extremely honest with themselves about challenges they're facing, and their abilities to contend with them. Their optimism doesn't lead them to overlook obstacles, it helps them to not fear them. Instead of letting a tough situation derail them, they feel confident that in the long run things will ultimately end up moving "up and to the right." Psychologist Kimberly Hershenson says, optimism "doesn't mean that you ignore life's stressors. You just approach hardship in a more productive way."

In the field of positive psychology, which has researched optimism extensively, optimism isn't defined as simply believing good things will happen. It's described as an explanatory style that leads people "to see the causes of failure or negative experiences as temporary rather than permanent, specific rather than global, and external rather than internal." Just as a growth mindset instills the belief we can improve our abilities, optimism helps us realize we can use those abilities to improve outcomes. Practicing optimism is a form of self-empowerment.

But isn't whether we're an optimist or pessimist a fundamental character trait that we're born with, baked into our personality? To some extent, yes, but not nearly as much as is commonly believed. Research has determined that genetic inheritance accounts for only about 25 percent of our tendency to be either generally more optimistic or more pessimistic. That means the influence of our upbringing and our life experiences factor into the other 75 percent. More importantly, we have 100 percent ability to override our genes *and* our life experiences to take a more optimistic approach to situations when we choose to.

We shouldn't think of ourselves as "an optimist" or "a pessimist." We're all a little of both. For example, most of us tend to be more optimistic in some areas of our lives and more pessimistic in others. We might be highly optimistic about raising our children well and pessimistic about finding work we love or staying healthy as we age. We can all choose to build up our optimism about things we're pessimistic about.

Martin Seligman, widely considered the father of positive psychology, has studied optimism inside and out, and he wrote that "a talent for joy, like any other, can be cultivated." That was the main theme of his 1990 book *Learned Optimism,* and a ton of research since in positive psychology has backed up his finding that optimism can be consciously developed. Seligman was also a leader in proving why doing so is hugely beneficial for selling.

The Optimist's Advantage

In the 1980s insurance giant MetLife asked Seligman to conduct a study on the potential effects of optimism on the performance of the company's salespeople. At the time, MetLife was hiring nearly five thousand new salespeople a year and training them at a cost of $30,000 each, only to have half of them quit after the first year. This is a huge loss on an even huger investment.

Seligman conducted his study with fifteen thousand new hires, assessing their level of optimism by measuring how hopeful they said they were about the future, how well they thought they could overcome obstacles, and how they felt about their chances for success.

Those who scored in the top 10 percent for optimism generated 88 percent more sales after two years than those in the bottom 10 percent for optimism. Seligman found that optimism was even a far more important indicator for achieving great results than high proficiency in sales techniques.

The strong link between being optimistic and success in selling has since been illustrated in over a thousand studies across many industries and sales organizations. Optimism has been found to boost success because it results in lower turnover, more motivation to take ownership of one's destiny, a willingness to intentionally jump into challenges, and greater perseverance in the face of obstacles.

We witnessed this when we were training a new batch of salespeople for a company that used a common practice among sales teams of giving brand-new salespeople leads to work on from the "icebox." These are typically old leads that were never converted into deals, but aren't considered completely dead, hence they've been put "on ice." The philosophy behind this practice is that it's good training, allowing the inexperienced salespeople to get their feet wet with real potential customers and hone their skills before getting in front of fresher opportunities with a higher likelihood of closing. Since icebox leads can be months, or even years, old, most new salespeople generally don't expect much out of these leads (nor do their managers). But that didn't deter one trainee.

Katie was such an optimist at heart she just *knew* there were sales to be found in the icebox. She looked through every lead she was assigned and studied their history. Before prospects ever picked up her phone call, she assumed there was something good brewing on the other side of the line. She was able to initiate incredible conversations with people who barely remembered what her company was selling, and her high expectations led to conversations that never would have been as effective if she had adopted the mindset that she was just "training" and not truly expected to close any sales. She converted so many leads that normally wouldn't get touched, let alone converted into customers, that the tenured salespeople decided they should start re-connecting with their old leads themselves. After all, they were the ones that had put in all the effort laying the groundwork (at least in their minds), only for this newbie to come in and get all the glory!

Another reason optimism in selling is so effective is that it has literally been found to be contagious. Business professor Scott B. Friend and his colleagues found in their research that a salesperson's optimism is often transferred to customers, and even co-workers. They call this the "contagion effect."

Garrett witnessed this firsthand while helping a growing tech startup build a program designed to strengthen relationships with distribution partners for their software. The company was trying to sell a very large distributor on carrying their product and reselling it to its huge book of customers. The partnership manager had inked deals with this particular distributor at a previous job and, frankly, he'd been burned. "This isn't worth it," he'd complain. "It's going to take months to get a deal done, and then once we sign nothing's going to come of it. They'll be on to the next thing and we won't be any better off." This pessimism was clearly carrying over into his conversations with the partner, which had stalled.

Unlike the pessimistic partnership manager, the founders of the company believed a partnership with the distributor would be huge for the company. They weren't ready to give up on it, and they had an idea. They took the partnership manager off that deal and gave it to a young, enthusiastic salesperson who had no experience with distribution deals, but was notorious for being positive and ambitious.

At first the representatives in the room for the distributor didn't understand why the young rep was so excited. Was there new information? Was there demand they hadn't seen before? What were they missing? They couldn't help but get excited, too. It wasn't long before they saw what they were blind to before; a huge opportunity to be an early adopter in an industry that was about to become commoditized! They started talking about potential market collaborations, joint press releases, and ways to incentivize the distributor's sales team to sell the company's product to the largest segment of their customer base. Nothing about the partnership had changed at all, those opportunities were there the entire time. The only difference was the level of optimism of the person leading the conversation.

Someone who has been able to harness the power of the contagion effect throughout his entire career is music executive Jeff Ayeroff. Jeff made it to the highest echelon of the music industry by selling ideas to iconic artists like Prince, Lenny Kravitz, and the Police; and then selling radio stations, publications, and TV networks on buying those ideas once they'd been created. When we sat down to interview him in his Pacific Palisades living room overlooking the Pacific Ocean, he told us, "I've always thought selling is a lot easier if you approach it like a fan." According to Jeff, giving himself permission to be a fan has allowed him to be authentically optimistic, the same way most fans are optimistic when it comes to their favorite artists. He illustrated exactly what he meant by this when he told us about the time he sold MTV on taking a shot on a relatively unknown artist signed to Warner Bros. Records, the label where he'd just been made a senior vice president.

When describing how optimistic he was about his new artist, he told us, "I *knew* how special Madonna was going to be. I called a couple of the executives at MTV and said, 'If you play this, she *will* be your biggest star, and *when* she is the face of your network, she *will* show up for you.'" Listening to Jeff recalling what he said on that call from forty years earlier, it's still obvious he meant every word. You could sense the admiration and optimism he had for who and what he was selling. By thinking like an optimist, genuinely believing Madonna's success was inevitable, he also tapped into what was important to the people he was selling to at MTV. He was confident that if they bought what he was selling, they'd be better off, too. "Trust me," he told them, knowing they could. His optimism was contagious, and the rest is history, of course; Madonna went on to become one of the defining icons of the MTV Generation, and Jeff became MTV's biggest supplier for many years.

Becoming a better seller is only part of the reason to work on building your optimism. Cultivating optimism has also been found to be extremely beneficial for health. Research has revealed that optimism is good for our hearts, reducing both heart disease and heart attacks, while also boosting the strength of our immune system. An analysis of the results of the Nurses' Health Study, conducted at Harvard and one of the longest-term and most respected studies in the field of public health, showed that over an eight-year period, the women who had scored highest on an optimism test were 30 percent less likely to die from a serious illness during that time.

When selling, building up our optimism is key to being proactively prepared to face the challenges most sellers will inevitably encounter. Without optimism, it's way too easy to default to a darker, more negative place.

It's Natural to See the Negative

Unfortunately, as humans we're hardwired to look for negativity. From our earliest days as a species, the intense dangers of daily life bred into us an adaptive tendency to be highly alert to potential danger. Over time, as our brains evolved, this led to a natural tendency to focus more on negative events, real or imagined, than on positive ones. This is called the negativity bias, and it's the reason we generally find it easier to remember losses, disappointments, slights, and mistakes than to remember accomplishments, achievements, and successes. We've seen it drag so many sellers down. One salesperson we worked with told us, "I can't remember all the deals I've won, but I'm pretty sure I can list every single one I've lost."

Psychologist Roy F. Baumeister has studied this phenomenon, and he explains that our brains process negative emotions more thoroughly than positive ones. This means we feel negative experiences more deeply. We even use stronger words to describe bad experiences, which is part of why we remember them more vividly. This explains, Baumeister says, why people get "more upset about losing $50 than [they] are happy about gaining $50."

The pressures inherent in selling, from managers breathing down our necks about numbers, to unrealistic goals, to the overall urgency to perform, can understandably trigger this bias. That all too often leads to a vicious self-reinforcing negativity spiral. Salespeople start dwelling on the deals they *didn't* close, engineers obsess over the feature that *didn't* get built, frontline employees focus on the incentive bonus they *didn't* achieve.

In his book *Flourish*, Seligman emphasizes, "We think too much about what goes wrong and not enough about what goes right in our lives. Of course, sometimes it makes sense to analyze bad events so that we can learn from them and avoid them in the future. However, people tend to spend more time thinking about what is bad in life than is helpful." We've certainly found this to be true for many of those we work with. They share boatloads of reasons why it's not possible for them to get better results. *The market is too small and there aren't enough potential customers. We're getting lapped by our competition. Our product is missing features. Our customers' habits are changing faster than the company can keep up. The executive team can't get out of their own way. Marketing isn't generating enough leads. The sales cycles are too long. We can't do anything until we close the next round of funding. Our customers walk all over us.* And on and on.

We've seen this negativity get a debilitating grip on people time and again. It undermines their ability to see how they might improve their outcomes and they become so focused on rationalizing why they're not getting better results that they aren't even really trying anymore. This is true even when it's clear they've got all the talent they need for success.

We saw this with the best trainee, by far, in a development course we taught for a client. He had incredible enthusiasm, huge ambition, and did everything right during classes, but once he was actually on the job, he couldn't close a door, let alone a customer. After a few months, he left the company.

Looking back, it was pretty clear he had made the all-too-common mistake of thinking that more activity would cure what ailed him. He became obsessed with pitching as many people as possible, employing the "spray and pray" method so many salespeople fall back on when things aren't going well. In doing so, he had completely skipped over the incredibly important step of checking in with the people to whom he was speaking to see if they could even *use* what he was selling. Instead of asking for guidance from his boss and colleagues, who would have easily been able to help him diagnose this problem, he grew embarrassed and began to check out, and after a few more months, he left the company, and gave up on selling altogether, instead becoming a project manager.

As it started to become clear his increased activity wasn't leading to more sales, he began making fewer calls and sending fewer emails every week. In fact, in his last month, he made 90 percent fewer calls than he did when he had first started. This huge drop in activity is a classic symptom of *sales burnout*. Often, when we first dig in with a company whose sales team is having challenges growing their numbers, we find a very high percentage of the team is at or near burnout, covertly exhausted and overwhelmed, acting cool in the office while desperately talking to any recruiter who reaches out about the next gig. The World Health Organization has recognized burnout as a legitimate medical diagnosis, and it's only one of a number of adverse health effects that can result from dwelling too much on the negative. They also include mental health conditions, like depression and anxiety, as well as physical health effects ranging from minor ailments to heart disease and even a shorter life span.

Clearly, for anyone who wants to sell well and enjoy doing it, cultivating an optimistic mindset is critical.

Flex Your Optimism

One of Colin's best friends, Kevin, believes in psychics. Once, when Kevin was walking in Venice Beach, a psychic who had a table set up on the boardwalk flagged him down. "I know you won't believe me unless I prove it to you, so I'm going to read your fortune for free. If

I'm right, then you come back and pay me for the next reading. If I'm wrong, we never have to see each other again. Deal?"

Kevin shrugged his shoulders. There was nothing to lose. "Perfect."

The psychic leaned in and gave her prediction: "Three great things are going to happen to you today."

Kevin called to tell Colin what she'd said, and Colin didn't give it much thought, hoping Kevin wouldn't either. But Kevin called again an hour later and said (we're paraphrasing because Kevin curses more than Samuel L. Jackson in line at the DMV), "You're not going to believe this! I was just at Chipotle and ordered my usual burrito with double chicken and a side of guac! The girl behind the counter only charged me for one scoop of chicken. When I pointed it out, she said don't worry about it, it was on her!"

Colin laughed. "I get it, that's one great thing."

A couple hours later Kevin called again. "How crazy is this? My meeting ran long, and when I was heading to my car I saw that a parking attendant was just about to give me a ticket. I ran over and got there just before she hit the 'submit' button on that ticket machine by seconds, bro! She told me, 'I guess this is your lucky day.'"

Colin laughed again, and humored Kevin. "Interesting."

Hours later Colin got a third call. "Okay, this is getting insane. I just got off the phone with my client. He canceled the call we had scheduled to talk about final contract details tomorrow because he came down with something, then out of nowhere he told me he didn't need the call anyway because he's ready to move forward and just wants me to send over the contract! Do you believe now?!? The psychic was right!"

Colin took a deep breath and said, "Kev, as your boy, let me ask you a question. If the psychic told you three *bad* things were going to happen to you today, what do you think would have happened?" He wished he could have seen Kevin squirm during the awkward twenty seconds of silence that followed. "I don't know, I guess I'd be more prepared for the bad stuff since I'd be on the lookout."

"The same way you were more prepared for the good stuff today . . . because you were on the lookout?"

Kevin's story illustrates two important points about the intentional practice of optimism. First, it's a perfect example of how if you look for the good, you'll find it, and if you look for the bad, you'll find that instead. It's also a great reminder that a single shift in our mindset can be the difference in how we view the world.

As we started digging in and asking more questions about how those with an Unsold Mindset sustain their optimism, we realized that they specifically *condition* themselves to stay so focused on the positive. If you ask a body builder how they maintain such a defined fourteen-pack, they'll look at you funny and then state the obvious, "I go to the gym every day." Optimism is no different; you have to continually flex your optimism muscles. Those with an Unsold Mindset focus on finding ways to "stay in the gym." They look for the good vigilantly, turning that practice into a habit they actively maintain. Even some great sellers who told us their default nature was more pessimistic recounted ways they shifted their mindset to prime themselves to see the positive. They made it clear it's possible to be intentionally optimistic.

The one who most colorfully shared his particular approach to training his mind to focus on the good was comedian and actor JB Smoove. JB was legendary for the way he was able to "sell" his ideas in the weekly pitch meetings when he was a writer at *Saturday Night Live.* JB told us a story about how, after three seasons with the show, he fired his agent, knowing full well that would mean his contract would not get renewed because the agency had strong ties with the show. "Sometimes you got to make moves that seem scary," he told us. "But if you believe in yourself and what you bring to the table, how hard you work, it doesn't fucking matter." This is pathological optimism.

JB knew that even though he wouldn't be returning to a job he loved, if he worked at his craft he'd find a way to come out ahead. "You've got to believe that even if you can't sell that thing, there's something else you can sell just as fucking good." (As JB's fans know, he never met a sentence he couldn't improve with an F-bomb or three!)

As we dug deeper into JB's philosophy on optimism, he shared some thoughts that can provide a boost of optimistic motivation any time one is tempted to get discouraged. "There are negative *fuck its* and positive *fuck its*," he said. "Negative *fuck its* are where you throw your hands up and say 'fuck it' because you feel like you have no other options. Positive *fuck its* are where you say, 'Fuck it, I'm gonna go for it. I'm going to build something amazing. I'm gonna fucking make this shit work.'"

Research backs JB up. Positive psychology has shown that this kind of self-coaching can have powerful effects. By leading us to take the positive actions we're striving for more often, the coaching creates a positive reinforcement loop. Or, to put it in JB's terms, the more often you default to a "positive *fuck it*," the more you'll prove yourself right, and the more you'll want to say, "Fuck it, why not try?!?"

There's an Indian proverb that says, "Sometimes the wrong train takes you to the right station." There isn't just one path to where we're trying to go. Even in the face of challenges, it's important for us to remember we all have the power to choose what we focus on and to set our own expectations for any situation, as long as we remain present enough during the thick of it to make the choice. People with an Unsold Mindset are fully *aware* that shitty situations, hell, even shitty quarters, happen sometimes. But it's that same awareness that empowers them to train themselves to acknowledge when they're focusing on what they *don't* want, call themselves out on it, and refocus. Optimism helps them accept that bad days, quarters, or even years do not define them.

Point/Counterpoint

Seligman advocates what he calls "disputation." Disputation—in other words, *disputing* your current beliefs—"centers on generating counter-evidence to . . . negative beliefs in general." This can mean reframing the cause of the event or its implications. It can also mean reminding yourself of the benefits that might stem from moving on from the adversity instead of dwelling on it. In a way, it's the practice of arguing with your own thoughts to talk yourself out of negativity, but it's really a form of reappraisal, of looking for the good and pushing back on negative thoughts with a positive response.

Say a contact at a company you've been trying to sell into for months suddenly ghosts you. No return calls, no emails, nothing. Your initial (pessimistic) thought might be, "Oh no, they decided not to buy and now they're ignoring me so they don't have to say *no* to my face." As a result, you freak out. Maybe you even send a desperate "save" email to try to win them back, or worse, get passive aggressive with one of those transparent "breakup" emails some salespeople are so fond of sending (*I haven't heard from you in a while so I'm going to assume your priorities have changed . . .*).

If you're able to label your negativity, you will be able to catch yourself and tell yourself a new story. *Stop jumping to conclusions. I'm not the center of their universe. There are plenty of reasons why they could have stopped responding; they could have their own problems I know nothing about.* As you do this more and more over time, you'll find yourself being proven right. You'll get energized when you acknowledge your thoughts are just thoughts, instead of reacting to them as if they were facts. In our experience, self-aware sellers will almost always yield better results than more knowledgeable, experienced sellers who lack that trait.

Start with "Yes"

We interviewed Jim Ellis who, during his tenure as dean of USC's Marshall School of Business, raised over half a billion dollars for the university. That's no small feat, since fundraising for a university is literally asking people for money even though they won't receive anything tangible in return (unless, of course, you're spending enough to get a building with your name on it!). We asked him how he was able to fundraise so successfully, and he talked about a simple mindset shift we've since heard echoed by others.

"Somewhere along the way I learned to start with *yes*. Maybe we'll get to *no* down the line, but that's not where we're going to start," he told us.

Conventional wisdom says a typical salesperson is going to get rejected approximately 70 to 80 percent of the time. Nonetheless, we've found that people with an Unsold Mindset optimistically start with *yes* in every sales interaction. They assume they're going to close *every* deal, and that leads them to treat every person they talk to *like they're a customer already.* When you assume every prospect will be a customer, you treat them differently. There's less of a sell/sold power dynamic, and there's no fear that the deal is fragile, because your relationship isn't based on closing a deal anymore. You push back when you know it's the right thing to do, you don't fear introducing a competitor into the conversation or discussing a feature your product doesn't have, and you say "no" when something isn't right for them without anxiety, because you're not scared of losing a deal you've already closed.

World-renowned artist Kelly Reemtsen told us that she assuages her anxiety about how many paintings she'll sell in a show by setting a simple, achievable goal to "sell just one painting," even though she always sells out. It's her way of making sure she quite literally starts with *yes* to get herself into a mindset where she's confident having conversations with collectors to sell herself and her work. She's usually able to hit her one painting benchmark before the show even starts, and she says having that *yes* allows her to "show up with confidence and enjoy myself rather than wanting to hide in the bathroom!"

Another welcome side effect of starting with *yes* is that when you genuinely believe every interaction with a prospect or customer will be a good one, you start to look for (and find) all the reasons the customer will buy. *The buyer doesn't know it yet, but I'm going to get her promoted! I've never seen a company more suited for our solution. This is going to change the way they do business forever.*

People with an Unsold Mindset know better than to pay any attention to the statistics about the percentage of deals they're "supposed" to close. If you only look for three out of every ten prospects to become customers, what do you think you're going to get?

Conscious Gratitude

Gratitude is having a pretty big moment these days, so much so that we almost didn't include it at the risk of sounding too much like everyone else. But the more we thought about it, the more we realized we'd be remiss if we didn't discuss it. Gratitude is a critical characteristic of the Unsold Mindset, it's not a coincidence, and it would be unfair to you if we left it out just because it feels like a buzzword. Lots of ways to practice gratitude have been tested, and the beneficial results are real.

Gratitude is the single most important sales activity that contributes to learned and sustained optimism. People with the Unsold Mindset know this, so instead of simply telling themselves to "be grateful," they *look* for ways to practice scaled gratitude. Most people view gratitude acutely—they see something they should be grateful for and acknowledge it in the moment. There is no way to scale this type of in-the-moment gratitude for long-term success because it's too situational, you can only be grateful for what's in front of you. When stuck in the myopia of acute gratitude, you might be grateful for the angel investor who just said they'd participate in your seed round, but not for the engineer who created the product that enabled you to raise that money in the first place. Or you might be grateful for the joy your kids bring to your life in a proud moment and forget to be grateful for your partner, without whom they wouldn't exist. To *scale* gratitude, it has to be integrated into the way you think about life, not just sales. You have to see reasons for gratitude even when they're not clearly visible, not just when it situationally benefits you. If you can scale gratitude, incorporating it into your default mindset, you can enjoy the benefits we've described in this chapter on a prolonged basis, in every interaction, and not just when things are good.

How do you become omni-grateful? Start by looking for and taking note of gratitude when it's difficult to do so. We suggest keeping a "Hard Day's Night Log." At the end of your most challenging days—days you've lost a deal, been rejected, feel unhealthy, gotten into it with a colleague, or just had a generally terrible day—write down everything wrong that happened. Even though it doesn't immediately focus your gratitude, it's cathartic. Then, on the next page, write down everything right that happened that day, or things that *might* go right tomorrow. This may not be as easy. It's easy to be grateful on good days, but if you can start becoming grateful on the not-so-great days, you'll realize they will come less and less often. The idea of keeping a log (we know you're thinking "Gratitude Journal," but this really is a different exercise) might sound too cheesy for some people, but many of the Unsold-minded people we spoke to have a similar way of scaling their approach to gratitude. Noticing gratitude in this way can enhance optimism just by forcing you to look for it.

According to psychologist and gratitude expert Rick Hanson, while negative experiences register immediately because of the survival implications we discussed earlier, we have to hold positive experiences in our awareness for somewhere between five and twenty seconds in order to register an emotional memory. Without registering the memory in this way, we can't enjoy the positive emotional effects over time. Hanson therefore suggests taking the time to focus on a half dozen positive experiences a day and lingering on them to properly absorb them. This should be especially easy now since we're already looking for reasons to celebrate the process!

Get an Objective Measure of Your Optimism

In any good training regime, you want to get a baseline against which you can assess your progress. A tricky thing about trying to increase optimism is that it can be difficult to know where you fall on the optimist/pessimist spectrum. Quite often, when you ask a pessimist to evaluate themselves, they'll just say they're "realistic." If this describes you, it's a good idea to more effectively assess your level of optimism, or lack thereof, with the simple list of questions below, adapted from M. F. Scheier, C. S. Caver, and M. W. Bridges' "Life Orientation Test."

Instructions: Put a corresponding number next to each statement. Be honest with yourself as you rate how much you agree with each, rather than worrying about how you think "most people" would answer.

5 = I agree a lot
4 = I agree a little
3 = I neither agree nor disagree
2 = I disagree a little
1 = I disagree a lot

Statements:
1. When most people are scared of an outcome, I'm confident everything will be okay.
2. When shit hits the fan, I assume it's happening for a reason.
3. Bad things happen to me less than most other people.
4. No matter the present situation, I know I'll get through it.
5. If I look hard enough, I'll find the silver lining.
6. If I work hard enough for long enough, good things will happen.
7. I handle rejection well.
8. I rarely get aggravated over things outside of my control.
9. My default level of happiness is higher than everyone around me.
10. I don't get too high on the highs or low on the lows—I'm content knowing I'll always have enough.

If you scored a 35 or higher, your default optimism is higher than most. Keep doing what you're doing and "stay in the gym." If you scored under 35, there's no need to freak out, you're in the majority, and the approaches described above will undoubtedly help you take steps toward developing a more optimistic outlook.

• • •

You've probably never heard of Dr. Katalin Kariko, but her work has almost certainly impacted your life. Dr. Kariko is a biochemist. In the early 1990s, she started working on technology that would eventually evolve into the mRNA technology used for vaccines, including the COVID vaccine. It's now being tested on diseases like cancer, multiple sclerosis, lupus, and malaria. She's won dozens of awards for her work. But her success wasn't a foregone conclusion. Early in her research, she suffered setback after setback.

She was denied funding, in part because she was "selling" her research against far more popular technologies and "working in the shadow of the gene therapy and people who work with DNA." Progress on her work was painfully slow and incremental, for which she was demoted or fired several times. Despite these roadblocks, she never stopped being optimistic. "You will see, every picture [from that time], I'm smiling. I was happy." In large part, this optimism stemmed from her genuine belief that what she was trying to do would work. "I could see that it would be good for something," she said, "that's what was driving me."

Dr. Kariko trained herself to remain optimistic in the face of her challenges. She didn't ignore reality when it knocked her down; instead she got back up. She figured it was just a matter of time, and trusted that if she did the work, sold herself and her ideas to people who cared about the work she was so vigorously optimistic about, she'd eventually accomplish the scientific progress she'd set out to accomplish. *This* is how people with an Unsold Mindset use optimism to change the way they sell.

One of the most important findings in the history of psychology, discovered over the past couple of decades by neuroscientists, is that the brain is malleable. It continues to grow new brain cells throughout our lives, and we can consciously shape how it grows, developing habits we want and suppressing ones we don't, such as anxiety or depression. If our thinking is dominated by negativity, we'll reinforce the neural networks of pessimism. The same is true for positive thoughts strengthening the networks that support optimism. We're never going to entirely avoid falling into bouts of negativity, but through activities like disputation, starting with *yes*, and practicing gratitude, we really can engineer our minds to look for the good much more often. Which, of course, means we'll start finding the good more often, too.

CHAPTER FIVE

Fall in Love, Actually

Lindsey Lanier has one of the most enviable selling jobs in the world. As vice president of A&R (artists and repertoire) at Motown Records, her job is to discover, sign, and develop new artists. While it may seem like she is the buyer (Who wouldn't want a record deal with Motown?!?), her business is highly competitive, and to sign great talent she has to sell artists on why they should work with her and her team instead of another label. That's not always easy. "I really believe in what I can do with an artist," she told us, "but I also can't do it for everyone."

Lindsey told us about dramatically different experiences she had recruiting two different artists while she was an up-and-coming music executive at Universal Music Publishing Group. The first was a young rapper who had a hit song out at the time and was looking for a new label. Lindsey's boss really wanted to sign him, and entrusted Lindsey to do just that. "You have to meet with him," she told Lindsey.

When the day arrived, Lindsey showed up for the meeting and waited. And waited. Over half an hour later, the rapper's managers came into the room. "He's not feeling good," one said. "He's in his car. He might be asleep." *Hmm, that's weird,* she thought to herself. A few minutes later, they came in again. "He's coming, but he doesn't feel great. He'll be here soon." Finally, the artist showed up, shook Lindsey's hand, gave her a nod, and walked out.

"He's just going back to the car," his managers said.

Lindsey was confused. "Is he okay? Do you need to take him back to the hotel?"

"He's fine," they assured her. "We can finish the meeting from here." But to Lindsey, blowing the meeting off and leaving it to other people without a real explanation was concerning.

The managers played Lindsey some of the new music the artist had been working on, which didn't sound anything like his previous music. It was still good, but she didn't love it. Lindsey had seen and heard enough. "Listen, I don't know if the kid is super talented or not, I don't know if he's gonna be great or not. But I can't, in good conscience, say to him that no matter what happens to him in his career, I'm going to be on his team, or that I completely believe in everything that he's doing. It wouldn't be fair to him." She passed on the deal.

Contrast that experience with that of another artist Lindsey courted. The second artist had some prior success in comedy and television but was relatively unknown as a musician. Her encounters with him couldn't have been more different. When they first met, he was completely engaged, talked with enthusiasm about his music, and vulnerably shared his grand vision of where he wanted to take his career. She loved his music and his ambition, and she wanted to sign him on the spot so they could immediately get to work on what she thought was going to be a very special musical career.

When Lindsey told her boss that she was passing on the first rapper her boss wasn't pleased. "He's got a hit song on the radio!"

"It's cool because I'm signing this other kid," she said, "I really believe in him."

"It's your call, but you might be making a big mistake," her boss warned her.

Ultimately, both artists were successful, though not nearly to the same degree. The first artist signed with a different label, had a couple more relatively popular songs, and was even nominated for two Grammys, though he didn't end up winning any. The artist Lindsey loved so much she felt compelled to take a chance on went on to have massive commercial and critical success. Donald Glover, better known in the music industry by his stage name Childish Gambino, has been nominated for twelve Grammys (so far) and won *five*! (For good measure, he also won two Golden Globes *and* a matching pair of Emmys for *Atlanta*, the TV show he created and starred in.)

Lindsey doesn't think of herself as a salesperson, even though she admits "that's what it is [I do] at its core." A huge part of her job is selling herself and her label to artists, and then selling them to the world. But she added that "I didn't feel like I was selling Donald because I believed in Donald. I *wanted* to work with him. Before I even committed to signing him, I *fell in love* with his music, his vision, and the idea of what he could become. Once I've done that, it doesn't feel like selling, it feels like 'let's do this *together.*'"

Time and again in our interviews, the "L-word" kept coming up. They weren't talking about romantic love, of course, but a no-less-real platonic connection that stemmed from genuine care for and interest in the other person. For example, Kelly Perdew, a longtime entrepreneur-turned-venture-capitalist, who "sells" his fund, Moonshots Capital, to founders he wants to work with, told us, "I pretty much fall in love with every entrepreneur I meet." He says that because he's been in their shoes, he can't help himself. The founders can feel it as well, which is part of the reason Moonshots attracts so many great investment opportunities for its partners, such as ID.me, Olive, and Gretel.

In another of our interviews, Amy Volas, founder and CEO of Avenue Talent Partners, one of the most admired enterprise sales recruiting agencies in the country, told us she started the company because "I *love* working with salespeople." She credits digging deeper into who her prospects are and finding something to truly fall in love with about them as a huge reason why her firm is so successful. "It's all about the people," she told us, "you want to help them solve problems and reach goals."

You might be thinking, *Yeah, right, they don't actually fall in love. Do these guys know how cheesy they sound?* You might even think we're being hypocrites, since a huge part of our message is about cutting the bullshit and now it seems like we're slinging some. We get it. We worried that writing a chapter about love might turn some people off. But we've felt the same love our interviewees have expressed in our various roles as sales leaders, professors, and speakers. We've also felt its spark when great salespeople sell to us.

So we decided to dig into what science might have to say about this sort of love. We wanted to understand whether the feeling we have experienced, and that was being described to us, can really be considered love. And if so, we wanted to find out what we could learn about its nature so we could help more people feel it when they're selling. Imagine how excited we were to learn that research has shown that, yes, it really is love we and the sellers with an Unsold Mindset have been feeling; a well-documented type of platonic love that can rapidly connect people. What's more, the science has shown why it's such a boost for success, and a powerful life enhancer in general, with benefits for both mental and physical health.

Love on the Brain

Barbara Fredrickson, one of the leading contributors to positive psychology, has specialized in studying the nature of love and how it makes us not only happier but healthier. She introduces what she calls "the new science of love" in her book *Love 2.0,* which explains exactly the kind of love we're discussing, and what leads people to experience it. Biologists have learned a great deal in recent years about the physiology and neuroscience of love. For example, the body releases a different cocktail of hormones when feeling romantic versus platonic love, which is why it's possible to feel a deep love for friends, family, and sometimes strangers, that has no romantic quality to it whatsoever. But Fredrickson posits that at the foundation of all love is a collection of what she calls "micro-moments of warmth and connection" between people. In some cases, those micro-moments result from romantic attachment or familial love, but more generally, they create a special sense of bonding and appreciation between people that is exactly what a lot of the Unsold-minded people we've interviewed have described, and which resonated deeply with our own experiences.

Fredrickson writes, "Love blossoms virtually anytime two or more people—even strangers—connect over a shared positive emotion, be it mild or strong." She is unequivocal that love is exactly the right term for this feeling of connection, even in work situations or with people with whom we've only had a brief encounter. "Do I really need to call that moment of connection I just had with my colleague *love?*" she writes. "Was that *love* I just felt when I shared a smile with a complete stranger?" Yes! is her resounding reply.

When we told our developmental editor, Emily, about this on a Zoom call one day, she said, "Oh, I had exactly that kind of experience with a cable company guy!" The story she then told us captures why seeking to spark this kind of loving connection with clients, colleagues, and audiences we're presenting to is so good not only for selling, but for living richer lives.

Emily's niece was scheduled to appear on a big national news show, live, for the first time. But twenty minutes before showtime, when Emily turned her TV on, excited to watch her niece, her cable service wasn't working. She frantically called the cable company's 1–800 number and the man who took her call did the impossible: He made her a fan of cable tech support!

Almost everyone has experienced those infuriating calls when a technician has tried all the obvious stuff and tells you they have to do a "system reboot." We end up waiting and waiting and there's either awkward silence or the tech puts us on hold so we can listen to the Spotify station of our worst nightmares until they check back in. But this technician was different. With what Emily took as genuine curiosity, he asked how her day was "outside of the cable debacle." She laughed and said he must be from a friendlier place than New York (where Emily lives), only to find out they actually lived in neighboring communities. He heard her cat meow and asked how many cats she had before admitting he was a cat parent as well. She responded that her cat liked to watch TV with her, and he shared that his own cat had somehow pushed his TV to the floor a while back so he had to buy a new one. They laughed and shared a couple more feline misadventures. Meanwhile the service was still rebooting.

A few minutes before her niece was scheduled to appear, Emily shared that she'd been hoping to watch her on a big news show and the tech asked, "What show?" He then turned on his own TV—he worked from home—turned it to the station, and cranked up the volume so she could hear her niece through his headset. Emily didn't miss a bit of it. The tech even described how poised and authoritative her niece appeared. Then, just as the interview was wrapping up, the service was restored.

She told us she'd been telling this story to friends for months. She couldn't stop herself. And when she told it to us, she expressed so much passion that we could hear her reliving the pure joy of that brief interaction. Her only regret, she said, was she wished she'd gotten his name so she could write to his company about how amazing he was. Just imagine how much more fruitful, and personally satisfying, so many business interactions, let alone sales, would be if they inspired that much joy!

Why is it we can experience such an intense feeling of connection with someone so quickly? Our bodies and minds have evolved to foster and reinforce these connections in a bunch of ways, because they're so good for us. In fact, Fredrickson writes that moments like these are "the most essential emotional experience for thriving and health." Neuroscience has shown that when we're getting to know someone we're interested in, the "happiness chemicals"—dopamine, serotonin, and oxytocin—are released in our brains, and as psychologist Marc Schoen writes in his book *Your Survival Instinct Is Killing You*, oxytocin in particular "is sometimes referred to as the bonding hormone or the love hormone . . . [It] makes people care for each other, promoting harmony, cooperation, and altruism."

The "for *each other*" is so important when it comes to the power of this feeling when we're selling. What's especially trippy is that when we're feeling this high from the rush of chemicals hitting our brain, we spark the same chemical release in the person we're interacting with. Research shows that our brains actually sync up with one another. This "neural coupling" has been described as a dance between brains, in which brain activity matches up, which also leads us to sync up physically. This is why in authentically engaged conversation, when the person we're talking to smiles, we tend to smile as well, or lean in more closely when they do, genuinely and subconsciously, rather than as a disingenuous tactic.

Neuroscientist Uri Hasson led the way in discovering this mind melding. He monitored people's brain activity while they listened to a recording of a woman telling an engaging story about an experience she'd had. While telling the story, she had been hooked up to equipment that monitored her brain activity. The brain activity of those listening to her immediately began to mimic hers, often within less than a second. Not only does this dance release a stream of oxytocin bursts, the chemical boost causes us to focus more on the person with whom we're talking, making better eye contact, listening more closely to them, and growing more attuned to their emotions. Fredrickson writes, "your awareness expands from your habitual focus on 'me' to a more generous focus on 'we.'" Oxytocin also builds trust between people. Studies show that it makes people "a whopping 44 percent more trusting with confidential information about themselves." We let down our guard and open up to one another.

We've all experienced this incredible sense of connecting with someone we just met, maybe sitting next to them on an airplane, chatting in a waiting room, or in line at the grocery store. We can find ourselves almost in a trance when talking with someone we find fascinating, admire, or who makes us feel inspired. If we continue to have these moments of micro-connection with someone, be that a client, colleague, or casual acquaintance, the bond we form with them keeps deepening; our trust keeps growing, our interest in them becomes more encompassing, and our understanding of and compassion for them flourishes.

It's pretty obvious why love is such a positive force in making selling not only more fulfilling, but actually joyful, healthy for us, and of course, effective. So how can we become better at fostering this sense of connection?

Let us be 100 percent clear: We are not suggesting using "pickup" techniques to appeal to prospects (though that book has probably been written). That would be the absolute antithesis of authenticity, not to mention unethical, if not worse. The connection *has to* be genuine. Fredrickson even addresses this, saying that if someone we're conversing with detects that we're faking our attunement with them, the positivity is immediately nixed; their levels of happiness hormones plummet and trust turns into a sense of betrayal.

The goal isn't to learn how to mimic connection, but to find ways to genuinely feel it, to cultivate a strong desire to know and be of service to those we're selling to. One of the things we've heard people with an Unsold Mindset say they love most about selling is getting to know so many people they wouldn't otherwise meet: being continuously surprised by how interesting they are, or funny or thoughtful or kind. That's what turned Colin's whole approach to selling around in his first job. Garrett also felt this during the earliest days of Bitium when there were only five people at the company and he was the one doing the selling. The product was still in its infancy and it wasn't easy to sell potential customers on taking a chance implementing a solution that wasn't fully baked yet. Then he met Brett, an operations leader at a growing startup, and even though their conversations were initially about business, they quickly turned into conversations between friends. The company Brett worked for eventually became Bitium's first paying customer, but the friendship didn't end when the contract was executed. Sure, the deal may never have happened if not for the connection they had built, but it was also deep enough that they remain friends to this day—they even shared a babysitter when their kids were very young!

Making these kinds of connections begins with opening our minds to the limitless opportunity there is to find them. We've found it's nearly impossible to interact with someone and not find *something* to love about them, but as you'll see below, sometimes you have to *look* for ways to become enamored. We've found a number of great ways to do this, and to make the most of the *potential* for a connection.

Love 3x3

One exercise has worked especially well for us in showing clients and our students how they can get themselves into the right mindset to fall in love with prospects. Many traditional sales trainers teach a research exercise called a "3x3." In their version, you spend three minutes researching three things about a prospect before each call. The point, as it's taught, is for the salesperson to find three things that they can leverage in the conversation to "build rapport," create the impression they've done deep research and created a customized pitch, and then potentially use as a means of persuasion. For example, perhaps the prospective customer wrote a blog post the salesperson can reference, or there's a news article about their company describing a problem the seller's product can help them solve. On the surface, there's nothing wrong with this. It's certainly a good idea to do your homework before making any kind of outreach, let alone a pitch. The problem is the focus on finding an "edge" to convince the customer to buy. That focus undercuts the potential for fostering a genuine interest in the person. To do it right, it's far more important to focus on the quality of the interaction rather than the outcome. Just think for a moment about how different you would feel, and sound, if you were talking to someone you genuinely want to learn about versus talking to someone you see as the fourth prospect on a list of twenty you've been told you have a 30 percent probability of closing.

To take the focus off persuasion and shift it to connection, we reimagined the 3x3 practice and turned it into what we call the "Love 3x3" (don't roll your eyes at the name, it works!). Instead of looking for information to leverage in a conversation with a prospect to get them to buy, look for three things you genuinely *love* about them, regardless of any bearing on whether that might mean they'll be interested in doing business with you. Your only objective is to catch a vibe, that's it. It's a pretty great way to spend your time, looking for reasons to love someone.

With a little practice, this becomes easy. When we do this exercise with teams, giving them the time to do some research, they always quickly begin reporting what they've found: *I saw on Facebook that they are huge advocates for foster parenting. I LOVE that!* or *I LOVE her career trajectory—so unexpected!* The points of interest don't have to be as major as social contributions or career achievements. After all, we bond with people in our day-to-day lives over all sorts of little things. One client, a huge Lakers fan, told us: *I LOVE that this guy's wearing a Kobe jersey on his LinkedIn profile pic!* Another person we worked with, Michael, told us he felt a strange connection with anyone who shared his name. He started intentionally prospecting people named Michael (*Hi Michael, it's Michael!*), and the funniest thing was, they seemed to share the affection. Lucky for him his name is so common! He converted more cold leads to opportunities than anyone on his team over the course of our three-month engagement.

In case you're skeptical that people would respond so well to something as banal as sharing a name, there's actually work in social psychology showing that even the slightest sense of a shared life experience can have a powerful effect on people feeling better about themselves. In a study involving college students who were struggling with a math class, those who were told they shared a birthday with a math major thereafter reported feeling better about their math abilities and worked harder on their next math test. The positive feeling that stems from finding these simple connections also often occurs when two people like the same sports team, have the same hobbies, listen to the same music, or share meaningful life experiences. Looking for yourself in others is a deliberate way to fall in love authentically.

So no, we are not telling you to prospect people that have the same name or horoscope sign as you; we're telling you we've seen firsthand that *certain* people genuinely felt connected because of these things. The goal is to find what drives *you* to feel genuine affection for the people you're interacting with.

We've found the Love 3x3 exercise can work even with people who are dead set against it. We once worked with a seasoned account executive who couldn't (or wouldn't) get his head around the value of attempting to fall in love. He thought the concept was too "hippy dippy" for him, and after we introduced the exercise to him and the rest of the sales force, he announced to the room that he was sure it wouldn't work. Because he was a highly respected senior figurehead in the sales organization, we knew this was an ideal teaching moment.

He was convinced the prospective customer he'd been assigned would have no interest in hearing from him based on the data he'd received about where the lead was located, the size of their business, and all the other signs that pointed to a barely qualified lead. Our exercise required him to do more research, of a different kind than he was used to, and to his credit, he did (though probably with the intent of proving us wrong). He looked into where the guy grew up, how many children he had, which sports teams he followed, what organizations he was a part of, and the interests he listed on social media. It turned out Jim and the prospect had graduated from college the same year. More interesting, though, was that the guy attended the University of Minnesota, where Bob Dylan briefly went before dropping out to pursue music full time. See, Jim was a HUGE Dylan fan. And just like that, he didn't just fall in love with the prospect, *he fell in love with an idea of who he wanted the prospect to be.* He hoped the guy loved Dylan as much as he did, and that he might have even heard a few Dylan stories about his time at the college.

When Jim made the call, the prospect didn't disappoint. After some initial introductions, Jim casually said, "I noticed you graduated from Minnesota. Impressive—not even Bob Dylan could do that!" It didn't take long before they were comparing favorite songs and the guy was sharing campus legends about Dylan. Jim ended up successfully selling to the "Dylan Prospect," as he later referred to the guy, and though Jim was quick to emphasize that he closed the deal because the product turned out to be a good fit, we reminded him how cynical he had been about that same product fit earlier. On a regular selling day, Jim might not have even called the prospect, or if he had he wouldn't have had nearly as much enthusiasm as he did that day. And he definitely wouldn't have heard those Dylan stories.

We've seen such astounding results from the Love 3x3 exercise that we now put our students through a version of it on the first day of class every semester. We tell them, "You're going to be paired with a random classmate and your job is to fall in love with them before the exercise is over." At first, they look at us like we're crazy. We imagine them thinking, *I thought this was a class about sales, now I have to sit here and "fall in love" with a stranger? I'm dropping this class!* Yet, without fail, the exercise is a huge hit with a major impact.

The only piece of advice we give them is to *focus on the questions* they would need answered in order to *actually* fall in love with someone, platonically of course. They always begin with standard conversation starter fare: *Where are you from? Why did you decide to take this class?* But they quickly begin asking deeper questions, getting more personal, and interesting, answers. *What was the hardest part about moving across the country to attend school? How do your parents feel about you switching majors?*

When everyone's had enough time to ask and answer questions, we get them all together as a group to share how and why they fell in love. It's always magical to watch the popular, outgoing collegiate athlete describing what she loves about the shy, introverted art history major, and without fail everyone is able to find *at least* three things they fell in love with.

Students are often able to pinpoint the exact moment their conversations shifted from awkward classroom assignment to sincere inquiry and a genuine connection. Almost always, it coincides with the moment they saw *themselves* in the person across from them. *I love that he is into sports cards, I have a huge collection myself . . . I love how honest she was about struggling when she was a freshman, I had a hard transition, too . . . I love that he switched from being a finance major to journalism, we talked about how hard that decision was, I made a similar decision sophomore year.* They're able to articulate how this connection led to a more meaningful, familiar, and valuable conversation.

You can do this exercise in any selling situation. Say you're pitching a campaign to your chief marketing officer. Why might you be excited just to be in the room with them, regardless of whether or not they approve what you're asking for? What if you're giving a presentation to a large group of people in an organization? Look into some of its members and keep things you find to love about them in mind as you take the stage. You're no longer speaking to nameless, faceless audience members, but a group of people you expect have so many more things about them you can love.

You'll know you've succeeded when you feel a little bit like the junior high school version of yourself when you had a crush on someone. You couldn't wait to get to school to see that person. You didn't talk more, you listened; you laughed at their jokes because you genuinely thought they were funny even when others didn't; you cared, and you found good in them everywhere you looked. Find a crush, be excited you *get* to talk to them, and you'll show up differently without having to put on an act.

The Larry King Effect

Never underestimate how appreciative people will be of you asking them about themselves, or how receptive they might be to answering more personal questions. Of course, in selling situations in real life, we typically can't just dive in asking people deeply personal questions. You don't want to come across as interrogating, or worse, as an intrusive weirdo. So how do you know when to ask a personal question in a selling conversation, and of what sorts? Let Larry King be your guide.

We heard a great story about a publicist who worked with the late Larry King, one of the most successful radio and TV interviewers ever, when he was on a book tour. The first day of the tour, King and the publicist had just met and were ushered into the green room at a TV studio waiting for him to go on a show. As soon as they sat down, he turned to her and started to ask her questions about herself. Where had she grown up? Did she like growing up there? She didn't mind the cold winters? Was she still an avid skier? Suddenly she thought to herself, *Wait a minute, he's the famous person here, why does he care about me?* She'd had some wonderful bonding moments with other clients, but what really struck her about this experience was how quickly she felt completely comfortable with King.

Soon, she was asking him questions about his own life; how he was able to be so direct, inquisitive, and honest with people he interviewed, whether he got nervous talking to influential public figures. When he responded warmly, she mentally froze for a moment: *Oh my god, I just "Larry Kinged" Larry King!!* What really stuck with her was that she felt like she'd known him, really, personally known him, for years.

One way King was able to get so personal was by starting with simple questions. He once said about his interviewing style, "The simple questions are the best." The key for him, he said, which carried him happily through over sixty thousand interviews, was that he was "insanely curious" about people, no matter what they did or where they were from. "When I was a kid," he recalled, "I would ask bus drivers, why do you want to drive a bus?" He wasn't asking questions condescendingly, or to show off how clever or knowledgeable he was. He simply wanted to know. He quoted an old mantra that he said had been his guiding principle: "I never learned anything when I was talking." His basic formula was "I asked good questions, I listened, and I followed up."

When you are genuinely curious about people and you start with broad questions about them that you actually want to know answers to, it doesn't take long before your interest in them grows, and so will the depth of the ensuing questions. When people sense authentic curiosity, they'll often open up with answers that will naturally lead you to even more questions that result in a deeper connection.

Every situation and every person is different, so unfortunately there isn't a hard-and-fast rule for knowing when it's the right time to ask a deeper question or know if you've asked one that seems too personal. It's similar to our "if you think you sound cheesy, you sound cheesy" rule from chapter 1; follow an "if you think it's too soon to ask the question, it's too soon to ask the question" rule. And don't forget you can always show your work. *I have this question I really want to ask you, but I'm worried it'll come off the wrong way, which is so not my intent.* Pause for a bit and see if they encourage you to go ahead and ask, and pay close attention to whether they seem glad you want to know more or maybe are put off but don't want to offend by saying so. If you're asking out of genuine curiosity, people feel it, and you'll be surprised how open they will be just knowing you are truly interested in them and what they have to say.

When you care enough about understanding someone in this way, answers to surface-level questions will sound different to you than they do to others. They will intrigue you to the point you'll *have* to know the answer to a follow-up question, which usually is a layer deeper. This normally sounds something like, "What!? Wait, I need to know more. Were you nervous?" Remember, this probing is not a tactic, it's you caring enough to *want* to know the things others don't care about, and that starts with falling in love.

Love Is a Two-Way Street

Another way sellers with an Unsold Mindset gain permission to go a layer deeper with their questions is by sharing information about themselves first. One of the powerful norms of human behavior is the ethic of reciprocity. For most of us, most of the time, if someone does something for us, we're inclined to return the favor. The same is true in conversations. If someone discloses something about themselves, we're generally quick to reveal something of similar depth. Think about a time a client or colleague told you about something embarrassing (like when Colin's headphone cord got disconnected and the whole room got to hear the oh-so-catchy sounds of Miley Cyrus's "Party in the USA" blasting from his computer); you were likely quick to share a similar awkward experience of your own (like Garrett then admitting his favorite pop song of all time is Carly Rae Jepson's "Call Me, Maybe," and trying to justify his opinion with science to boot). Maybe they shared details of a challenge they faced in their personal life, and you felt inclined to return the gift by telling them about a time something similar happened to you. This isn't done as a manipulation, it's heartfelt vulnerability rooted in the desire to understand the other person.

When Colin was engaged and in full wedding planning mode, Margot would book time on his calendar between his meetings to talk details. Because of this, Colin would occasionally show up for scheduled calls a couple minutes late. "I'm *so* sorry," he'd be forced to say, "I'm usually really punctual but I'm planning a wedding and my fiancée called to ask for some opinions on wedding stuff just before I was supposed to call you." Almost without fail, people's responses would fall into one of two camps. Either something like "Don't worry about it, I've been married a long time and the saying is true: happy wife, happy life," or "No problem, I get it, it'll be easier on your second marriage!" In either case, Colin later realized, he'd authentically formed an instant connection. Without even officially starting the conversation, customers were comfortable talking about their marital histories and they were already connecting on a deeper level. Colin's candor led customers to be candid themselves.

We think one reason this kind of self-revelation can create such a connection in selling situations is that it cuts through the ultraconfident salesperson stereotype. We become, in a word, human; a fellow traveler rather than a marksman taking a shot. This is another reason why showing your work can be so appreciated; we're often opening up about doubts or challenges we've had, being vulnerable, and that encourages others to open up to us.

When we first met the team at XX Artists, a fast-growing digital marketing agency in Los Angeles that boasts corporate clients like YouTube and Robinhood, and celebrity clients like Oscar winners Brie Larson and Jennifer Hudson, we had just started to gain momentum booking large speaking engagements and workshops. A friend introduced us to a contact at the agency to see if they might be a good fit to help us build up our online presence. We set up a call and started the conversation by vulnerably telling the three people on the call that we had avoided social media as a platform because we were scared of how we'd be perceived. We shared that we didn't want to be forced to act like anything other than ourselves to make an impact online, and we feared losing control and becoming something we're not since our mission will always be way bigger than likes or follower count. We didn't know much about their approach to working with their clients and worried they might find us naïve or maybe self-righteous. But we wanted a real relationship with whoever was going to help us articulate our brand and guide our presence online. The XX Artists team asked us a lot of great questions and assured us it was normal to be scared about building a social media presence, and we left the meeting feeling heard.

XX Artists sent us a proposal a week after our meeting, and when a member of their team called us two weeks later, we assumed they were following up to see if we'd accept, but that wasn't it at all. Instead, they wanted to hire us to be the keynote speakers for their leadership offsite! We later learned that the connection they felt as a result of our vulnerability was a big factor. They needed to trust that whomever they invited to speak with their team and lead workshops would be able to make their employees feel comfortable being vulnerable themselves during the offsite so they could connect on a deeper level with one another.

In opening up about ourselves with prospects, or anyone we're "selling" to, there is a big difference between offering up appreciated vulnerability and making our issues someone else's burden. The conversation has to be one of give and take, and if that back and forth isn't happening, move on to another way of conducting a conversation. The key is to aim for *transformational conversations*.

Conversations That Transform

In an article written for *Psychology Today* called "The Neuroscience of Conversations," psychologist Judith E. Glaser wrote about three types of conversations, and the impact they can have on our brains. The first, transactional conversations, revolve around the exchange of information, like a typical discovery conversation where a seller is asking questions to learn about the buyer's budget, needs, timing, and so on, while the buyer asks about pricing, product features, and the buying process. Or if you're selling yourself in an interview, a transactional approach would lead you to offer various descriptions of the value you think you can bring to the company while asking your interviewer what you can expect in terms of promotions, raises, stock options, or other perks.

Second are positional conversations, which focus more on advocating for ideas. In a selling context, this involves shifting into persuasion mode and would be where you make the case for your product or service in hopes of consummating a sale. A non-traditional selling example might be trying to convince a friend to agree with you about a political issue or convincing your partner to go out for Thai food for dinner instead of Italian.

The third type, transformational conversations, are characterized by a mutual interest in discovery, deep listening, and free-flowing sharing of insights and wisdom. Glaser describes them vividly as a process of *co-creation* between the parties.

Garrett still remembers the first time he had a transformational conversation in a sales setting. He was working at his first startup, Fastpoint Games, where he'd been selling branded fantasy sports games to properties like Turner Digital, Major League Soccer, and NBA.com. For months, he'd been working hard on a deal with The Sporting News (TSN), which was looking to outsource production and management of some of its most popular games. Landing the contract would supercharge Fastpoint's growth.

Up until that point, all the conversations had been either trans-actional or positional, with Garrett asking what TSN wanted and, in return, telling them how Fastpoint could help and making his case for why his company was the best option. Garrett thought he was doing everything a good salesperson should do, and yet, he couldn't get TSN to commit.

Then one day the TSN decision maker, Geoff, announced he was coming to Los Angeles and was going to make time to visit the Fast-point offices in person. Garrett was thrilled, not only because Geoff was the one who could finally agree to a deal, but because Garrett had grown to admire Geoff as he learned more about his climb up the ranks in the highly competitive digital sports media industry. He wouldn't have called it this at the time, but Garrett had fallen in love with Geoff, or really the *idea* of him since they hadn't met. The in-person conversation they were about to have was to have a massive impact on Garrett's approach to sales.

When Geoff arrived, Garrett couldn't wait to talk to him. He asked questions he hadn't thought to ask earlier in the sales process; questions about Geoff's goals for the project, personal and profes-sional, about the company's history and the significance of the games to TSN's readers. Most importantly, they discussed collaboration. In-stead of just talking about pros and cons and product details and tech-nology specs, they talked about what working together would look like, how they'd grow the brands together, and how to solve poten-tial roadblocks as a team. At times, they challenged each other and identified potential showstoppers, but then worked out ways to solve them. To Garrett, it didn't feel like a sales conversation at all. It was a transformational conversation, which was invigorating, strategic, re-warding, and downright fun. Two weeks later, Garrett got word that

TSN was moving forward with the deal, which was, at the time, the largest of its kind in the industry.

Sell Yourself First

Before we turn the page on falling in love, there's one more trend we noticed in our conversations with Unsold-minded sellers: It's not just their prospects they fall in love with. A question we're often asked is, "Do you have to believe in what you're selling in order to be a great seller?" There's no way around this; the answer is *yes*. Unfortunately, there are plenty of people out there selling products they don't believe in to customers who don't really need them. They're often the ones perpetuating the stereotype of the "typical salesperson," saying whatever they need to say to convince customers (and themselves) that the purchase is a good idea. They might think the product is fine, but they know deep down (or, sometimes, not-so-deep down) if the customer knew what they knew, they wouldn't buy. Maybe they don't actually need it, the quality isn't where it should be, there are competitors with a better option, or they just flat out won't get more value out of it than the money they're putting in. Even those who are generally honest and trying their best to do the right thing can leave us with a bad taste in our mouths in situations where they don't believe in what they're selling and try to fake it.

On the other hand, people with an Unsold Mindset wholeheartedly believe in whatever idea, product, or service they're selling. It's impossible to be truly great at selling, and feel proud doing it, without being excited about how the customer will benefit from what you are selling. We're not saying you have to be passionate about the product you sell, or even be a potential customer yourself. There are plenty of people selling products and services to people and businesses that they would never use themselves. We even spoke with a team that sold refuse services (we're talking high-volume trash pickup!) and their top salesperson LOVES her job, and she's damn good at it. What we *are* saying is that you need to know that what you're selling is right for the person you're selling it to and *love* that you have the chance to share that with them.

This rule is important if we want to be great at selling anything, even in non-traditional selling situations. Robert Simon, the trial lawyer we met in chapter 1, told us it's important for him to fall in love with his clients (yes, he used those very words) before he gets in front of a jury on their behalf. He told us about a client who had been injured in a car accident. Unfortunately, even though the client had a compelling case, Robert wasn't relating well to him. The client had engaged Robert to represent him in a case that was almost certain to go to trial. "Selling" to a jury might be as difficult a sale as there is. Imagine if you were not only selling against a competitor, but that competitor was there in the room with you, trying to poke holes in your "sale" in real time while the customers (jury) sit right there watching! Any sign of doubt or insecurity about what you're selling can be the difference between a huge win for your client or walking away with nothing.

Robert knew this, and because he wasn't really connecting with his client or his story, he was considering dropping the case and referring him to a different attorney. But before he did this, he decided to dig deeper and go to the client's home to learn more about him and the impact his injury had on his life. While there, they got into a surprisingly deep and candid transformational conversation. Robert learned that the client and his wife had struggled through years of infertility before having their daughter. Coincidentally, Robert and his wife were going through the very same struggle. They talked about the emotional toll of the experience, and the client gave Robert advice and support that only someone who'd been in the same position could give. "When I first met him, he wasn't the type of person you just fall in love with. But once I heard his story, I knew exactly what he'd gone through because I was going through it myself, and I just wanted to fight for him," Robert told us that one conversation, and the loving mindset it fostered, led him to take the case, which he ultimately won for the client and his family.

Robert's need to believe in what he's "selling" isn't unique. One salesperson we interviewed told us, "Every job I've ever had has been the best job I've ever had." What he meant was, every time he works for a company, he intentionally falls in love with the product he's selling, the company he works for and its culture, and, most importantly, the customers he gets to work with. Imagine the difference between a conversation with someone thinking that way, versus someone who is merely going through the motions selling something they don't actually believe in to people they don't actually care about.

• • •

We once had a speaking gig at a sales kickoff meeting for ADS, a company that sells equipment to the US military. The sales team consisted of about two hundred people, many of whom were veterans who had become salespeople after reentering civilian life. Leading up to the event, we had some serious debates about whether we wanted to talk about *falling in love* with a group of hardened ex-armed forces. *Will they just tune us out?* we wondered. *Or worse, will they laugh us out of the room?* In the end, we opted to go all in with our lessons on love and sales. *If we can get this crowd to fall in love with falling in love, we'll* know *we're onto something,* we decided.

After the event, we spoke with the CEO of the company, Jason Wallace. "When you guys started talking about love I was nervous," he admitted. "I thought the room was going to eat you alive. But a couple minutes in I realized, 'this is exactly what my team needs to hear.' Everyone could relate to how great it feels to interact with someone where both parties are *giving each other energy* and watching them realize they could do that intentionally was really something to see."

From the briefest loving connections made in a sales call to the most profound transformative experience, all the bonds we form through selling become uplifting ballast in our lives. The more we're actively cultivating an authentic feeling of love for our clients, for colleagues we're selling to, and also, of course, with all those we encounter in any situation in our day-to-day lives, the happier we'll be; so much more energized and eager to have the next conversation, so much less focused on worries about how calls and speeches will go or whether we'll close the next client. We'll find we are living more in the moment in every selling experience, and in the rest of our lives, too; more attuned to the opportunities for connection, which inevitably leads to making more and more of them every day. All of this, of course, leads to a more enriching and textured life.

CHAPTER SIX

Be a Teammate, Not Just a Coach

During the early days of the COVID-19 pandemic, just days after the world had been sent home from work in hopes of curbing the spread of the virus, we watched a recording of a Zoom call between a salesperson and a prospect at the request of a client of ours. The client had asked us to help the company's team cope with the stresses of their new daily routines, which had been profoundly changed by the effects of the virus. The salesperson started the call, introduced himself, and then said something to the prospect we weren't expecting. "I'm not really sure how to have this conversation, or if we're even *supposed* to be having it. I know we both have jobs to do, but this is crazy and a little scary, if I'm being honest! I guess all I'm saying is, this is my first pandemic, and I felt the need to acknowledge how weird it feels to be talking business right now."

As if the seller's genuine opening statement wasn't refreshing enough, the prospect's response was even more unexpected. With a warm, relieved smile, she said, "Tell me about it, we're in the same boat. I started this job just a couple of months before COVID hit, and I haven't even met most of my co-workers yet!" She then uttered five of the most beautiful words a potential customer can say: "We'll figure it out together."

Just like that, the typical dynamic of the seller taking control of a conversation, focused on nothing but the close, was flipped on its head. Instead of the usual seller-versus-customer way of thinking, the conversation that followed was rooted in camaraderie and understanding. From that point forward, they spoke about their time in quarantine like two friends. Then, *twelve minutes* into the call, the prospect took the initiative and cheerfully said, "Well, how about we get down to business so we can keep these jobs we're complaining about?" They both laughed and went on to have a great conversation *from the same side of the table*, even though they weren't even in the same state, let alone the same room.

As we compared this exchange to other examples we'd seen of sellers and prospects coming together in a united front, we realized we had discovered another key to the success, and happiness, of people who sell with an Unsold Mindset: They see themselves and the people they're selling to as members of *the same team.*

The Culture of Me versus the World

Thinking this way might sound like an obvious thing to do, but it isn't always easy, or natural. There's often an inherent distrust from customers when they know they're speaking with a salesperson, and this is often met with pushback from the seller as they fight to change the other person's mind. On top of this, sales trainings, the dynamics of managing business teams, experiences being sold to, and cultural depictions of selling have all conspired to instill the widespread notion that selling is a competition. Most sales team cultures breed a me-versus-them mindset, often intentionally. Even though we're said to be on a *team*, an elaborate infrastructure of carrots and sticks is geared toward driving us to behave like lone wolves with both colleagues and customers, each with our own goals, working independently of each other.

We've all been part of it in some way, either as an audience member or the one whose results are being compared to others via leaderboards plastered on giant flatscreens for all to see who's at the bottom. We love our commission check ceremonies, unless we're not the ones being celebrated but the ones being demoralized by being forced to see how much more money other people are making than we are. It's no secret compensation plans too often drive the exact opposite behavior customers want sellers to engage in. We heard about one manager who rearranged desks every Monday in order of highest performer to lowest. Imagine how inspired the underperformers are when they come in to take their seats for the week with one leg of their chair poking into the men's restroom. All of this encourages a mentality that we've got to be out for ourselves. *If it's not going to contribute to my commission, I'm not doing it.*

This built-in culture of antagonism isn't just limited to sales professionals. In many fields, colleagues are measured against one another, with managers often admonishing team members when they're not matching up to others. At most companies, we're siloed off from each other into functional groups—marketing, product, engineering, customer success, finance, human resources, and of course, sales, to name a few—which often leads to an adversarial culture that undermines getting the best overall results. If you work at a company like this, the marketing group might seem to exist purely to blame sales for not converting enough of their leads. Sales, in turn, might constantly gripe about the engineering team focusing on building the wrong features for the wrong customers. The operations team might blame the product team for making too many changes to the product roadmap.

And these are just the people who are working for the same company. Among the unfortunate effects of cultivating this me-against-them mentality in the workplace is that it carries over to customer interactions as well. We're expected to "win" the deal, "overcome" objections, "beat" our forecasts, "crush" the competition. This mentality isn't just the result of mental osmosis; countless books, blogs, and podcasts on sales and marketing explicitly promote methods of gaming potential customers into buying, treating them like adversaries to be outwitted, or duped.

When Persuasion Becomes Coercion

Many of the game-like selling techniques touted in books and trainings are based on psychological studies of persuasion. They often have clever little names, like the "Door in the Face" technique. That one is based on research by psychologist Robert Cialdini but had been used in many shapes and forms prior to his findings. The essential tactic goes like this: If a salesperson makes a request that is considered by the prospect too much to ask for and the prospect turns it down by (literally or figuratively) slamming a door in the face of the seller, the seller then makes a lesser ask, and the prospect is much more likely to agree to it. Say the first ask was that someone pay $2,000 to attend a political figure's fundraising dinner, for which, in addition to a five-star meal, they'll receive a set of commemorative wineglasses. The second ask might be that they donate $200, for which they'll get the glasses and reserved seating at an upcoming rally. People will accept the second request far more often than if the fundraiser has made that request in the first place. Why does the tactic work? Cialdini argued that it's due to the strong ethic of reciprocity we discussed in chapter 5. Because the seller is seen as having made a concession, the prospect feels an obligation to return that favor.

Another popular gamesmanship technique is the "if I could, would you?" tactic. Imagine the seller is discussing pricing, and the prospect doesn't see enough value to justify the cost, so they decline. The seller then says, "I'm not sure I can, but *if* I could get $X approved, *would* you move forward then?" The seller actually knows they can offer the lower price yet *acts* as if they don't have the power to approve it. Not only do they not want to offer it until the prospect commits, but they also want to come across as having really gone to bat for the customer. They're acting like they're bending over backward for the customer while in fact they're playing them better than a Jimi Hendrix guitar solo.

These tactics, and so many more that can be weaponized by unscrupulous sellers, generally exploit irrational cognitive biases wired into our brains. In chapter 4 we talked about how and why we are hardwired to process negative emotions more thoroughly than positive ones. A side effect of this is the bias of loss aversion that sales authority Zig Ziglar described when he wrote our "fear of loss is greater than the desire for gain." Many studies have proven this, including a 2016 study by Simon Schindler and Stefan Pfattheicher, which concluded that people are more willing to take risks (or even behave dishonestly) to avoid a loss than make a gain.

Other win-no-matter-what tactics have emerged with the evolution of technology. Companies pay good money for tools that make it look like the salesperson is calling from the same area code as the phone they're calling in hopes of tricking the prospect to pick up. Some salespeople presumptively send calendar invites to prospects with the objective of getting them to show up on a call they never agreed to. Automation makes it *seem* like emails and social media messages are personalized (until you get one that begins, "Hi [FIRST NAME] . . .").

These methods obviously perpetuate the stereotype of salespeople being manipulative, and while they are sometimes effective in the short term, they weigh on the psyches of sellers (and customers) over time. Many people we've worked with have expressed discontent about these practices, which contributes to why so many aren't proud to be in sales. This shame, of course, also triggers stereotype threat and its various negative consequences.

On top of those psychological punishments, the "win by manipulation" tactics often backfire. One study found that marketing and sales pitches designed to persuade (as opposed to merely inform) can lead to a significant decline in the desired response by prospects. Assessing the results of a Centers for Disease Control campaign to encourage people to get a vaccine to protect against the flu, the study found that the overtly persuasive pitches led to a 39 percent drop in expressed intent to get vaccinated among those who were wary of the vaccine. The negative response to persuasion efforts is thought to be due in part to "psychological reactance," the tendency for people to respond negatively to attempts to get them to do things that they perceive are hampering their agency and freedom of choice.

Those selling with an Unsold Mindset aren't adversarial about selling. They're not looking to find a weak spot in an opponent's defenses to exploit. They approach conversations with a *Same Team mentality*, in which they see themselves in alignment with prospects, working together toward a common goal. Their job is to support prospects, have their back, and ultimately do right by them. They don't see sales as a zero-sum game. If something isn't good for a prospect, then it isn't good for them.

To be clear, this isn't us sitting up in an ivory tower casting stones at people who employ the selling tactics we describe in this chapter (or anywhere else in this book). We get it. We've been there, and it's not always easy to avoid the path of least resistance when things are working just fine and you don't feel like you're hurting anyone in the process. We know the psychology of influence really does drive behavior, and that's not easy to ignore. We also understand what it feels like to not only have the company depending on you, but also your family, your team, and their families, too. We didn't write this book to judge other people's ethical comfort zones, we wrote it because, based on our research, the *real* reasons people are successful and happy (or not) at selling have nothing to do with tactics like the ones we just described, and we hope you agree. If we all know we have a choice, why *wouldn't we* choose differently when it benefits us and the people we're selling to?

As Simon Sinek wrote in his bestselling book *Start with Why*, "There are only two ways to influence human behavior. You can manipulate it or you can inspire it." If you're on your prospect's team, there's no incentive or benefit to manipulation, so inspiration is the only option.

Why "We" Works

As we interviewed successful (and happy) sellers, we saw that the Same Team mentality had become second nature to many of them.

It's built into the foundation of their work habits, and they reap the rewards daily. You can hear it in the way they speak to people, conveying a genuine desire to help, and in the way they react to challenges or objections without getting defensive or deceptive.

One top selling cardiothoracic medical device salesperson told us he once met with a doctor who loved the *Godfather* movies. "Not only did he reference them often, but you could tell they informed a big piece of who he was, how he viewed the world, even possibly how he made decisions," the salesperson told us. But that wasn't the point; he genuinely enjoyed working with this doctor. They had built a relationship and he wanted to understand the doctor better, not because it would help him sell more products, but because he actually cared about his "teammate." He couldn't appreciate the doctor's affection for the movies because he had never watched them. He decided to check them out and ended up *loving* them. Because of this, he didn't just watch them, he read commentary on blogs and message boards, collected his favorite quotes ("A man who doesn't spend time with his family can never be a real man"), and had a bunch of questions! The next time he saw the doctor, he told him, "Hey Doc, finally watched the Trilogy . . . I get it! Let's catch up soon." They went to lunch soon after, and the Corleone Family was the main topic of conversation. From that point on, they were on the same team, not because the salesperson watched the movies, but because he authentically felt a desire to put in the work to understand something that mattered so much to someone he viewed as being on the same team.

One company we worked with intentionally tasked its sales team members with serving as their customers' points of contact for frontline support issues. Even though the company had a customer support team to handle any issues that couldn't be immediately resolved, customers would always communicate with their sales representative first. Many businesses would consider this an unwelcome distraction, taking salespeople's precious time away from clear revenue-generating activities, but a huge part of this company's business was renewals, and communicating with each customer before the end of each contract period was critical. By having their sales rep helping customers with support, the company ensured that its reps and customers were constantly communicating from the same side of the table, with reps positioned as advocates fighting on the customer's behalf whenever they required resources to resolve an issue.

Treating prospects like team members, with whom you're working to advance toward a common goal, is effective and psychologically rewarding for lots of reasons. For one thing, it breaks through the invisible wall most prospects put up when they sense they're being sold to. Asking someone questions with the intention of understanding how to join them in their cause, as opposed to merely trying to gather enough information to sell them on something, creates a whole new dynamic. Selling with a Same Team mindset makes each step of the sales process a collaboration, not a competition. The seller's job shifts from convincing and persuading to teaching and empowering. When you're on the same team, a decision isn't *your* idea, it's *theirs.* Or better yet, *ours.*

The Natural Impact of Collaboration

Another reason the Same Team mentality works is because it satisfies our innate desire to work together, to pool our complementary talents for the greater good. Many argue that humans are naturally combative, but biologists and anthropologists who've probed into the roots of human behavior have emphasized that our natural inclination to try to get along, collaborate, help each other, and even sacrifice some of our own good fortune for the sake of others, is at least as powerful.

Modern hunter-gatherer societies are considered representative of the earliest form of human civilization and therefore prime examples of our most natural way of living. Good teamwork seems to be a core value for them. In a number of these groups, like the Hadza people of Tanzania and the Agta people of the Philippines, researchers have found a strong ethic of combining forces in the work of foraging and hunting. The best hunters don't go off on their own and keep their prey for themselves; they lead hunting parties and the groups divvy up the meat among their families. Group members also work in teams when foraging for fruits, nuts, and grains, and caregivers share responsibility for all the tribe's children.

Psychologists studying young children have also found evidence of an innate desire to help others and to join in teams. One study found that nineteen-month-old children were eager to share a piece of fruit with a stranger, even though every parent knows kids *love* sugar in any form they can get it, including fruit. The children were seated at a table with strawberries placed on a plate in front of them. Then, a man they'd never seen before entered the room, sat down near them, and reached for a strawberry, which he dropped, seemingly by accident, but really by design, so it was out of his reach. When the children saw that he was struggling to pick up the strawberry, they handed him one. And they did so even when they were very hungry.

More evidence comes from the study of how children choose to play. By the age of three to four, children begin spontaneously playing in groups with one another, engaging in what's called "associative play," sharing toys and often collaborating, making up games, even with kids they've just met. They've already learned a lesson that the stresses of work life and its pressures to compete can make us quick to forget: working together toward a common end is simply more fun—and rewarding—than watching out for ourselves.

Redefining Empathy

Usually when we're teaching teams about the benefits of a Same Team mentality, someone will suggest that the reason it's so effective is that it forces sellers to have empathy for those they're selling to. It's not surprising this comes to mind; in traditional sales training, the word "empathy" gets thrown around profusely. The internet is also flooded with commentary about it. In fact, as of the time of this writing, if you google "empathy in sales" you'll get almost 37 million results! Almost universally, when people write about empathy in sales, they're talking about putting yourself in the customer's shoes, trying to get a sense of their pain and frustration, and seeking to understand their perspective. That's great, as far as it goes. But there is a problem with the way being empathetic is often presented—as another means of manipulation.

Scrolling through articles about sales empathy on the internet can be an exercise in cringiness. "Empathy is like a sales superpower," proclaims one headline, "*use it right* [emphasis ours] and you'll build rapport with buyers, get insights into their business, and box out the competition." The implication is that empathy can be weaponized. An article in the *Harvard Business Review* titled "What Makes a Good Salesman" even compared having empathy for prospects to the precision-guided power of heat-seeking missiles, allowing sellers to "home in and hit their marks."

Using an awareness of others' feelings to get them to agree to a purchase or give you the buy-in you're looking for isn't empathy at all. When you're feeling stressed or upset, are you hoping that a seller will come along and take advantage of that? Obviously not. So a seller who perceives that someone is frustrated, worried, lonely, etc., and consciously thinks about how to use that perception to close a sale is not really feeling what that person is feeling. Also beware that feeling genuine empathy is often much trickier than the torrent of articles suggests. Has someone ever said to you "I know how you feel," when you know damn well there's no way they know how you feel? Recall our earlier discussion of authenticity and how acutely sensitive people can be to bullshit.

Does this mean you shouldn't try to be empathetic? Not at all. The key is your mindset about what being empathetic means and how you try to develop it. While we probably all have a general notion of what empathy entails, science has shown it's not just feeling what someone else does. In *Unleash Your Primal Brain*, Tim Ash nicely summarizes a vast amount of research on empathy, introducing the finding that "To be empathetic requires three distinct processes to come together":

- Mind reading—mirroring and mentalizing to understand what another is thinking
- Affect matching—synchronizing your mental state and outward actions and gestures with theirs
- Empathic motivation—proactively wanting to help the person with little regard for one's own needs

Ash highlights that "If the chain is broken at any point, *empathetic behavior* will not occur" (emphasis ours). In other words, if we aren't motivated to take action to help the other person, we don't have true empathy.

That's why we don't teach people to *have* empathy, we teach people to *give* empathy. *Having* empathy for someone is about you. It's you changing the way *you* think and feel about a person and their situation in order to understand them better. That's only a first step, and it doesn't earn you the right to be on the same team. *Giving* empathy is all about them. It's about making the other person *feel understood* and working with them to make sure you really do understand what they're feeling and how you can help them. Which brings us to why a Same Team mentality helps cultivate true empathy for prospects; it turns our focus toward helping prospects rather than working them.

So, if thinking like you're on the same team works but isn't always natural in selling situations, how can we cultivate this mentality, and then convey it to those we're selling to?

Act Like a Teammate, Not a Coach

We've seen so many sales efforts fail largely because the seller dominated and controlled the conversation, acting more like a coach to prospective customers than a teammate. We know this can be confusing since being a "coach" has positive connotations, especially in the sales world. And there is certainly a time and a place to be a coach, teaching the prospect what you know, saving them from their own biases and shortcomings, and pushing them toward the best outcome.

But even better than having a coach on your side is having a teammate. Like a coach, teammates also want what's best for you, but instead of telling you what to do, they're in the trenches *with* you. They're learning as you learn and have just as much at stake. Yankee legend (and human quotebook) Yogi Berra once said, "When you're part of a team, you stand up for your teammates. Your loyalty is to them. You protect them through good and bad because they'd do the same for you." Sellers with a Same Team mentality feel this way, and it changes the way they interact with those on "their team."

We can develop our Same Team consciousness by labeling and acknowledging when we're showing up too much like a coach, at best, or adversarial, self-interested, or manipulative, at worst. With intention, this is easy to do in the moment, or in hindsight when reviewing calls or past conversations. Can you identify times in your conversations when you're feeling the need to be "right," as if you have all the answers and the person you're talking to does not? Usually, this is easiest to spot when an objection pops up. You might find yourself interrupting or waiting to speak instead of truly listening. You might then rattle off a rebuttal that, even though technically correct, doesn't really address the actual concern.

If this sounds like you, try stepping back the next time a customer voices a concern and ask different questions, ones you really want answers to so you can understand. Is what they're saying really the issue, or is there more to it? Maybe they're saying they don't need the solution right now, when in truth, they would like to purchase it but don't quite have the budget to. Maybe they see all the value in the world in what you're selling, but they worry purchasing would made them look bad. What questions do you need to ask, do you *want* to ask, and what do you need to fully understand, to act as a teammate helping solve a problem instead of a salesperson trying to win a deal?

The advice to ask clarifying questions in the face of objections has been around since the first caveman salesperson tried upselling his neighbor on "premium" stone wheels, but when you shift your mindset to ask them from a Same Team mentality, genuinely looking for ways to win together, the tone and depth of your conversations might change completely. In time, you'll progress from hearing yourself inadvertently trying to win, to more naturally showing up as a teammate. When you meet someone like this, you're grateful because they treat you as an equal. They're kind, and not dishonest, so you can count on them to be real with you, do the right thing, and have your back.

Level the Playing Field

When you think about people who sell for a living, doctors aren't likely the first people that jump to mind, but in reality, many doctors are selling patients on life-and-death decisions every day as they work with them to select treatment options or make lifestyle changes that sometimes last for life. Dr. David Agus is a world-renowned cancer doctor who has treated everyone from singers (Neil Young calls him "my mechanic") to celebrities (Howard Stern swears he saved co-host Robin Quivers's life) to titans of business (Salesforce.com CEO Mark Benioff anointed him "a prophet") to political figures (he's treated Al Gore and Ted Kennedy). He's even credited with adding seven years to his late friend Steve Jobs's life. When we spoke with Dr. Agus, he talked a lot about his version of the Same Team approach to sales. "There is no one right way to treat a patient," he told us. "My job is to educate, and together with the patient make the right decision for them. It's not to tell a patient what to do. There's a misconception that you have to go and get an opinion from a doctor. What we really have to do is give them all the data to let them make the right decision for themselves. So in a sense it's a joint decision."

To make his patients comfortable and truly convey to them that they really are on the same team, working *together* on a treatment, Dr. Agus eschews anything that might create the perception of rank or status. "I don't wear a white coat and I don't set a division between myself and my patients. At my office and my clinic I'm not behind a big desk. Instead, I have a table because I want us to be equal."

His orchestration of a level clinical playing field was no accident. "Steve Jobs told me once," Dr. Agus recounted to us, "that if you go into a room with a patient and you stand up versus sit down, they perceive half the amount of time you spent with them. If you actually sit, you'll have a much deeper conversation with them."

MindMedium CEO Jon Dahan also strategically crafts the setting of his meetings with prospects to impact his mindset. Whenever he's hosting an important sales meeting, he brings food and serves people himself. He told us he thinks of clients like family, and eating together is how his family shows love and connection. He says serving them food also takes him out of "sales mode," so he feels freer to be himself, and his customers respond in kind.

Another way to establish Same Team rapport is with "walking meetings," a practice both of us have borrowed from Steve Jobs because it changes the dynamic of our conversations. Instead of sitting in a conference room or office, we'll head outside and take a stroll. Walking meetings can break down hierarchies between people, and we've found we much prefer the connection that comes from walking side by side rather than sitting across a table. Both parties are, quite literally, on equal footing and not subject to the power dynamics that come from who's sitting in what seat or behind a fancy desk or on their "home turf." An added benefit is that walking meetings have been found to inspire more creative discussion. And hey, even if the meeting doesn't go well, at least you get to burn off the calories from that fifth slice of pepperoni mushroom pizza slathered in ranch you had for lunch! (Or maybe that's just us.)

Next time you have an in-person sales meeting, try setting the location in the calendar invite for a walk around the block instead of a physical location. They may or may not accept the offer, but at the very least they'll appreciate you tried, be pleasantly surprised, and feel grateful you gave them the opportunity to get outside and away from their screen. The effort alone would say more about your uniqueness as a seller than any pitch you'll ever give.

There's No "I" in Sales

When we first met our literary agent, who was instrumental in getting this book published, it was our last meeting at the end of two long but exciting days of meeting with potential agents. Candidly, we thought we'd already decided to work with someone else based on an amazing meeting we'd had earlier, but all of that changed when we met Lisa DiMona. The entire conversation was special, but afterward, when people asked us how the meeting went, we cut straight to the end: "We hugged goodbye." Who hugs? Families hug. Friends hug. Teammates hug. Not usually people who just met at a business meeting. Lisa didn't hug us to sell us on working with her and the team at Writers House. Quite the opposite, she told us we had a whole lot of work to do before that could happen. It's what she said right afterward that made hugging at the end of the meeting feel natural. She said if we were willing to do the work, she would help get us to where we needed to be. We left that meeting feeling like we had a new member of our team.

Don't hesitate to be explicit about your desire to work with a prospect and support them. We've seen time and again how expressions of this intent transform sales interactions into collaborations. One great seller we know had a very mistrusting prospect. No matter what he said, the prospect would question the validity of the claim. Then one day, when the seller had had enough, he calmly asked what he'd been thinking: "How *will* you know I have your back?" The question opened up a beautiful conversation about setting success milestones and the importance of advocating for someone, even when they don't know it's happening.

Even just being inclusive in your language can be remarkably powerful. The word "we" is in heavy rotation in conversations Unsold-minded sellers have with prospects. The difference in the effect between *"you're* going to . . ."* and *"we're* going to . . ."* is palpable in the tone and body language when we observe sales interactions; we can feel people removing barriers, leaning in, and effectively rolling up their sleeves to work together. Both parties feel the impact of the shift, in part because the word "we" sends an important signal that the person selling has made a mental shift from trying to win to being on the other person's side.

Find Common Ground

In *Think Again,* Adam Grant points out that the best negotiators spend more prep time looking for opportunities to agree with their counterparts and identifying concessions they can make than they do on crafting arguments about why they're right. Similarly, instead of focusing on building a case against any possible objections or misgivings a potential customer might have, sellers with an Unsold Mindset turn their attention to looking for *common ground.*

We've found that in preparing for sales situations, people often obsess over what could go wrong. When researching their prospects, they want to identify as many potential roadblocks as they can. Do they already work with a competitor? Are they going to have issues with our pricing model? Are there other decision makers that need to be included? Asking these questions and preparing for how to discuss them is an important part of preparation, for sure. But for every minute you spend planning for these concerns, spend three minutes looking for things that you *already* agree on.

One salesperson we worked with used a simple-but-effective way to keep herself focused on common ground. She kept notes for every call on a yellow legal pad, and before each call she drew a vertical line down the entire page about a third of the way across. Her normal call notes went on the right side of the line, but the left side was reserved for what she called "handshakes"—the things she and her customer agreed upon. Some of them were clearly related to the sale. She might write, *Building a solution internally would be costly, but it is an option,* or *Ensuring this has 99 percent uptime during business hours is non-negotiable.* Other things on her list showed that she had engaged in a wide-ranging conversation and discovered entirely different types of commonality, such as *Election Day should be a holiday,* for example, or *hot dogs are actually sandwiches.* She was conditioning herself to look for all of the ways she was *already* on her customer's team, and not only did she close a higher percentage of her prospects than her peers, she also received more referrals from her existing customers than anyone else on her team.

Put Some Skin in the Game

Think about instances when you asked a server what was especially good on a menu and they suggested the most expensive options. Then think about when a server suggested the cheap, greasy-yet-delicious option and told you it's what they had for lunch right before starting their shift and they loved it. Whose advice did you trust? When a waiter suggests that the $14 fish and chips is better than the $34 lobster roll, he's well aware that you would rack up a higher bill if he pushed the lobster, but he's willing to sacrifice some tip to help you have a more satisfying meal.

When customers feel supported by you in this way, knowing that you're making a genuine sacrifice, no matter how small, for their benefit, the entire dynamic of the relationship shifts. Most people have heard of real estate agents giving up a portion of their commission to get a deal done, but we've also seen agents invest *their own money* in projects they're working on with their clients. Shahin Yazdi, managing partner at George Smith and Partners, a prestigious commercial real estate group in Los Angeles, reinvests a portion of his commissions back into his clients' projects. "It creates the type of balance I long for in professional relationships," he told us. "Their success is my success, and vice versa." This is also the fundamental premise of deal-making in venture capital; founders are willing to give VCs a literal seat at the table in the boardroom of their beloved enterprises where key decisions are made largely because the VCs have put up a substantial sum of their fund's money.

When Will Smith was first making the transition from rapper and TV star to movie actor, he told his manager, James Lassiter, known as "JL," that he wanted to be "the biggest movie star in the world." With this goal in mind, JL got to work reading every script he could get his hands on. One day JL showed up at Will's house with some big news. "All right, look—there's a studio that wants you to costar in a gangster movie called *8 Heads in a Duffel Bag.* They're prepared to pay you ten million dollars." Will freaked out. It was more money than he'd ever made before, even as a successful musician. But JL wasn't done. "And I came here to advise you *not* to take it," he said. "It's not right."

Will couldn't believe it. As his manager, JL stood to earn a 15 percent commission—$1.5 million—for *himself* (he was also still living in his childhood bedroom at his mother's house). But he was telling Will not to take the job. "Tom Cruise wouldn't take this role," JL said. As a manager, Will was JL's customer, and JL knew that to truly be on his customer's team he needed to have his back, believe in the same vision, and take the risk *with* him. Will said no to the $10 million and took a role in the movie *Six Degrees of Separation* for $300,000 instead. He more than held his own among a cast of award-winning industry pros, and had taken the first major step toward his goal to become the biggest movie star in the world.

We're not suggesting that you have to invest your own money or leave seven figures on the table to put yourself in the Same Team mindset. There are plenty of non-monetary ways to put skin in the game. It can be as simple as resisting the urge to sell someone more than they need, disagreeing with a prospect at the risk of upsetting them because you know it's in their best interest, allowing a customer to make a decision in their own time without pressure, or committing to spend extra time with them to help them after a sale is made to ensure their success. For non-sales sellers, you likely have even more opportunities to creatively drive alignment, ensuring that you only win when the person you're selling to does. The long-term benefits of finding ways to put skin in the game make it easy to make these short-term sacrifices; more customers, more referrals, and, most importantly, the psychological benefits that come from acting with integrity and doing the opposite of what the salesperson who hates their job would do.

Partners, Not Customers

One of the first things we advise early-stage startups to do when they need to optimize for revenue is define their ideal *partners*. An ideal partner is different from an ideal *customer*. A perfect customer might be a certain sized company with a certain budget. A perfect partner, on the other hand, might be an early adopter willing to put up with frequent product updates and provide candid feedback. It might be an angel investor with a large network of other potential partners. It might be a big company whose logo on the website provides just as much value as a contract would. Thinking of those we're selling to as partners rather than customers, believing it, and truly treating them that way, is a powerful means of showing up with a Same Team mentality and manifesting a true teammate dynamic.

One of our clients' enterprise sales reps approached every prospecting call as if he was assembling a team of superheroes like Nick Fury recruiting the Avengers. He knew having the right partners by his side in each of the verticals into which he was trying to sell signaled to the market that his company was on the rise, was trusted by industry stalwarts, and had the ability to handle the specific challenges that vertical represented. Yes, these partners would help boost his firm's growth more than displaying a haphazard bunch of logos on the firm's website, as so many service companies do, but they would also change the way his company did business. He knew that he could be open about this strategy with his chosen partners. He told them something his CEO had impressed upon him, "We're creating an industry, and we believe that starts by picking the right partners, ones that are representative of their entire vertical, who define innovation in the space, who know what leadership looks like and want a seat at the table."

Because he had shifted his mindset to look for partners instead of customers, the way he spoke to his prospects changed. He wasn't just talking the talk. Instead of handing off his clients to his company's account management team and never speaking to them again, as so many sales reps do, he created a quarterly forum where he got all of them together to discuss not only the product and the future roadmap, but general challenges they were facing in their industry. He lived up to his end of the partnership bargain by providing them a place to be heard, and by introducing them to peers at other companies so they could compare notes and build up their own networks. He also provided regular updates about how their feedback was being implemented.

Look for ways you can offer a seat at the table to clients so they can help drive the vision for you and your company's success. Create your own "Partner Advisory Board," a coalition of partners who can give you candid feedback on a regular basis to help you improve your strategy, product, or support. Find ways to let your partners celebrate your success. One startup we knew of hosted events with customers to celebrate together whenever a milestone in the firm's growth was achieved. Another went out of their way to mention partners by name in press releases when big things happened so the partners benefited from the company's wins in the form of some free publicity.

Don't just look for customers to sign a contract, pay their invoices, and then move on to the next one. Dedicate time during your work-week to reach out to old customers, check in, and elevate surface-level relationships into authentic partnerships. It can lead to amazing relationships, and results.

Picking Teams

Former sports agent and current founder of Sports 1 Marketing, inspirational speaker, and philanthropist David Meltzer told us he became more successful and happier in sales when he realized that he should only spend his energy working with people who were open and willing to work together as teammates. After that epiphany, he told us, "I refused to talk to closed-minded people." If prospects are negative in response to your outreach to them, without even listening or sharing any information that might help you understand how you could help them, move on rather than dig in to try to persuade them. Nobody wants to be persuaded, and normally they're taking precious time away from you finding true partners.

We get that moving on from a prospect is not an easy thing to do when your compensation is dependent on selling to as many customers as you can. But when selling with an Unsold Mindset, people know that in the long run the selectivity pays off. Take the case of investment adviser Dan Conway. Early in his career, he worked at global financial behemoth Shearson Lehman Brothers. He describes the atmosphere there at the time as highly competitive, with no attempt to hide the importance of closing as many clients as possible, no matter what. Every day he was expected to arrive early, make hundreds of calls to wealthy individuals and business owners while reading from a script, and signing as many of them as he could to be clients. For Dan, this felt counter to who he wanted to be as a salesperson. "I wanted to do things differently," he said. "I felt my clients wanted a different level of service. I also wanted to choose the people I worked with as much as they were choosing me, because great advisory relationships go on for decades, sometimes across generations to clients' children and grand-children. So I came up with a new question to ask myself while talking to prospects: Is this a person I would enjoy being stranded on a desert island with? If the answer was 'no' I wouldn't work with them." He says that once he drew that line in the sand, he never had to cold call again because so many of his clients referred others to him. When he decided to leave to open up his own firm, nearly every one of his clients stuck with him.

Others have shared similar yardsticks for selecting their custom-ers: *Would I have a beer after work with this person? Does this person give me energy or take it away? Would I hire this person if I knew I had to work with them every day?* Coming up with a benchmark of your own can be a valuable exercise, especially if you have lots of customers who drain your time and energy. Many people don't believe they have the luxury to be selective about who they work with, but one glaring com-monality across those with an Unsold Mindset is they know they can.

Selling shouldn't require taking a beating from prospects, and this is another way that approaching sales with a Same Team mentality is so effective. In our experience, every prospect you connect with that becomes a teammate is much more valuable to your success than the begrudging prospect you finally convince to make a deal. Team player prospects offer great insight into the future; they tend to help you find other prospects and spread the word; they're a whole lot more fun to interact with; and they provide much needed camaraderie for so many sellers who feel like they're on a team of one.

• • •

In his book *Wanting*, Luke Burgis says, "Transcendent leaders don't insist on the primacy of their own desires. They don't make them the center around which everyone and everything must revolve. Instead, they shift the center of gravity away from themselves and toward a transcendent goal, so that they can stand shoulder to shoulder with others." In the same way the leaders Burgis describes "shift the center of gravity" from themselves to a bigger goal, sellers with an Unsold Mindset take the focus away from themselves, their company, or their product, and shift it toward the outcome that's best for their customer.

Being on the same team and conditioning yourself to stay in that mindset consistently will almost surely take some practice. The cultural conditioning to treat selling as a game, with prospects as adversaries we're supposed to defeat, is programmed into most of us, even if only subconsciously. But as you keep reminding yourself to be on the same team, not because you have to, but because you enjoy the interactions that result from it, the approach becomes a habit. You'll start seeing all sorts of opportunities to partner with prospective customers and unexpected ways to work together toward common goals. They'll also start to reciprocate. More importantly, the act of selling will shift from being an endless series of contentious battles into a collection of meaningful connections that make the entire process a whole lot more fulfilling.

CHAPTER SEVEN

Transform, Don't Transact

I n cities around the world today it's common to find enterprising chefs hanging out the back windows of food trucks, selling niche cuisines from virtually every country on Earth to long lines of hungry diners. Food trucks are *everywhere,* and it's hard to remember it wasn't always that way. In the mid-2000s, however, most of the world didn't have easy access to the diverse range of reasonably priced cuisines the food truck revolution has offered. Chef Roy Choi was a major force in kicking off that revolution when he brought his Kogi BBQ trucks to the streets of Los Angeles in 2008.

Serving innovative gourmet Korean/Mexican food at street-food prices, the Kogi trucks were unlike anything the food industry had seen. Choi cultivated a close personal relationship with his customers, Tweeting where the trucks would be each day and giving them a sense that they were part of a special group of followers and devotees of his mission to make inventive cooking more accessible. His emergence as a leader of the movement was improbable. Choi is a graduate of the prestigious Culinary Institute of America in New York, and he had worked at four- and five-star restaurants, including at the posh Beverly

Hilton, but when the 2008 recession left him out of work, he took a friend from the Hilton up on his idea of selling tacos from a truck. That might have seemed a major step down, but he was inspired by a vision of how he could help transform the food world.

"It was like what Virgil [Abloh] did with haute fashion," Choi told us. "In the beginning, houses like Louis Vuitton, Chanel, and Christian Dior would look down on streetwear, but eventually they had to succumb to the cultural shift . . . The more chefs I could get to embrace social media and lower pricing and inclusion, the better the world could be, for me *and* for them." To do this he had to get others to buy into his concept, and that wasn't easy at first.

As he described his journey, we were struck by the amount of selling he found himself doing, especially since he'd never thought of himself as a salesperson. First, he had to sell diners on the concept that street food could be something special, and that they didn't need the confines of a restaurant to have a memorable dining experience. Next, to get his idea off the ground, he had to sell investors on the promise that they could get a great return from such an unconventional business model. Lastly, he knew that for his concept to be truly successful, he needed other highly trained chefs to join the movement, so he had to sell them on the idea, too.

"In the beginning, the old chefs were like, 'get off my lawn,' " he recalled. "A lot of the gatekeepers thought we would just be a flash in the pan, that we were just a trend. I was constantly telling them the world is changing. It wasn't a sale of convincing them, closing the deal, and moving on. I was selling a cultural shift. It was getting you, even though you might be a critic of who we are, to understand that this is real, and I care for you, and let me show you how you can come over and be part of this." Choi wasn't just selling a dining concept, he was selling a large-scale transformation of an industry.

The lessons he learned while sparking the food truck revolution have served as the building blocks for one of his latest restaurants, Best Friend, in Las Vegas. It flips the script on the traditional Vegas model of pricey celebrity chef sanctums featuring bouncers, ridiculously expensive cocktail and wine lists, and menus featuring $175 Wagyu beef steaks and $240 caviar sushi rolls. Instead, it's inspired by the casual vibe of Mexican taco joints and Korean dim sum parlors, enlivened with the energy of L.A., celebrating, Choi says, "the culture of the streets, of immigrants, of hip-hop, of the 'hood." The menu features his famous tacos and other food truck specialties at family-friendly prices. He wanted Las Vegas locals to frequent the restaurant, not just tourists up for a splurge. "That's a big sell to a place like Las Vegas," he told us, "but it changed the whole trajectory of what future restaurateurs and entertainment developers are doing for Vegas."

Selling isn't traditionally thought of as a catalyst for major shifts in beliefs, circumstances, or culture, but great sellers don't let that stop them from seeing the potential for those types of changes. They seek opportunities to go beyond the bounds of what's expected of them, and of what conventional wisdom says they should offer to their prospects or buyers. They think beyond the typical notion of selling as a bounded value-equation transaction where "I provide you with this and you compensate me with that." In fact, they don't think transactionally at all. They think *transformationally.*

The Trap of Tit-for-Tat

No one could be blamed for thinking in a purely "this for that" transactional way about selling. After all, at its core selling is about a literal transaction of some kind—I offer you something of value and if you agree it has value to you, you should be willing to provide me with some sort of value back in return for it. The return value might be money, but it might also be things like time, support for an idea, an introduction to a contact, advice, or just about anything else. The trouble is we're taught to think that in any selling exchange we should receive at least as much return value as we've given, otherwise we've been taken advantage of.

This thinking stems in part from how we perceive the most common value exchange we take part in each day, our jobs. In a sense, any job is about this basic sales proposition. We do our work in exchange for compensation, and in that transaction, we expect to get back from our employers an amount commensurate with what we've given. But when it comes to selling to customers, clients, and colleagues, we can find our work much more fulfilling and rewarding if we're *not* keeping a tit-for-tat tally of what we're getting back from them and focus instead on the impact we can have and the transformations we can make.

This is a challenge because, in most types of work, companies encourage us in all sorts of ways to focus intensely on the dollar value of our output. We're told to keep to standards for how much time we devote to customers for each transaction, or to focus our time and efforts on "high value" customers. We're given monetary targets and our performance is quantified. In short, we're made to feel like human cash registers. The implication is that our job isn't to do our best work, our job is to collect money.

Back when Garrett was an associate at a law firm, he was required to track and bill for the time he worked for clients in tenths of an hour. That means he literally had to account for every six minutes of his day! Talk about feeling like a cog in a money-taking machine! He was also judged by the firm's partners, in large part based on the hours he worked rather than the quality of service he provided clients. In one instance, Garrett had been assigned to draft a cease-and-desist letter for a client, a fairly standard form, and it had taken him thirty minutes to write. When he submitted his billing for the project, he was called into the managing partner's office.

"Why did you only bill a half hour for this letter?" the partner asked.

"Because that's exactly how long it took me to write it," Garrett earnestly replied.

"A letter like this should take two hours," the partner admonished. "You need to take more care in your work and not rush things."

But the quality of the work wasn't the issue at all. In fact, the letter was sent on behalf of the client with virtually no changes to Garrett's version. The clear message was: *We are selling time here. Make sure the client doesn't get more value than they are paying for.*

Within a few months, Garrett left the legal profession and never looked back.

We work for so much more than just a paycheck. We want to be proud of our accomplishments; we hope our job will offer us opportunities for rewarding relationships with colleagues and clients; we'd love for it to give us the chance to learn and express our creativity; we want to climb the ranks and achieve status and impact in our industries; and we want to believe that we have an opportunity to make a meaningful contribution to people's lives. This is why we resent it when companies make us feel our work is really all about extracting value (money) from customers and redistributing it to the company and ourselves.

Manipulating Value

In some types of work, the encouragement to think in tit-for-tat terms is especially pronounced, and in traditional sales, it's drilled almost constantly into our awareness. In fact, it's overtly expressed in one of the linchpins of traditional sales training, the Perceived Value Equation:

Perceived Value = Customer's Expected Benefit – Customer's Perceived Cost

The idea is that if a customer isn't buying, it's simply because they don't perceive enough value in what's being offered. Your job as a seller, it's said, is to change their perception. As soon as a customer's expected benefit outweighs their perceived cost, they'll buy. *That's it!* they'll tell you, as if the art of selling could be reduced to three simple variables.

This has led salespeople to manufacture all sorts of ways to lower *perceived* costs and increase *expected* benefits to inflate *perceived* value, often in lieu of *actually* increasing value. These tactics include endlessly evolving types of special offers like sales, volume discounts, or favorable terms; adding bells and whistles like "premium customer support" (as opposed to what, mediocre support?); "white glove" onboarding (aka "regular" onboarding that costs more); or even raising prices to create a perception of luxury or exclusivity.

When these tactics are employed solely for the purpose of artificially boosting perceived value, it's only a matter of time before customers see through them and trust can be irreparably damaged. Even when ancillary add-ons like these are offered altruistically, there's risk. Discounts can lead to a perceived cheapening of what you're offering, or an influx of "bargain hunter" customers who drain resources and aren't good for the long-term health of the business. Special offers tied to claims of scarcity—*Offer only good for the first 20 customers. Act now!*—can turn off customers who know about the discount but don't qualify. Special "improvements" to a product often come across as just salesy gimmicks, rather than real value add-ons—how many times can things be "new and improved"?—and they can even negatively impact the way a company's products are viewed. It's kind of like the fast-food commercial touting a new "hormone-free" chicken sandwich. While the goal is getting customers to think, *Nice, a healthier chicken sando!* many instead ask, *"Wait, so all of your other chicken sandwiches have hormones in them?!?"*

Another problem is that the bar for customers' expectations keeps moving. When someone is buying a car, they *expect* the salesperson to go to their manager and get them a lower down payment. When they're buying software, they *expect* onboarding costs to be waived. And with online comparisons now so easy to make, customers can find out how good (or bad) an offer is instantly. It's offensive when someone acts like they are doing you a favor when they're actually just doing their job.

We saw this up close in a sales team we worked with in the staffing industry. Their large sales team was given permission to offer potential customers up to a 20 percent discount on first engagements "in extreme cases where a discount is required to get them over the hump." The salespeople didn't need approval for the discount, so what do you think happened? *Every* single salesperson ended up giving the maximum discount on *every* single new deal they closed. New customers expected the discount, old customers ended up hearing about it and demanding that *their* contracts be adjusted to the lower prices, and everyone the team spoke to knew the discount was really just a sales tactic.

Even when tactics designed to influence the perceived value equation do produce results, who's proud of resorting to them? Talk about reinforcing the "by any means necessary" sales stereotype. People with an Unsold Mindset don't resort to manipulation of perceived value; they shift their thinking, looking for ways to offer substantive, qualitative value that has the opportunity to be *transformational* and go beyond the transaction at hand. They don't think in tit-for-tat terms. They view their job as being as valuable as they can, always looking for more ways to give away that value, even (especially!) when doing so isn't part of the expected equation. Finding ways to *be valuable* to customers is part of the excitement for them, and hugely satisfying.

The Gift of Giving

In *Give and Take: A Revolutionary Approach to Success,* Adam Grant writes, "Every time we interact with another person at work, we have a choice to make: do we try to claim as much value as we can, or contribute value without worrying about what we receive in return?" He talks about "givers" who, instead of thinking in terms of reciprocity, focus on helping people by *giving value away.* With an Unsold Mindset, giving becomes part of the process.

One example is Jason Wallace, CEO of ADS, the military products distribution company we mentioned in chapter 5. Their products can make the difference between a service member coming home from a deployment or not. Wallace tells his sales team that being genuinely valuable to their customers is their overriding responsibility. Every decision they make about serving customers has to live up to that responsibility. And he walks the talk himself.

He told us about a time he was working with the CEO of a large supplier. Deep into the sales process, Jason realized the supplier's business model was not a fit for ADS, and he was forced to tell the CEO that they wouldn't be able to move forward with their deal. Instead, he introduced the CEO to a smaller competitor to ADS, one with a slightly different business model, which *was* a great fit. The supplier and the competitor made a deal. Jason didn't receive any immediate direct benefit, other than the intrinsic reward of doing right by a potential customer he'd built a genuine friendship with.

As Daniel Pink showcased in his bestselling book *Drive,* research has proven we are more powerfully motivated by intrinsic rewards, and a good deal more fulfilled by them than by extrinsic ones. Other research has found that giving freely to others is one of the greatest sources of intrinsic reward. A wealth of studies have shown that giving to others, whether of our time, money, attention, advice, or even just a little bit of recognition, is a major contributor to our own well-being. For example, a team from Harvard Business School led by Michael Norton conducted an experiment in which they handed envelopes full of money (either $5 or $20) to students on campus. The students were told they had to spend the money by the end of the day, either on themselves or on others, as a gift or a donation to charity. Using a survey, researchers asked subjects to rank their happiness levels at the time they were given the money, and again later in the evening after the money was spent. "We found that people who spent the money on themselves that day weren't happier that evening," said Norton, "but people who spent it on others were. The amount of money, $5 or $20, didn't matter at all. It was only how people spent it that made them happier."

In another experiment, scientists at the National Institutes of Health took magnetic resonance images of nineteen test subjects' brains as they elected to make charitable donations to causes that were important to them. They were able to detect physical changes in the brain in the regions associated with pleasure, trust, and social connection. When contrasted with the fMRI results of subjects who made less altruistic decisions, the results clearly showed the positive impact was far greater as subjects did things for others and not themselves. This positive feeling that stems from giving to others has been called a "helper's high."

As ever, we're hyper-cognizant of the fact that all of us who sell in any way to earn our living still must walk the line between doing things that will benefit us intrinsically and doing things that keep a roof over our heads. We have to be closing deals, or getting buy-in for our ideas, or funding for our startup, or making whatever "sale" is required of us to accomplish the things we want to do in our lives and careers. But we don't have to "always be closing," as the cringey mantra says, and we don't have to keep a constant tally of monetary or other extrinsic payoffs we're getting back for the value we're giving.

We can rest assured we'll get plenty back if we're being valuable— more joy in our work; the fulfillment of living in tune with our values; higher-quality relationships; feeling trusted or significant; and, yes, more financial rewards. When we stop constantly keeping score, we are playing a long game, the game of living a more meaningful, textured life. Over time those with an Unsold Mindset will get back disproportionately more in quality of experience than they would by being trapped in the transactional mentality, and they often find gifts coming back to them in ways they might never have anticipated.

This is exactly what happened to Jason, the CEO at ADS. He kept in touch with the CEO of the supply company he'd introduced to a competitor, and over time their friendship grew, and they became advisors to one another. Years later, the CEO moved to a huge company with a household name that was an ideal partner for ADS. The two have since done millions of dollars of business together. Sometimes the rewards of giving without concern about getting will far exceed whatever compensation you might have calculated you should receive.

We found this out ourselves as we were growing our company. When we were starting out, we said *yes* to any speaking event that came our way. Most of them (let's be honest, *all* of them) at the time were unpaid, but we didn't care. We loved the experience of speaking to audiences, and how rewarding it felt to help as many people as we could change the way they thought about sales. We ended up speaking in some really, shall we say, "interesting" places to diverse kinds of audiences. Our favorite was an event we agreed to do for a campus entrepreneur organization at a small university. They told us it was a hugely popular group and said they expected a large crowd of enthusiastic young founders. When we arrived, the event was in a dingy campus breakroom and we were greeted by five students staring at us awkwardly with mouths full of free doughnuts. *Were they just there for the free food?* we wondered. It didn't matter! We gave them everything we had. As it turned out, someone in the tiny audience knew someone else with a business that needed help building a sales team and made an introduction. That new client eventually referred us to another client. We landed the business with those companies because we chose not to quantify the value of the time we were putting into our speaking events, but to give it freely to those we knew needed it. And in a nice bit of synchronicity, the people who referred us to others *they* knew were doing so because they, in turn, were thinking about how they could be valuable themselves.

Thinking Beyond Bounds

By thinking beyond the confines of "giving this for getting that," we can also discover ways to provide value we and the people we're selling to have never considered before. Rather than simply securing our piece of the pie, we may be able to make a bigger and better pie, to the benefit of everyone involved.

One field where sellers are often seen as stereotypically pushy and cutthroat is real estate. (Flashback to Alec Baldwin and those *Glengarry* steak knives.) But according to a *Business Insider* article, there's a new breed of real estate players that has been changing the terms of the game. These agents understand that "Real estate isn't all about money . . . and some of our rising stars are fighting to fix what's wrong with the system." One of them, Christine Wendell, worked in real estate development for years and took a strong interest in affordable housing. She saw that people seeking to move into these buildings often face daunting amounts of paperwork as part of an application process. This and other factors lead to long delays in units being filled. Wendell co-founded a company, Pronto Housing, that provides a simple means of completing the process, through an easy computer program akin to those used for tax preparation. It's helping people in great need of better housing to get it faster and easier. Through Pronto, Christine is still in the business of selling real estate, but she's trying to make huge improvements to the way it's done for the benefit of her clients and the industry at large.

Another business that can be brutally competitive is the recording industry. Jeff Ayeroff, the record executive we introduced in chapter 4, is another example of someone looking past industry norms and seeking to be transformational in unexpected ways. In 1990, Jeff was frustrated with the political landscape, and more specifically, the apathy he perceived young people had about politics. He wanted to do something about it. "People were saying MTV unplugged an entire generation . . . I was going to plug them back in," Jeff told us. To do this, Jeff co-founded Rock the Vote, an organization aimed at increasing turnout for voters between the ages of eighteen and twenty-four. His goal was to empower a generation to exercise their rights and represent their interests to drive meaningful change. To truly make it work, he needed to sell his competitors on offering up their artists to the cause. He also needed to sell the artists themselves to take a stand, and he needed to sell MTV to get on board and be the platform the cause needed. All these stakeholders would be contributing time, money, and resources to a cause that wasn't going to contribute to the bottom line. On top of that, they didn't even know if the effort would work.

Spoiler alert: It did. In creating Rock the Vote, he set in motion a powerful mechanism that's been responsible for registering over 12 million young voters, and has even gone beyond its initial aim. Rock the Vote has spearheaded and built support for a wealth of initiatives critical to young people and has raised awareness about issues like global warming and gun violence. Meanwhile the participation of big-name artists, like Madonna, R.E.M., and Aerosmith, helped many less-established artists get great exposure, and Jeff raised his stature in his industry and gave his label a new level of credibility with artists and partners.

We realize that as inspiring as these stories of transformative selling may be, the notion of pursuing such bold, paradigm-shifting opportunities can also be intimidating. Depending on what you're selling, it might even seem ridiculous to think in such bold terms. The good news is we can take much smaller steps through our selling and still have a transformational impact on our customers.

Make It Personal

Shirley, a salesperson at a robotics e-commerce company, told us about a time she realized she could break free from purely transactional selling. She was working with a high-ranking executive at Ikea trying to sell them her company's on-demand shipping fulfillment solution and had a great relationship with him. But she had been waiting for what felt like forever for him to provide her with specific information she needed to move the deal forward. She didn't want to become a stereotypical pestering salesperson, but she also really didn't want to drop the ball, so she stepped back to take stock of the situation and realized something. In every recent interaction, she was trying to *take* something from him. She was asking for time, responses, updates, and, of course, the information she needed. As far as adding value of her own, she'd followed the traditional sales playbook—she'd offered favorable payment terms, enticing features, and flexible timetables. Because of all this, she had convinced herself it was okay for her to be extracting the value she'd been asking for. She had done her part and it was time for him to do his.

Realizing that she'd slipped into this transactional way of thinking, she decided to hit pause on pressing for the information she was looking for. Instead, she remembered a conversation they'd had in which he had shared his frustration that he had a big vacation planned for his family, but to go they all needed to pass a COVID test. He'd been banking on having everyone take in-home rapid tests, but at the time it was easier to find a grain of sugar in a saltshaker than it was to find one of those tests. The kits were sold out everywhere and time was running out. One of Shirley's customers was a massive pharmacy with stores across the country, so before calling Ikea's executive, she reached out to her closest contact at the pharmacy to ask when the next shipment of rapid tests would be arriving at the stores near him. When she finally spoke to the executive, she was able to let him know, almost down to the minute, when the testing kits would be available so he could order them to be sent to his house later that day. The executive later sent Shirley a screenshot of his order confirmation and reported that one hour later the kits had arrived at his doorstep. He also asked if her company's technology was behind the fulfillment and delivery of his order. Yes, on both counts, was the answer. Shirley didn't do this as a tactic. She took stock and realized she had slipped into the transactional mindset and consciously made the shift to a giving mindset instead. She felt fulfilled in having helped her customer with something that was important to him, and also in working for a company that she'd realized was offering a service that could be so meaningful.

Think about the person you're selling to and consider how to be more valuable to them in a personal and consequential way *without expecting anything specific in return*. Think about challenges they're facing and how you can help them overcome them. Consider how to help them get better not just at whatever's written on their job description, or at understanding what you bring to the table, but better in the purest sense of the word. Help them become better professionals, better parents, better partners, better employees, better human beings. Think about what you know about their lives, their interests, their family life, any difficulties they're dealing with, like caring for an elderly parent or contending with the stress of taking care of their children while also keeping up with work. What other challenges are they facing in their jobs? What information do you have that might provide you with an opportunity to be helpful to them, even if it has nothing to do with what you're trying to sell them?

Greg, a salesperson we talked with after an event we spoke at, did this beautifully. He sold office management software that helped enterprise companies keep track of employee scheduling, travel planning, and inventory management. He was having a hard time getting one of his prospects on the phone because the guy was neck deep in strategic planning and financial forecasting for his company. He'd voiced his frustration about the process, and Greg deeply understood what that felt like because he had hated every quarterly planning session he'd been forced to suffer through at previous companies. Since he'd felt that pain before, he compiled a library of templates that could be used for the planning process and shared them with the customer. The gift was so well received that Greg put together more templates and shared them with *all* his prospects and existing customers. These planning documents had absolutely nothing to do with the office management software he was selling—he made them because he knew many of his prospects were facing similar challenges and he felt good about supporting them. Greg not only found creating the templates intrinsically rewarding, which was one reason he'd created them for himself to begin with, but he liked that his clients and prospects came to see him as more than just "the guy selling software to me." He enjoyed that they started to view him more holistically, as someone with talents beyond his expertise in software and in pitching his product, and as a peer with similar pressures and experiences.

A successful real estate agent shared another great example. She was working with a couple who had their heart set on buying a home in the neighborhood where the wife grew up. She remembered the rare sense of community she felt there, how her neighbors all knew each other and spent time together, and she wanted that for her own children. The problem was, people hardly ever sold their homes in the neighborhood because they never wanted to leave. The agent proactively crafted a beautiful letter on behalf of her clients expressing their desire to move into the neighborhood in hopes of connecting with a current homeowner who might be interested in selling their home *if* they knew they were paying it forward by selling to a family who would create a home full of memories, like the ones they might've made while living there. Since the agent had spent a lot of time falling in love with her clients, she was able to include stories about why the neighborhood was special to the family, what they do for fun, and even added a picture of the family corgi, Booger. She shared the letter with her clients and asked for their permission to give it to home-owners in the neighborhood in hopes of landing them the house of their dreams. She then hand-delivered a copy to every house in the neighborhood, knocking on doors and speaking with homeowners whenever possible, and made her clients' dreams come true when a homeowner who was planning on moving but hadn't listed their house yet sold the couple their home before it ever hit the market. Plenty of realtors write bulk letters for their clients; few do it with such passion-ate attention to their clients' personal stories and the commitment of personal, door-to-door delivery to each and every house in a neigh-borhood.

The only way to understand someone enough to make something personal for them is to truly get to know them. As is so often the case when selling, the best way to do this and uncover opportunities to be transformational on a personal level is by asking the right questions.

Ask Impactful Questions

The ability to ask great questions is one of the most important skills for selling. For salespeople thinking transactionally, the questions they ask are often selfishly designed to get them what *they* need to make a sale. *What is your budget? When do you need a solution? Who is involved in the decision? How can I sell you?* These questions are designed to extract value (information) from the customer. What if, instead of always taking, you asked questions that *gave something* to the person answering? Original questions you asked not because you thought they didn't know the answer and you did, or because you wanted to look smart or prove a point, or because you needed information to leverage for a sale, but because you were genuinely *interested* in gaining their perspective about something they've never considered before and helping them do the same? Sellers with an Unsold Mindset ask questions like this constantly. We call them Impactful Questions.

Impactful Questions are always open-ended, never leading, and they often lead the person answering them toward valuable insights or new ideas they'd never thought of before. They are never used solely as a tactic. If you're asking one you must genuinely *want* to know the answer. You're not driving to a quick close; not looking for what *you need* from them, as with standard sales playbook questions like those above. When you ask an Impactful Question, you're giving someone the gift of ideating *for the first time, in real time*, and making sure they leave the interaction knowing more about themselves than they did before it began.

Mark Roberge, former chief revenue officer of HubSpot, currently managing director of Stage 2 Capital, and author of *The Sales Acceleration Formula*, says all the best salespeople he's ever interacted with are masters at asking questions that lead buyers to new understandings. "At the end of a call, buyers might say, 'I feel like I'm in therapy!'" Mark told us. "All a therapist does is ask a bunch of questions that reframe your world. Great salespeople do the same thing."

Impactful Questions can invoke honest and vulnerable reactions in otherwise veiled conversations. A great way to do this in a selling context is by asking people to narrow their focus on a subject on which they typically don't take a narrow view. One hugely successful seller we know sold a product to chief technology officers (CTO) and had conversations with them every day. He knew that the typical CTO was constantly inundated with countless issues, projects, and fire drills, and that many had a hard time prioritizing because of it. "What are the one or two numbers you measure and focus on consistently, and why?" he would ask them. This might seem like a straightforward question, but in reality most CTOs don't focus on just one or two numbers, they have a huge data set and track dozens of metrics at a time.

When he asked this question to a CTO, they'd typically answer the question in one of two ways: either they'd acknowledge they've never actually been able to narrow their focus to one or two, or they'd posture, pretending they had the answer at the ready, and throw out a couple of metrics. In either case, the person answering gets the gift of hearing themselves think *I can't easily answer this and I should be able to. It would help me prioritize if I could.* In cases where CTOs would make up an answer, the salesperson was able to truthfully respond, "Wow, I talk to CTOs every day and I've never heard that answer before!" Most of the time, the CTOs who responded in that way would turn to him and ask, "Well . . . what have you heard from others?" Just by asking an Impactful Question, the buyer was able to identify a possible area for growth, and the seller became a thought leader, not because he called himself one, but because the minute his prospect asked him what other CTOs were doing, he *was* one.

In our work with sales teams and our interviews with the Unsold, we have collected a small set of our favorite Impactful Questions, listed below. Those that are particularly appropriate for you will likely vary by what you're selling, the industry you're in, and, maybe most importantly, what you feel most comfortable asking. Remember, we've got to allow ourselves the space to be authentic, and we also have to trust our instincts to know when we sound like someone we don't want to be. Hopefully some of these will work for you, but even if they don't, let them inspire your thinking about other questions you *can* ask.

- What do your customers *actually* say about your company, and what would you *like* them to say?
- How do you think your team talks about you when you're not there to listen?
- What type of leader do you want to be remembered as?
- If you could focus more resources on only one problem your company is facing, what would it be?
- What is the smallest action you could take today to have the biggest impact?
- What does failure look like?
- What characterizes the best partner you've ever had? What do they do differently than you?
- Reflect on a specific time you were being the person you were "born to be." How can you repeat that behavior today?
- What rules should we be breaking?
- What are people/you thinking but are afraid to express?

If you've truly asked an Impactful Question, it will serve as a form of giving in itself. Asking someone about the kind of leader they want to be, for example, might help them commit to developing a particular aspect of their leadership they want to work on, that they otherwise hadn't thought of. Asking about a time someone was acting as who they were born to be might hearken them back to an activity they used to love but had allowed their busy schedule to crowd out of their life. And fundamentally, taking the time to ask people such thoughtful questions about themselves is a form of caring, helping them to feel seen and worthy of that attention.

In a selling context, Impactful Questions can serve many purposes. They can lead a customer to open their mind to new possibilities or help them think about their situation in a new way. They can provide perspective on why making a purchase is the right decision for them. They can reframe challenges, reveal blind spots, or spark urgency. Sometimes, the right question at the right time simply serves to strengthen the connection between a buyer and seller. In any case, Impactful Questions give agency to the person answering because whatever insight they glean, it's not someone telling them something, it's them arriving at that understanding for themselves.

Just remember, if an Impactful Question doesn't come from a place of genuine curiosity, it might not spark anything but annoyance. As we've discussed before, you never want to cross over the boundary of being intrusive. As long as you are thoughtful and intentional, asking questions you genuinely want to know answers to, you can unlock great realizations, for them and for you.

Assessing Your Value

Another great way to spot opportunities to be more transformational in selling situations is our Value Assessment Exercise. We developed it while working with a sales team that hired us to figure out why they had such a low closing percentage with qualified prospects who seemed like "perfect fits." We quickly identified a trend in their customer interactions: They were constantly asking for things, extracting value, without providing anything of significant value in return.

We asked the team to do an exercise to make a point about how many of their interactions were about giving and how many were about taking. Here's how it works:

Print any documented communications you regularly use with customers—email templates, scripts, follow-up cadences, call transcripts—and tape them all up on a wall. Under each document, tape a blank piece of paper divided into two columns. In one column write down everything you were seeking to *extract* with that communication (such as asking for time, money, or information). In the other column, list any value you were *adding*, ranking the value-adds on a scale from one to ten for their significance or impact. For example, recommending a relevant article to a customer might be a two, and introducing them to a contact who can help them with their business might be a six.

For the sales team we first had do this, the exercise produced a glaring portrait of how much more extracting than adding they were doing. The team worked together to find ways to flip the ratio and give substantially more than they requested in return. They hired an outsourced resource to scour the internet for content their customers could use in their businesses and created a series of "Industry Q&A" web events with experts where their customers could come to learn and interact. They scaled back on their "asks," making sure that anything they were asking for was critical to driving the sales process forward, and only done after significant value was added first. Within two months their closing rate on those "perfect fits" improved dramatically.

This exercise can immediately help you start thinking more

transformationally by revealing opportunities where small, simple changes in your interactions can make a disproportionate impact. And speaking of disproportionate impact, there's one last practice we recommend for making sure you're giving more than you're getting.

The 100/20 Rule

As much as we coach ourselves not to think in transactional terms, the cultural messaging to do so is so strong, and we've been exposed to it for so long, that we can all too easily find ourselves slipping back into that mindset. One way to stop ourselves from backsliding is by following the 100/20 Rule, which David Meltzer, the sports business leader turned inspirational speaker, author, and philanthropist we briefly introduced in chapter 6, shared with us. It was his ticket to falling in love with selling, and to transforming his life, and those of many others.

His original concept for the 100/20 Rule was that in every sales interaction he had, he would seek to provide $100 in value for every $20 he asked for in return. It didn't have to be literal value. He just wanted to make sure that whatever he gave in the interaction—products or services, time, information, knowledge, introductions, entertainment, experience, and so on—felt to the customer like five times what they were providing in return. It didn't matter if the value was literal, so long as *he* believed that he was giving it. This worked, and gave him a deep sense of fulfillment, so he eventually adopted the rule for *all* his interactions with people, not just those he was selling to.

He initially made the commitment after a profound realization that the way he'd been selling had led him to become a person he didn't want to be. He told us he started his career as the embodiment of the stereotypical salesperson. "I was a complete chameleon," he told us. "I would oversell, backend sell, lie, manipulate, and cheat. I had the old car salesman attitude." In much the way we have discussed, this shortsighted outlook on selling served David for a time. He became a millionaire only nine months after finishing law school and taking a sales job, and a multimillionaire by the time he was thirty-two years old. He owned dozens of properties including homes, a golf course, and even a ski mountain. But then he found himself embroiled in a lawsuit, and he told us he let his ego drive him to spend a ton of money defending himself simply to "prove that I was right." Those expenses led to defaults on payments to banks that, over the course of two years, forced him to file for bankruptcy. This crucible experience led him to take a hard look at himself and how he'd been living. And in the process, he came to the realization that for him to live a meaningful life and find a lasting and truly rewarding type of success, he'd need to think about how to give value to others, not just take it. "I had to retrain myself that [the way I was doing things] was not beneficial," he admitted. "I realized, what if elevating others elevates myself? What if, for every deal I wanted to do, I was capable of articulating the actual value by being honest?"

He adopted a new life philosophy based around helping others, and says he now wakes up every morning with the goal of finding opportunities to help ten people that day. This has proven transformative, both for those he's helped and for him. This new philosophy eventually led to a friend he had helped coming to him and saying, "You're a great negotiator. Can you help me negotiate a deal?" He did, and the lawyer on the other side of the negotiation was Leigh Steinberg, the legendary sports agent who served as the inspiration for the film *Jerry Maguire.* David impressed Steinberg, and he was quickly hired as the COO of Leigh Steinberg Sports & Entertainment agency, one of the most successful sports agencies in the world. Six months later, he was made CEO.

Fast forward to today, and David is a hugely successful business-man (he co-founded Sports 1 Marketing with NFL legend Warren Moon), has a vast following as a speaker and author, and is widely respected as a philanthropist and humanitarian who uses his massive platform to try to achieve a truly transformative mission: to empower over *one billion people* to be happy.

• • •

The Hebrew word *mitzvah* means a "good deed." As two guys raised by amazing Jewish mothers, we heard the word *mitzvah* a lot grow-ing up, but it wasn't until a student of ours sent us a blog post by Rabbi Alexander Seinfeld that we realized how well that word de-scribes the transformational giving of the Unsold Mindset, and the positive effects that so often follow. "A mitzvah," the rabbi wrote, "is a certain type of transcendent connection that you create when you do some actions (such as good deeds) *with the right frame of mind*" (emphasis ours). The frame of mind he's referring to is one of con-sciously choosing to do something for someone else, not because you feel you're supposed to, or because you'll benefit from doing it, but purely with the intention of doing good. Each *mitzvah* you offer someone, he says, "is a unique opportunity to give your life transcen-dent meaning."

We thought immediately of how an Unsold Mindset helps tran-scend the limits of transactional thinking, and of the "transcendent connection" it allows sellers to make with the people they sell to. By going beyond what's expected and instead seeking to be a catalyst for transformation, big or small, they don't just make deals better, they make *us* better. In the process they lift themselves up too, enriching their lives through the relationships they build and the impact they have on the people they encounter along the way.

CHAPTER EIGHT

Creative Selling

O ur first Sales Mindset for Entrepreneurs class of the semester had just ended and several students had lined up to introduce themselves to us and ask questions. We noticed one student letting others go before him, as if he had a secret to share with us he didn't want anyone else to hear. When everyone else had left, he shyly introduced himself with his hands in his pockets and head turned slightly downward. "Hi, I'm Chris. Um, I'm not really sure if I should take this class. I really love startups and entrepreneurship and I want to learn as much as I can, but I'm a huge introvert and I'm nervous I might not be a good fit in a class about sales."

We looked at each other and smiled. There's at least one student in every class who comes to us early on with similar doubts. One of our favorite things about teaching is seeing these students who worry they may not have the personality for selling realize that what they perceive as weaknesses are actually strengths and that they have the potential to be the best sellers in any room, not just our classroom.

Chris didn't disappoint. While he didn't speak out in class as much as his more outgoing classmates, when he did, he always added to the conversation in meaningful ways. He also scored among the highest on our written assignments. But what impressed us most was the way he leveraged one of his strengths—creativity—to adapt a sales outreach email we'd shared in one of our lessons to his own life.

Midway through the semester, Chris was applying for internships at technology startups, and he was especially excited about an e-sports company called 100 Thieves. As a big admirer of one of its co-founders, Jackson Dahl, Chris had been following him on social media. He'd reached out to Dahl a couple of times by email asking to meet for an interview but hadn't received a response. Then he got creative. Since he knew from social media that Dahl, based in Los Angeles, was a Lakers fan, Chris fired off his own version of an email we had discussed in class:

Subject: Wager

Hi Jackson—

It's obvious you're busy. Looks like the Lakers are playing the Nets tomorrow night.

If the Lakers win, I'll send 100 Thieves a large pizza and never contact you again, but if the Nets win I would love to talk to you for 10 minutes about the career moves that most contributed to your success. Deal?

Dahl was so impressed that not only did he write back immediately to set up a meeting, he tweeted a screenshot of the message after the game with a link to a headline showing that the Nets had held off the Lakers at the buzzer to win 104–102. "Was sent this email by a college student on Monday, ahead of last night's game," Dahl tweeted. "Reminds me of my favorite quote from [billionaire investor and occasional *Shark Tank* shark, Chris] Sacca: 'It may be lucky, but it's not an accident.'" Of course, Chris hadn't even needed the luck of the win to snag the meeting, and neither do most people who have used the "pizza bet." (We can count on one hand how many pizzas we've paid for over the years.) Prospects normally respond like Dahl did, rewarding creativity.

Dahl's tweet was retweeted dozens of times (including by Sacca himself), inspiring over a thousand likes and lots of impressed comments, like "Wow! The harder you work, the luckier you get!" Chris landed the meeting with Dahl *and* eventually got a job offer from 100 Thieves, one of many he received that semester. One of those offers was from us, and Chris graciously served as our teaching assistant for three semesters!

When we ask people to name the top characteristics of a great salesperson, creativity rarely, if ever, makes the list. But for sellers with an Unsold Mindset, creativity is a key part of their job. They've realized that coming from a creative place can have outsized benefits, for both results and quality of life. Giving themselves permission to be creative makes their work more engaging, a more intriguing challenge to tackle in some new way every day. We've found that they've come to appreciate something about creativity that is generally misunderstood: We *all* have the capacity to be wildly creative.

The Three Myths of Creativity

One myth about creative work is that it's reserved for, well, "creatives"— artists, performers, inventors, and perhaps marketers and advertisers, who write brilliant copy and create ads that make us laugh. Maybe some would also include software engineers and product designers who dream up futuristic new things we didn't even know we needed. As for selling, it's generally seen as taking what *others* have created and persuading people of its value.

In keeping with that view, most of the emphasis in sales training is on "how to" techniques, like scripts for phone calls that are supposed to decrease your chances of getting hung up on. *Do exactly what we say,* is the message. *It's worked for other people so it will work for you, too.* Except too often it doesn't. One study found that cold calling has a 2.5 percent "success" rate. In our experience, it's clear that removing the ability to be creative isn't the answer as some of the most successful cold callers we've ever seen are the ones who ditch the script and get creative.

People love to label sales as scientific and data driven, pointing to statistics and formulas as the reason for their success and LinkedIn influencer stardom. You've got to make fifty calls a day, according to one post, and seek to spend an average of 9.6 minutes on every call. That's awfully precise! And absurd. Characterizing advice like that as scientific is an insult to science, which is one of the most creative endeavors you can undertake. Science requires experimenting with things that have never been tried before; testing new ideas, even if they seem crazy; rejecting conventional wisdom and constantly asking *What if?* and *Why not?* Einstein said, "The greatest scientists are always artists as well."

As in science, great sellers thrive on trying approaches that haven't been tried before, flexing their creative muscles whenever and however they can think of ways of doing so. They love the challenge of dreaming up original content, crafting unexpected experiences, and rethinking so-called rules of selling that are ripe for breaking. They relish putting their unique personality into their interactions with other people, speaking in their own distinctive voices. It keeps them engaged, it makes selling fun, *and* it drives results. Research has shown that salespeople assessed as being more creative dramatically outperformed colleagues ranked lower in expressing their creativity.

The second myth about creativity is that some people are more creative than others because they're "right brainers." The popular notion that creativity is a product of the right brain, with logic and analytical thinking coming from the left brain, has been debunked. According to leading creativity researcher and cognitive scientist Scott Barry Kaufman, "the creative process draws on the whole brain." Neuroscience has revealed that as we engage in creative endeavors, an intricate web of connections among a vast number of brain regions are activated. In fact, science has shown that we *all* have the capacity for vast creativity; the impulse to create is woven into the genetic fabric of our basic human nature. As psychologist Peggy Orenstein writes, "Rather than a rare gift, [creativity is] more akin to kindness or compassion—an innate human trait." What's more, the more frequently we engage in creative thinking, the more readily we're able to "turn on" the creativity network. The more we express our creativity, in other words, the more natural it feels to do so.

Admittedly, as anyone who's heard Colin rap or Garrett play guitar can attest, some people simply aren't as talented in their creative output as others. Why that's so is a matter of much dispute, though. Producing the highest quality of creative work, of any kind, may well entail a greater degree of innate ability, but experts on creativity and many of the world's most esteemed artists—be they writers, painters, composers, dancers, inventors, or designers—agree that conscious effort and the relentless challenging of one's talents have been the key to their success. Maybe that's because, over time, their brain's creativity networks were so constantly fired up. Which speaks to the third great myth about creativity.

A final myth is that being creative is synonymous with being artistic and has to result in output in the form of traditional artwork, like a painting or novel. This just isn't true. Everything we do can be done creatively, and our daily lives offer an abundance of opportunities for creative expression. Psychologist Ruth Richards, one of the most influential researchers on creativity, pioneered the concept of "everyday creativity." She describes it as our great hidden potential, and she emphasizes that we "can be creatively present to life in writing a report, teaching a class, landscaping the yard, fixing a car." While we might think that being creative is easier said than done, Richards has shown that being creative might actually be easier done than said. It's a natural proclivity built into us by evolution and, as Richards writes, it's really fundamentally about problem-solving, not artistry. "Our creativity helps us cope and survive," she writes, "and also to find out what we are surviving for." Being creative even in the small things we do each day gives them more meaning, both for us and for others, and gives us much more joy.

Creativity Boosts

Research shows that engaging in everyday creativity helps people feel better about themselves, work harder, and lead more purpose-driven lives. One study had subjects spend thirteen days tracking all their creative pursuits, no matter how seemingly inconsequential. Hundreds of participants rated their level of creativity each day, and simultaneously tracked their overall mood. "A clear pattern emerged in the diary entries," the researchers write. "Immediately after the days participants were more creative, they said they felt more enthusiastic and energized." Even better, the researchers have found that frequently expressing our creativity leads to an "upward spiral" of positive emotions, psychological well-being, and feelings of "flourishing" in life, with flourishing being defined as "an overall sense of meaning, purpose, engagement, and social connection." It improves our health, too, with many studies showing it lowers depression, decreases stress and anxiety, and boosts the power of the immune system.

Why, you might ask, are everyday acts of creativity so good for us? Happiness expert Mihaly Csikszentmihalyi (pronounced chik·sent·-mee·hai) argues that our joy in it makes perfect sense from an evolutionary standpoint because creativity was critical for devising ways of fighting off threats, improving living conditions, and ensuring our early ancestors had the best chance to survive. He hypothesizes that evolution may have programmed us to "feel good whenever something new is discovered, regardless of its present usefulness." Indeed, whenever we experience something novel, our brains release the beloved "happiness" drugs dopamine and serotonin. No wonder, as one researcher writes, "people are designed to crave the unexpected."

That also points to why others get joy from our expressions of creativity as well. In fact, we're literally attracted to it. One study found that people rank creativity as one of the most desirable qualities in a partner, and another showed that creative individuals across a variety of professions report having more sexual partners. (Oh, *now* we have your attention!) This innate attraction to creativity is why buyers respond so well to sellers who approach the process with a creative mindset.

So why, if even simple everyday creativity gives us such a boost in life, have so many of us convinced ourselves that we have to stay confined within the boundaries of what's expected of us?

Our Creativity Has Been Caged

Many of us have the joy of creative pursuit squashed out of us early on in our school experience. If you want to see unfettered creativity in action, spend a little time with a happy four- or five-year-old; you'll get a master class in imagination and innovation. We've seen our boys create entire fantasy worlds out of an empty shipping box and a handful of toothpicks! But as psychologist Sir Ken Robinson lamented in the most watched TED Talk of all time, "Do Schools Kill Creativity?," children's innate joy in being creative is often muted by feeling the pressure of being graded and being reprimanded for not following rules. Education specialist Ron Beghetto dubbed this "creative mortification," the killing off of one's creative spirit.

Colin experienced this himself in a moment that was seared into his psyche. He has color vision deficiency (CVD), commonly referred to as colorblindness, which causes him to mix up greens with browns and blues with purples (which explains his collection of mauve hoodies!). As a second grader in art class one day, he was tasked with drawing a sun in the sky, and his teacher came by and scolded him, "Why is the sky purple? It's supposed to be blue." Today, Colin will argue that he's the one seeing true colors and everyone else is wrong, so fortunately he got some of that stifled creativity back.

The mortification doesn't stop in grade school. Spanx founder Sara Blakely said early on she never told a soul about her idea for Spanx because she was afraid people would belittle it and reduce her enthusiasm. She feared comments like *Aren't they just pantyhose with the feet cut out?* or *You'll never compete with L'eggs.* Thank goodness she protected herself from those creativity-dampening criticisms and created a product that allowed so many women to feel empowered by what they were wearing.

The carrot-and-stick approach many companies take in hopes of motivating people with bonuses or commissions, which is endemic in sales jobs, can also curb our creative sparks. Teresa Amabile, a Harvard specialist on creativity in the workplace, highlights, "people will be most creative when they feel motivated primarily by the interest, satisfaction, and challenge of the work itself." Csikszentmihalyi backs that up, writing, "Creative persons differ from one another in a variety of ways, but in one respect they are unanimous: They all love what they do. It is not the hope of achieving fame or making money that drives them; rather, it is the opportunity to do the work that they enjoy doing."

Bring Your Creativity Back to Life

So the question is, how can we ignite our inherent creativity and use it in our own selling? We've established that you don't have to become a Birkenstock-wearing hipster or a tortured artist with a face tattoo (for the record, we love both), and you certainly don't have to paint a masterpiece or compose a magnum opus. In our own work and in many of our conversations with Unsold-minded sellers, we've discovered a wealth of simple but powerful ways to be more creative with any element of selling.

Make the Tried and True New

Being creative doesn't always mean being completely original. When Slash plays the "Sweet Child O' Mine" guitar solo for the millionth time at a show, he still finds a way to make it sound fresh. Successful painters often zero in on a style of work that they then replicate many times with some variation. Chris, our student who sent the "Pizza Bet" email to 100 Thieves, didn't create that email template, but he put his own stamp on it. Likewise, we've found many Unsold sellers find ways to make more creative use of tools they, and others, already have at their disposal.

Take LinkedIn for example. LinkedIn is one of the most ubiquitous tools for prospecting leads, and has been for some time, yet we *still* hear about people using it in new and creative ways that others haven't thought of. A salesperson we once worked with impressed us with his own novel approach. He used the company's customer relationship management (CRM) software, but instead of just using it to track his sales pipeline, as it's designed to do, he ran a report listing all the decision makers who authorized the purchase of his company's product for *existing* customers. Most people might think, *why is he wasting time with existing customers? They've already purchased. There's no opportunity there.* But that's where the creativity comes in. He took his list of buyers and cross-referenced all of them (there were hundreds) on LinkedIn to see if any had moved on to new companies since making the purchase. Sure enough, a lot of them had. He now had a list of individuals he *knew* liked his product enough to buy it before, who were at new companies that were not yet customers. He called them all, entering those conversations as a trusted and familiar voice rather than starting cold, and was able to convert several of them into customers again.

Creating with New Technology

As new technologies emerge, which is just about *always* these days, truly creative sellers will experiment and think about ways to use them for selling. One salesperson, Justin, approached us after a talk we'd given and told us how he'd harnessed Cameo, the website that lets you purchase personalized video messages from celebrities, to get a prospect's attention. Justin was convinced his prospect fit his ideal customer profile, so he made several attempts to connect but hadn't made any inroads. Then he remembered that in his research, he'd discovered the prospect was a *massive* Texas football fan. Justin went on Cameo and found a former Longhorns wide receiver who was doing custom messages for $30. "Justin knows you love Texas football," the receiver said, "so he reached out to have me say 'hi' and see if he can grab ten minutes on your calendar to see if he might be able to help you out. Hook 'em!"

Did Justin get a response? You bet he did, and without spending much time or money. His company would have happily authorized a whole lot more than the $30 to use traditional ways of getting in front of the prospect.

Of course, when someone comes up with a great new way to use technology, others pile on, and before long the dopamine hit you're delivering diminishes. But as with the salesperson who came up with the CRM/LinkedIn twist, don't underestimate the novel ways you may be able to think of to use and combine technologies; old with new; analog with digital; Garrett with Colin. Keep in mind that Sergey and Larry, the founders of Google, had no idea at all when they launched their version of a search engine that they'd end up building one of the biggest companies in the history of humankind, one that generates revenue from dozens of products far beyond the scope of their original idea. Any use of new technology requires evolution, and the challenge to "make it new" is part of the fun.

So often in selling, people simply follow the rules of engagement foisted upon them. Contract provisions, payment terms, timelines for delivery, and so many other aspects of a potential deal seem strictly prescribed. But you may be able to find opportunities to break out of those constraints.

Jon Dahan, the CEO of MindMedium creative agency, told us a story of a great case in which he did this. A consumer beverage client of his, which typically paid all their bills on time, had stopped paying for three months. "These were large, six-figure invoices," he told us, "and when I called, they told me they had no intention of paying them." Jon's first instinct was to call his lawyer to have him demand the money more forcefully. But he discussed it with his team and decided that option didn't align with the company's ethos or even his personal ethics—Jon and MindMedium see their clients as family. They aren't in the business of threatening to sue them.

Not long after, Jon received a call from a third-party acquisition company. "We're sorry," they told him, "but the company has filed for bankruptcy and will not be able to pay your full invoices. Our team will be taking over their remaining assets." Most people would have gone into a victim mentality here (remember chapter 3?), but Jon is a natural creator. *How do I find a way to make something out of this?* he asked himself. He decided to hear the takeover company out.

"Nobody's getting paid the full amount of their invoices," the company representative said when they spoke. "We're giving ten cents on the dollar for all vendors, regardless of who you are or what your relationship *was*. Take it or leave it."

"Time out," Jon responded. "Forget about the money for a second. Put aside the marketing work we've already done for the old regime. What are you trying to do with the brand *moving forward?*"

The representative told him their ideas. "That's not going to work," Jon candidly told him. "The previous company already tried that." More than just telling him, Jon *showed* him. He outlined why the previous plan didn't work, gave the company representative incredibly valuable advice on what would, and said, "Why don't we just start over? Let's build this company together. Let's look at the logo, look at the bottle, look at the marketing, look at everything and see if what we have is even worth rebuilding."

"I wanted them to know that I was here to help because I genuinely was here to help," Jon said. To show this, he called them regularly, giving ideas, making introductions, and serving as a resource. Eventually, Jon learned that the new company had a budget that they told him was "not to go to the past, but to go to the future. We're going to do X, Y, and Z."

Jon had an idea. "Okay," he said, "that all makes sense, and we can help. X and Y are free, we'll do that because we want to see the brand succeed. Z is where the work comes in, and we're going to do that work for you, too, but we're going to set up payment so that the work we do over the next six months equates to the amount the company owed us from before."

Surprised, the company representative said, "You're essentially going to work the next six months for free, and all we have to do is pay you your debt? Let's do it!" Jon creatively shifted the new company's mindset from viewing the money owed as a debt from the previous regime to payment toward the future. Over time, Jon and the new company rebuilt the brand together, and MindMedium ended up collecting far more in receivables than the original amount they almost didn't get.

We love Jon's story because it combines so many of the topics we've discussed earlier. He drew on a growth mindset, optimism, and a Same Team mentality. But most relevant here, he *created* a way forward where one didn't appear to exist. How many other companies got the same call he did and took the 10 percent payout? Probably most, if not all of them. But because Jon was creative, he not only got the money he was owed, he also got a long-term partner.

Thinking creatively like this can make an impact no matter what industry you're in, or what your circumstances are. A literary editor who read our manuscript told us about the time she was able to get an old academic publisher she was working for years ago, who was stuck in their ways, to agree to breakthrough new terms with authors. When we say old, we mean hundreds of years old; the company had been offering the same basic terms for ages. She was a young editor, without a reputation, and she was finding it extremely difficult to sign big-name academics. That was in part because the company charged a good deal more for its books than her competitors.

Then she had an idea. The books always came out in hardcover first, with a paperback to follow no sooner than about two years after. Almost all the hardcovers were bought by libraries because they were so expensive that individuals held off for the cheaper paperback. The authors hated this; they wanted as many people as possible to be reading their books as soon as possible. The strategy she wanted to sell made sense: If the company put out a paperback edition at the same time as the hardcover one, it could make significantly more money sooner, because most of the libraries would still prefer the longer-lasting hardcover. The company could sell simultaneously to both markets. She made her case, using revenue projections and a sincere request for the company to break their own rules for the benefit of its authors. She was shocked when management agreed, but less surprised when prestigious authors started flocking to her. A whole new revenue-generating model that changed the company's growth trajectory for decades to come was born out of a simple creative thought about a "rule."

You may have exciting possibilities for rewriting rules and finding new pathways out of your constraints that may only become clear to you if you dedicate some time to experiment creatively. When we say "experiment" we're not referring to what you did in college, we're talking about giving yourself permission to be creative without expectations, just for the sake of being creative, and seeing what happens. You might surprise yourself.

Then there's the creativity of working *within* your constraints. One of Teresa Amabile's empowering findings is about how operating under constraints can actually *enable* creativity. She highlights that sometimes a lack of constraints can squash our creativity because we can get analysis paralysis. For example, if people are given a blank piece of paper and asked to draw something, many have an extremely difficult time crafting anything. But if they're given a piece of paper with a squiggly line on it and asked to draw something that incorporates that line, many readily create inventive drawings.

Even seemingly daunting impediments can fuel our creativity. Business consultant Michael E. May writes about a study in which people played a computer game that required them to make their way out of a maze. Some of them played a version with a major obstacle in the way of one of the best routes, while others played a version without that extra challenge. Those who had to contend with the obstacle subsequently scored 40 percent higher on a well-established creativity test. He explains that "tough obstacles can prompt people to open their minds, look at the 'big picture,' and make connections between things that are not obviously connected . . . a hallmark of creativity."

Who hasn't sometimes felt, at least on occasion, that their company has put them in a maze, presenting them with all sorts of obstacles to doing their work well, whether that's inordinate paperwork or red tape, disadvantages compared to competitors, or the widely common lack of basic resources or budgets. Unfortunately, all too often, we really do have little or no ability to do away with these hindrances. But often we can find creative ways to work around them. Think about the enormous popularity of TED Talks. Speakers are given strict constraints of time and provided an elaborate set of guidelines for how to write and deliver their talks, and yet they've produced an astounding range of mind-altering results. Successful people adopt an Unsold Mindset that embraces defying constraints.

Bring Your Hobby to Work

Almost everyone has something creative they do outside of work, whether it be writing, carpentry, scrapbooking, knitting, painting, playing music, or being an influencer (you know who you are). Whatever your creative pursuits might be, look for ways to bring them into your sales process.

We heard a great story about a seller who did this from Gabriel Moncayo, CEO of AlwaysHired Sales Bootcamp, a company that trains sales development representatives and helps them earn jobs at large companies like Salesforce.com and Yelp. The people Gabriel works with are tasked with getting prospects on the phone, which can be one of the most challenging tasks for anyone who sells for a living. He told us about one seller, Kate, who decided to lighten up the load of the work by bringing her love of songwriting into it.

Outside of work, Kate was an amateur songwriter and guitarist.

One day, on a whim, she wrote a song about why clients should book a meeting with her, and then recorded it and started emailing it to prospects. Immediately, she started booking more meetings. A lot more. When she later posted the song on LinkedIn, it went viral. The success of that simple creative act that she did to incorporate her hobby (and personality) into her sales process ultimately led her to a new career helping other salespeople creatively generate leads of their own.

An old saying goes, "Find three hobbies you love: one to make you money, one to keep you in shape, and one to be creative." Why not find ways to combine them? Many who sell with an Unsold Mindset have figured out a way to blur the line between hobbies that make them money and the ones they pursue purely for fulfillment. Some turned a passion for writing into a hobby and applied those skills to launching successful blogs. Others took a passion for meeting new people that they developed through selling and used it to create podcasts. We've personally seen the benefits. When we first started speaking about the Unsold Mindset in front of audiences it was purely as a creative outlet. We had no idea it would turn into a class, a speaking and consulting business, and then this book.

Find Creative Collaborators

Reams of research on creativity has shown how powerful it can be to combine the perspectives and talents of multiple people. Collaboration takes pressure off, frees us up if we're stuck, helps us think about things through a new lens, and is frankly just a lot more fun. Neither one of us would ever have written a book like this alone. If Colin had tried it himself, you'd just be reading an emotional diatribe referencing Jay-Z as the single research source in the entire book, and if it was Garrett, you'd be falling asleep to a logical tangent of neurological jargon referencing every scientific journal known to humankind. By working together, we were able to bring our different perspectives to bear while calling each other out about our excesses, constantly bouncing ideas off each other, making fun of each other when those ideas were, well, not very good. There have also been plenty of times we've helped each other see where an idea we weren't sure of had the potential to turn into something meaningful. We've enjoyed every moment of powering through writer's block together, looking for inspiration together, conducting interviews together, and creating together.

On teams we lead, we build this collaborative creativity into the sales process in the form of "deal swarms," similar to the concept popularized by Tim Sanders in his 2016 book *Dealstorming*. These are some of the most popular meetings for companies we work with. Each month, members of a sales team bring their top prospective deals to a meeting to identify challenges and opportunities they might be missing as they work them on their own, essentially looking for blind spots they might have. What makes these meetings special is that the sales team is not the only audience. We invite non-salespeople to listen and weigh in on the deals. People from the engineering team, the product team, the accounting team, the HR team, the marketing team, you name it, all sit together and offer insights from their perspectives. Moreover, we try to include people from every level in the organization, from executives to interns. The more diversity the better. We kick things off with salespeople talking about their deals, describing what's going well, but more importantly, explaining the challenges they're having. The group then collectively tries to offer ideas to move things forward and poke holes in the deal that the salesperson may not have even thought of.

We've seen many a frustrated salesperson bring a deal to the "swarm" only to have an ultra-logical engineering-type or a creative marketing director completely remove a roadblock by bringing a new idea to the table. One salesperson brought a huge opportunity he'd been working on for over a year to a deal swarm. The prospective buyer had agreed on a price for a custom IT infrastructure build out, only to come back in the eleventh hour and claim that his research showed he could get it for half of what they agreed on. He said he was going to invite competitive bids. The salesperson had already discounted the project heavily and there was no more room to lower the price. The buyer's new numbers seemed unfathomable.

In the deal swarm, the salesperson's fellow sales team members were telling him to convince the client to honor the deal based on the commitments they'd already made. Then, from the back of the room a structural engineer raised his hand and said, "Steel and labor prices are higher now than when you gave him that deal, and they're poised to go up even more." The salesperson looked perplexed. "How is that going to help me?" he asked. Someone from the finance team spoke up, "Because you gave him a great deal whether he realizes it or not. We know how our competitors price, and now we know their prices will probably be even higher with the labor shortages in the industry." The engineer chimed in again, "Just tell the prospect the truth; tell him that with cost of raw materials and labor rising, it's unlikely any competitor would be able to beat our price, and if they extend the process much longer there's a very real chance we'd have to pull our current bid in order to reprice as well." After the meeting the salesperson called the prospect and presented the information. Once the buyer looked at the bid through the lens of the new facts provided, he quickly committed to the deal.

Selling is way better as a team sport.

Let Your Mind Wander

One of the most important findings in recent years in neuroscience has been that letting our minds wander can be a great source of creative inspiration. When we think of daydreaming, or "mind-wandering," as it's called, there's a negative connotation—it's implied we're being irresponsible by letting our minds drift off task. As it turns out, there's a method to the mind's wandering madness. Mind-wandering is so good for us that, if left to its own devices, our minds have been found to engage in it for 47 percent of our waking hours. It is our brain's default preference, which is why the neuronal network that is responsible for it has been dubbed the default mode network. The constant activity of this network is responsible for the phenomenon of sudden flashes of insight we get when engaged in activities that require little to no concentration, like showering, driving, and going for a walk. Scott Barry Kaufman calls the default mode the "Imagination Network," and he recommends carving out regular time to allow our minds to wander, like by taking a five-minute mind-wandering break every hour of the workday. Ruth Richards also commends the practice, suggesting that we "exercise deliberate and 'loose control' to let [our minds] 'run' for a time."

Start off by calling to mind a challenge you're facing and then just stop focusing on it and let your thoughts take their own course. Bonus points for hopping in the car for a drive, strapping on your sneaks for a run, or drawing a bath for a soak. A writer we interviewed told us she spent a half-hour every morning staring at the wall and letting her mind wander while having her wake-up coffee, and she swears it was her secret to coming up with all her best ideas for creative ways to start her chapters and to weave in unexpected stories and tantalizing facts that greatly enlivened her book.

Put on Six Hats

A final way to foster the creative mindset is by using the "six hats" technique, as introduced by Dr. Edwin de Bono in his book *Six Thinking Hats*. The exercise requires you to consider a problem from six different perspectives. The premise is simple: For any situation that needs a solution (for example, how can I cut through the noise to connect with more customers?), you put on different hats (metaphorically speaking, unless you have a ton of colorful hats in your closet, in which case, you, Garrett's five-year-old, and Colin all have something in common!) to look at the situation from vantage points you might not normally take. By doing this, many people are able to come up with far more ideas than they would if they only looked at a situation from one or two points of view. Huge companies like Prudential Insurance, IBM, FedEx, and DuPont have used the six hats technique to foster creativity and generate ideas that have led to measurable returns on investment.

The "hats" are:

Blue Hat: Think broadly. What is the best overall solution?
White Hat: Think objectively. What are the facts?
Red Hat: Think emotionally. What do your feelings tell you?
Black Hat: Think negatively. Which elements of the solution won't work?

Yellow Hat: Think positively. Which elements of the solution will work?

Green Hat: Think creatively. What are some alternative ideas?

Thinking about your own sales process or challenges from each of these different angles can unlock some creativity you wouldn't normally have if you're limited to your default way of thinking, and lead to some great ideas.

• • •

It's often said that selling is part science and part art. Allowing ourselves to exercise our creativity when we're selling helps ensure that we don't neglect the back half of that equation. Being creative is great for results and it makes selling *way* more fun, especially for those who have a natural aversion to "sales" altogether.

Expressing our creativity also helps us fill our work with more meaning, allowing us to make it our own, offer more of ourselves, and show up as deeper, more well-rounded people. Ruth Richards points out that being creative drives us to feel more sense of meaning in our lives, writing, "our creativity helps us . . . find out what we are surviving *for*." Which leads us to the last distinctive feature of the Unsold Mindset approach to selling: being motivated by a sense of purpose.

CHAPTER NINE

Set Goals on Purpose

One of our favorite things to do when we're speaking to a group of salespeople is to ask, "How many of you have goals?" Virtually every hand in the room will go up. Then we say, "Keep your hands up if those goals are written down and you review them often." More than half the hands typically go down (in an honest crowd). Then we say, "Now keep them up only if you have your *purpose* defined and written down." At this point, all but a tiny fraction of hands are typically lowered. Lastly, we try to offer a lifeline. "Okay, you can put your hand back up if you have your purpose defined, even if it's not written down." People chuckle uncomfortably as they realize how few of them have defined their purpose, the reason they do what they do. Of the hands that *are* still up, the people in the audience who have defined their purpose, it's almost always the top performers of the group. This isn't a coincidence.

One of the best examples for illustrating this point is Oprah Winfrey, of all people. If the Unsold had a Mount Rushmore, Oprah would almost certainly be one of the giant faces staring out at you from the side of the mountain. Even though she's not a salesperson by trade, Oprah has managed to sell more products, boost the growth of more businesses, and help create more millionaires than just about anyone else on the planet. Measuring the full extent of her economic impact would be impossible, but no doubt it's in the tens of billions of dollars.

Her Midas touch is so well known it has a name: the Oprah Effect, which is what investors started calling the inevitable lift in sales an endorsement from Oprah would lead to, whether she's "selling" the talents of people whose work she's featured (like Rachel Ray, Dr. Phil, and Nate Berkus), turning untold products into "overnight successes" by featuring them as one of her "Favorite Things," or boosting books picked for her book club to major bestsellerdom, with twenty-two of them reaching the number one position, usually within hours of her announcing them. When news broke in 2015 that Oprah was taking a 10 percent ownership stake in the weight-loss company WeightWatchers (now called WW International), the stock went up 105 percent in a single day.

You could say that Oprah is one of the greatest sellers ever, and yet almost no one would say she's "in sales." The question is, how has she been able to sell so much, with such a huge impact, without being labeled as a slimy, self-interested salesperson? She is seen as authentic and is revered for the fervor with which she sells, not labeled a manipulator and branded by the stereotypes. As we dug into interviews and other stories about her life, we realized that, like others with an Unsold Mindset, a huge reason she can accomplish this is because all her selling is done in the service of a specific, defined, meaningful purpose that guides her, inspires her communication, and fuels her drive.

Oprah has said that early in her life she realized her purpose, the thing she believes she is meant to do in life, is "to be a teacher . . . inspiring my students to be more than they thought they could be." Looking at everything she's done through that lens—creating a television show, personally curating products she believes will bring people joy and improve lives, amplifying messages of growth, positivity, and personal development—you find she has stayed scrupulously true to that mission. She has consistently educated her audience and inspired them to believe in themselves and pursue their *own* goals, instructing by example as she's constantly stretched herself to master new challenges, from becoming an actor—nominated for the Best Supporting Actress Oscar for her first role, in *The Color Purple*—to producing movies, launching a magazine and a TV network, and opening a school for girls in South Africa. Her goals appear to have been in seamless alignment with her purpose, which reinforces her authenticity, giving her powerful credibility and building enduring trust among her fans. She promotes setting ambitious goals, but only ones that are true to a larger life purpose, something she credits as a reason for her success.

It might seem as if Oprah was a natural at selling her audience on tuning in to her when she went on TV, but she didn't rocket straight to megastardom. In fact, she was fired from one of her early broadcasting jobs as a newscaster for a station in Baltimore. It wasn't until she was thirty, as she recalled in a commencement speech at Smith College, that she had an epiphany while interviewing white supremacist skinheads for her fledgling show in Chicago. She had thought that having them on the show would expose the ugliness of their beliefs, but when she noticed them smirking to one another as she questioned them, she realized they were using her show as a vehicle to promote their abhorrent ideology. She determined that day that "I would no longer be used by television; I would figure out how to let television be used by me, to turn it into a platform for service," and recalls, "I said to my producers, I will only do shows that are in alignment with my truth . . . *I will not fake it.*"

As we know by now, every element of the Unsold Mindset ultimately circles back to the power of authenticity. It's fitting that we're returning to the topic here, at the end, because knowing the purpose that drives us when we're selling, having clarity about the impact we are trying to have with it, is a driving force for staying true to who we are, in all aspects of our lives.

One of the most difficult things about selling is that many of our goals are set for us by other people, usually in the form of quotas or revenue targets. For many sellers, these financial goals can feel like the ultimate be-all and end-all of selling, its true purpose, no matter the lip service some give to building relationships or being in service of others.

Financial goals are a daunting presence for non-sales sellers, too. In marketing, all campaigns are tied to revenue. Startup founders selling their ideas are doing so in search of funding, whether from investors or customers, including when they're selling their story during board meetings. Engineers have to justify the business impact of the products they build. In selling ourselves in interviews, we're pitching that in addition to being qualified to do great work for a company, we deserve a certain salary or fee. Selling in charity work is largely about chasing donations. To some extent, it's almost always all about the money.

To be very clear, there's nothing inherently wrong with the pursuit of financial goals, *at all.* Without sales the lights don't stay on and people don't stay employed. Top salespeople in many organizations are among the highest paid employees, and that's how it should be. Oprah has made billions from her selling. Many of those we interviewed have also earned life-changing financial rewards. The problem is when financial goals loom so large that they overwhelm our true purpose for selling, hanging over us, making us anxious, and causing us to act like the salesperson we don't want to be.

Over and over, great sellers have told us financial goals, while important, are not what drive them. Instead, they view selling as a catalyst for achieving goals that are purposeful to them, and vitally, also, to the customers they're serving. They don't fixate on the performance goals imposed on them, which are usually all about numbers—revenue targets, usage metrics, billable hours, new account signups, fundraising dollars, and so on. They focus on the qualitative value of attaining goals, for themselves and others, and set goals that are inspired and motivated by their unique purpose, their reason for doing what they do.

We call these *purpose-driven goals,* and replacing your traditional goals (financial or otherwise) with them will have an outsized impact on your success. They will change the way you interact with your customers, inspire you to do things others won't do, and give your selling more meaning.

When Goal Setting Goes Awry

One of the problems with traditional sales goals is that they're held over our heads as "incentives" to perform, a not-so-subtle implication that we might not be self-motivated enough without them. While incentives tied to the profusion of performance metrics we're held to can certainly be motivating, and can be a good way of assuring that those with the best performance are recognized and ideally compensated appropriately for their contributions, for many sellers they backfire, motivating through fear instead of aspiration. That's because goals are often unrealistic, set by higher-ups, with little or no input from the people who have to go out and achieve them. Sometimes those setting them have no actual knowledge of how much time it would take to do the work to meet the goals, the nature of the work required, or the obstacles that need to be overcome to achieve them. Too often, sales goals are calculated by working backward from larger company targets established to satisfy performance demands of investors and market analysts, and not from a bottom-up assessment of realistic results. The authors of a *Harvard Business Review* article on the ways sales goals go badly wrote, "We often see company-level sales goals based on wishful thinking rather than on market realities." Ironically, one effect of these unrealistic goals may be lower results, as the authors highlight. They cite the case of a computer hardware company that gave its salesforce an unrealistic goal for selling a new line of servers. The sales team, realizing they couldn't meet the target, didn't bother to try. Instead, they turned their attention to other products they knew they *could* meet the numbers for.

Choosing to ignore the unrealistic objective is a form of what's called *completion bias*, the tendency to focus on completing relatively easy tasks rather than devoting the time we should to more difficult, and more important, ones when we feel overloaded. This might show up as spending far too much time going through our email inbox; writing quick answers to messages that aren't urgent; sending bulk emails rather than personalized, targeted versions; or knocking out busy work rather than tackling a bigger job of real consequence. When it comes to meeting quantitative goals, completion bias can lead to focusing too much on easy wins and neglecting opportunities that will have the largest impact.

Researchers who studied this problem found an example in doctors choosing to treat patients with less serious conditions, who could be treated more easily and quickly, while making patients with more complex problems wait longer for care. This is a great case of how flawed performance metrics can be: On paper, doctors increased their productivity, successfully treating more patients, even as they may have been putting the health of the patients with more serious conditions at risk.

Salespeople aren't born smarmy. When the pressure to hit sales numbers is intense, as it often is, the fear of missing them takes over and people may resort to pushy or unethical tactics. As we've shown, this reversion to the stereotype can eat at them with shame and fear that they'll be discovered and can cause both buyers and companies real harm. In one newsworthy example, thousands (yes, thousands!) of Wells Fargo employees created millions of fake credit and debit card accounts and charged customers bogus fees for them in an attempt to "meet unrealistic sales goals." This practice ultimately led Wells Fargo to be forced to pay $3 billion in fines. Were all of these employees bad people, dishonest frauds by nature? It's highly unlikely. A US Department of Justice investigation concluded they had succumbed to inordinate pressure from top-level management to meet targets for new accounts, and many convinced themselves they were doing something that benefited their customers. That case was so extreme it was eventually exposed, but countless people are suffering from intense, often debilitating anxiety about meeting goals, internalizing shame for not reaching their sales goals, and beating themselves up for not getting the job done.

When it comes to traditional selling, due to the commission compensation system, goals constantly weigh on the mind. We've known some sellers who love the pressure and wouldn't have it any other way, but we've also seen people melt down when things get intense. Meeting commission goals may, in fact, be the single most psychologically challenging aspect of selling.

Even if performance goals are realistic, they can have negative effects. In a paper titled "Goals Gone Wild" (university researchers love a good pun!), the authors cautioned that "systematic harm caused by goal setting has been largely ignored." Studies have shown that for many, the message that they should be driven by monetary rewards undermines their drive. It saps their intrinsic motivation about their work, which, to recall, is more powerful and more fulfilling than extrinsic motivators like bonuses. A friend of Garrett's was so offended by the elaborate performance targets and bonuses she was held to at a new job she'd started that she exclaimed to him over dinner, "They think I'm a rat in a maze! I don't need a piece of cheese to incentivize me. I want to do my job well because I want to be good at it!"

Beware the Hedonic Treadmill

As positive psychology has shown, the boost to life satisfaction from achieving material gains, over and above a base level of income security, has been greatly exaggerated. Colin learned this in his early twenties, when a key goal of his, his benchmark of success, was to be able to afford a fresh pair of Nike Air Force 1 sneakers every time he went out. In those days, the epitome of success in hip-hop culture was to have enough money to never have to wear the same pair of Air Force 1s twice. Once you could see a crease or a smudge of dirt, the shoes weren't "crispy" anymore; they were done. So what did he do when he started to see some success in sales? He bought dozens of pairs of Air Force 1s (which, incidentally, is why Garrett is responsible for our company's finances!).

The problem was, once Colin hit his goal with the shoes, he barely got to enjoy the accomplishment before realizing that his fresh shoes would feel a whole lot fresher if he had a fresh car. His new goal was to buy a Cadillac Escalade. (He'll be the first to admit now he was a walking cliché!) But the instant he achieved that goal and drove the car home to his apartment, he realized a cool car isn't that cool unless you're parking at a cool house. He was chasing materialistic extrinsic rewards, which, because they weren't satisfying in and of themselves, led him to focus increasingly on achieving more of them, all the way up to his lifelong goal of buying his own home. The saddest part about that purchase was as a kid growing up in an apartment, all he ever wanted was a house, so that was all he thought he needed for a lifetime of satisfaction. Yet no more than a week after escrow closed, he was stressing about how much money he just spent, and how he needed to build up more savings for retirement. He spent his whole life wanting something, finally got it, celebrated for less than a week, and then started thinking about a goal that was thirty years away, if he ever retires at all!

There's an inherent paradox in performance goals: You spend so much time and energy pursuing them, but, like Colin, once you finally get there you'll likely find yourself wondering, "Is this it?" In the 2020 documentary *Miss Americana*, Taylor Swift showed that even world-famous pop stars aren't immune from this feeling. "That was it," she said of winning the Grammy for Album of the Year for the second time. "My life had never been better. That was all you wanted.

That was all you focused on. You get to the mountaintop and you look around and you're like, 'Oh god, what now?'" She conveyed a sense of emptiness in not knowing what she'd do next.

In positive psychology, researchers explain that too much focus on the pursuit of material rewards traps us on the *hedonic treadmill*, which is "a metaphor for the human tendency to pursue one pleasure after another." The idea is that even though we think material gains will bring us enduring happiness, the boost we get from any plea-sure, big or small, eventually reverts to our default, baseline level of happiness. (Ditto for negative experiences, by the way.) This tendency to revert to the mean is why hedonism, the pursuit of pleasure, is so unfulfilling in the long run. You keep running after pleasure (i.e., the dopamine hit that comes from hitting goals), thinking it will bring happiness, but you're really just running in place rather than advanc-ing toward any meaningful boost in well-being.

Psychologists show that the way out of this revolving door is to stop focusing on the ephemeral pleasure of extrinsic, materialistic goals and start working toward achieving goals that are intrinsically motivating and have long-lasting meaning. Doing so is the best way to raise our baseline level of happiness permanently. If we don't find the work we're doing satisfying *in itself*, the material compensation we re-ceive for doing it eventually loses its power to enhance our well-being.

It's important for us to say again that we're not suggesting that getting well compensated for hard work is a problem; in fact, we endorse that 100 percent. And we're not saying that all commission structures and incentive-based bonuses are inherently flawed—setting realistic company goals and rewarding people well for their role in achieving them is the right thing to do. The key, which those with an Unsold Mindset have discovered, is that we should not be chasing *purely* quantitative targets; the measure of our contributions should be tied to something bigger.

We feel so much more positive well-being when we are highly engaged in our work and fulfilled by it in ways that have deeper meaning. Too often, the pressure to meet quantitative targets diverts our attention away from the more enriching aspects of our work. Many of those are hard to measure, and even if they could be measured, companies haven't formulated ways of doing so. When we're constantly reminding ourselves that we have to hit our sales targets or we won't make rent, we end up feeling we don't have time to enjoy conversations with clients and prospects, don't have time to develop relationships that might not result in any immediate "payback" that can be quantified by goal metrics, don't have latitude for expressing our creativity, and don't feel we have permission to focus on our own purpose.

For all these reasons, the authors of "Goals Gone Wild" write, "goal setting should be prescribed selectively, presented with a warning label, and closely monitored." But it's not all types of goals that need labeling. If we set *purpose-driven goals*, they can motivate us *and* provide the fulfillment we're all looking for.

The Remarkable Power of Purpose in Selling

Often in our interviews, we'd hear elite sellers tell us they are motivated by a specific purpose that inspires them every day to pursue each of their incremental goals tied to that purpose. They emphasized that this is a key reason they love selling—it is a powerful means to achieving things that really matter to them. What truly sets them apart from everyone else in this regard, however, is the fact that they can easily *articulate* their purpose for others. When we interviewed

Robert Chatwani, chief marketing officer of Atlassian, a global tech giant with over 250,000 customers, we didn't ask him about purpose specifically, but within the first three minutes of our conversation he articulated his, and its importance in his professional success. "When I'm most fulfilled and happy, the work I do is aligned with my purpose. For over two decades," he told us, "my purpose has been to work with high-performing teams to build meaningful businesses that create hope and opportunity in the world." Every goal he sets, every task he undertakes in his career, is colored by this purpose. "I could be working in any type of industry, on any type of business, any type of role—as long as it aligns with that purpose, I feel that I'm thriving."

Chatwani wasn't the only successful person we spoke with who let their purpose drive their careers. Influencer marketing legend Jon Wexler told us, "I've always felt clarity of purpose up front is critical—it defines your every move and forms the context for every decision you make." This clarity shines through in many of the interviews we've done with people who had their purpose clearly defined. Amy Volas, the salesperson-turned-entrepreneur we met in chapter 5, said the people she works with are what drive her. She told us her purpose is "to leave the sales ecosystem better than when I came into it through walking my talk and paying twenty-plus years of lessons learned forward." Comedian JB Smoove said, "My purpose in the end is to make people happy, to make them laugh, and to give them great memories." And entertainment executive Alex Avant said his purpose is "to create an atmosphere that will allow my sprit to align with others so trust is the dominant feeling. Whether I'm talking to one person or a million, my purpose is to foster true connection."

And it's not just true for the people we spoke with. A large study of top sales performers by Lisa Earle McLeod, author of *Selling with*

Noble Purpose, found that this kind of focus and clarity on a specific purpose that their selling serves was a striking characteristic of the top 10 percent of performers.

Being driven by purpose instead of simply closing deals and hitting targets gives you the opportunity to view selling as an opportunity to bring good to the world by uplifting the lives of the people you are selling to. A bank manager we talked to said she chose to work for a relatively small, community-based bank that focuses on small business loans because she is driven by helping local entrepreneurs and the neighborhoods they're based in. We might think of banking as the quintessential business whose purpose is making money, yet she sees her bank as a vital conduit to supporting business owners who bring much needed value to their communities. That makes every loan she signs off on deeply meaningful to her, not just another contribution to her numbers. Our book agent sees her purpose in helping develop and sell authors' book proposals, giving them a platform and helping to bring new ideas and valuable information into the world. And the reason we love teaching so much is because every week we get to see the impact we have on our students, through their assignments, their questions, their epiphanies, and their job offers. Every week they help push our mission forward.

Set Purpose-Driven Goals

We should all set goals that motivate us, but any goal we set should be tied specifically to achieving our purpose. Just as we have systems (like reviewing our goals every day) to help us push our goals forward, our goals help push our purpose forward. We even suggest, as goal-setting experts do, writing them down. This has worked for us in countless ways. A few years ago, after we decided to team up on our mission to change the way the world thinks about salespeople, we got together and wrote down a list of very specific goals, including achieving an exit for Bitium so we could afford to do what we're most passionate about, teaching other people to find meaning in a type of work we know is so rewarding, speaking in front of audiences in order to share our mission with as many people as possible, and writing a book for a major publisher to affect change at scale. It's important to note that every one of these involved selling something meaningful to us—the upside of a company we believed in, our ideas for the class, the book concept, and, at heart, ourselves.

We honestly thought we'd set some of these goals unrealistically high, but for us the magic was in the process of trying to achieve them because they were so tied to our purpose. The longer it took to hit a goal, the more time we had to discover new ways to move our purpose forward. We had come to feel a calling about putting an end to offensive sales stereotypes and giving people both a practical and theoretical take on how fulfilling and valuable selling authentically can be. And that made all the effort, all the false starts and stumbles, so much more than worthwhile. We've found our work engaging every step of the way, and we're almost always having fun doing it. Now we've made a career out of making fun of each other, spreading our message, and doing many of the things we'd been doing for free for years! We hadn't expected to find this sense of calling, and we were lucky, because we had each other to help us recognize how much we both wanted to pursue it.

One reason articulating purpose-driven goals is so powerful is that it's motivating, even during the hard times. It helps you enjoy the entire journey toward your goals, not just the destination. We've found that as we've chased our own goals. If we just had performance goals, we would have been failing the entire way, until the moment we weren't. But because we had articulated purpose-driven goals for ourselves, it was easy to celebrate the process because every win and every loss were moments worth celebrating.

Many have told us they see their purpose in every part of their work: the deals and the rejections; the amazing customers and the a-holes; from the beginning of the sales process to the inevitable relationship they have with their customers after it's over. Purpose removes fear and scarcity from the equation, because the highs *and* the lows become part of the greater good; they feel like they're happening *on purpose*, because they are. Areas of tension become moments of validation because the tension is an opportunity to exercise your purpose; it's why you do what you do.

This speaks to one of the more underappreciated side effects of articulating purpose-driven goals: They make you more productive. You have more resilience because you're more intrinsically motivated to keep working to achieve what you set out to do. This is another finding from the research on purpose in business. As Lisa Earle McLeod also points out, business professor Valerie Good conducted a study of sellers who scored high in expressing a sense of purpose about their work and discovered that they were more resilient and put in more effort to achieve their goals. When a salesperson's *goal* is to make fifty cold calls in a day, and they've been hung up on or rejected forty-one times already, how much more motivated and enthusiastic will they be for those final nine dials if they genuinely believe that one of the people who answers will get them closer to their purpose? We know from experience those conversations sound a lot different from the ones where the seller is simply making calls to hit a number because they *have* to.

When sellers set purpose-driven goals, decisions are also easier to make because any choice that doesn't align with their purpose is an automatic *no*. You don't interview for just any job. You don't take venture funding from just anyone. You don't even have to consider whether you'll use a smarmy sales tactic or do something that just doesn't feel quite in line with your morals or ethics. If it's not aligned with your purpose, it's not happening.

We once had an opportunity for a lucrative consulting project with a large software company whose numbers were leveling off. The chief revenue officer wanted us to come in and "fix" their sales team. As we discussed the situation with him, we realized that the problem started with the CEO, whose harsh style and obsession with unrealistic growth had put enormous pressure on the CRO, who in turn put inordinate pressure on the sales team. We asked to meet with the CEO to get his perspective on the problem, and it quickly became clear to us he was proud of the fear-based sales culture he'd created. In fact, he wanted us to reinforce it! Doing so would have violated *our* purpose, so it was an easy decision when we respectfully declined the gig.

Being clear on your purpose-driven goals can also help combat the completion bias problem. One of Garrett's friends is the CEO of a tech company who expresses his purpose in the form of a question: "What can I be doing at this moment that best serves myself and others?" He asks himself this question throughout each day, and it works. Instead of killing time scrolling Instagram on his phone, he'll catch himself and switch to watching an educational TED Talk. Instead of procrastinating by sorting through pointless emails, he reaches out to partners and customers he hasn't connected with in a while.

One last benefit of articulating your purpose was highlighted by

Simon Sinek in *Start with Why*, in writing about what he calls the "Celery Test." If you go to the supermarket and put healthy items like celery and rice milk in the same cart with junk food like Oreos and M&Ms, nobody can see what you believe in. You're not being guided by any discernible purpose. But if you truly commit to a healthy lifestyle as part of your purpose, then at the market you'll only have items in your cart that align with that purpose. You won't waste time looking for a bunch of items that don't fit with your purpose, or waste money on things you don't actually want or need. If people can identify your purpose, you can communicate it effectively, and you're more likely to get support from people who can help you with it, because they'll clearly understand what's important to you. As Sinek says, "With only celery and rice milk it's obvious to people walking by what you believe [when they look in your cart]." It works the same with the Unsold Mindset. By making your purpose clear, you'll "miraculously" attract more customers, partners, and referrals than everybody else.

This happened to us while sitting at a restaurant waiting for our dinner when a woman sitting at the table next to us commented on how much she loved Colin's shoes (for you sneakerheads who are wondering, they were Nike SB "Hawaii" Dunks with the hidden suede). Colin thanked her and mentioned that while he wanted to take all the credit for them, our college students often inspire his footwear. "What?! You guys are professors?!" she asked with the same look of disbelief most people have when they realize that we don't exactly fit the university professor stereotype. In the conversation that followed, we talked about our class, our book, our business, and everything in between. As we were talking about what we love doing through the lens of our purpose, she blurted out, "I want to help!" She told us that in her line of work, authenticity in selling is everything, and she was inspired to spread that message to others.

Her "line of work," it turned out, was public relations, and Jessica Sciacchitano leads a division at PR giant Rogers & Cowan PMK. In the weeks and months that followed, Jessica introduced us to some huge names in sports and entertainment because she believed they were perfect examples of the Unsold Mindset. We caught up with her recently and she said, "I've got to tell you, every time I talk about your book with someone it reminds me how important your purpose is. I want to help more, let me help you promote it. You don't have to pay me!" Because we knew our purpose, we were able to convey it to Jessica. She, in turn, saw *her* purpose in ours, which has led to collaboration that wouldn't have happened otherwise.

Knowing Your Purpose Is Easier Said Than Done

Here's the thing: You can't set fulfilling, purpose-driven goals without a clear sense of your own purpose. Experts have been touting the importance of purpose for years in books, on shows, in articles, blogs, and podcasts, and yet when we ask people to describe theirs, most struggle. The fact is, articulating a purpose you really, truly believe in (as opposed to generalities like "my purpose is to serve others") can be difficult. That's due in part to all the unhelpful cultural messaging we're bombarded with about materialistic markers of success. It's also partly because, through the course of our lives, we're *told* what our purpose should be: to get good grades; to raise a happy family; to make a good living . . . all perfectly admirable *goals*. But they aren't specific to a particular aspect of our being, some distinctive drive within us, that we want to express and develop.

During what she describes as her transformational senior year of college, a student of ours set a goal to land a job, and she assumed that once she accomplished that she would be happy. But to her surprise, when she was finally offered a good job, she found herself scared, unhappy, and confused. She couldn't accept that this version of "happy" was as good as it gets. She quickly realized that she needed something less situational and external, more internal and deep-rooted, to achieve true happiness.

We asked her what her purpose was, *why* she was taking the path she was on, and she stumbled trying to define it. She spent the next few weeks doing the internal work required to identify her purpose, and watching her transformation was incredible. She went from seeing herself as "just" a college senior with a job in marketing to, as she put it, "a daughter, friend, artist, comedian, student, teacher, influencer, coach, historian, entrepreneur, chef, and marketer." She realized what most of us find to be true at some point in life: What we're good at isn't necessarily the same as what we're meant to do. When it was all said and done, she crafted a strong, clear purpose: *To use my voice to speak up for people who can't speak for themselves.* She recognized that her purpose was evergreen—she could use it as motivation forever, whether she reached her goals or not. She started an online newsletter as a side project, which eventually turned into a source of income for her and, more importantly, connected her to like-minded people with similar purposes of their own. She continues to build her path, through marketing, in the social justice arena.

So how do you first define your purpose and then articulate a meaningful set of purpose-driven goals? We've found the following three exercises to be remarkably effective, so much so that we do them with nearly all our clients and students.

The Third Why

First, ask yourself the obvious: *What is my purpose?* Once you have an answer, act like a five-year-old and ask "why?" based on that answer.* When you get the next answer, go back into toddler mode and ask "why?" again, and then be the persistent kid that asks "why?" a third time. By the time you answer the third why, your actual purpose should be a lot clearer. (Quick aside: You may want to have someone else ask you the questions. We've found that a different perspective can lead to more targeted "why" questions that you wouldn't think to ask on your own.)

Nine times out of ten when we lead this exercise, people answer the first question with a goal, not anything to do with their purpose. They might say something like "to be independently wealthy," or "to crack six-figures this year." Sometimes they'll answer with something more personal, like "to make enough money to buy my family a house," or "to get promoted," but these are still just goals: extrinsic, tangible, easy to measure. It takes a second or third *why* to start revealing a deeper purpose.

Here's how the exercise unfolded when we did it with a growing company that had an eighteen-person sales team. Each salesperson was expected to convert ten new customers each month, but when we were brought in, only four people were consistently hitting that target. We asked each of them "What's your purpose?" and most answered with generalities. One said, "to help my customers find

---

* As best we can tell, this concept originated with Sakichi Toyoda in the early 1900s. He called it "5 Whys." We know from experience that the Unsold see tremendous value in three "whys," but feel free to ask as many "whys" as it takes!

a solution." (Uh, really, is *that* what's getting you out of bed in the morning?)

We responded: "Why is that important?"

"Because if I can help my customers find a solution, they'll buy from me, and we both win." (At least that's a bit more honest.)

Then the second why: "Why do you need to 'win'?"

"If I win, I get paid. That's important when it comes to things like paying my kids' tuition and taking them on family vacations. Getting paid helps me to focus on the stuff I want to do instead of what I *have to* do. In general, as long as I'm making money I'm a happy man, and the more you're paying me the happier I am." (Getting closer . . .)

Then the third why: "And why do you think you'd be happier?"

"Because I'm happiest when I'm being an awesome father to my kids and husband to my wife. If I could do that more, I'd be a lot less worried about the future. I could just be there with them in the moment." (Hell yes!) Being motivated to do all the things it takes to be a great seller is a lot easier when you see yourself furthering your desire to be a present parent and loving spouse, as opposed to telling yourself that you're "helping customers" as a means to a paycheck.

We're recommending doing this exercise to pin down your own purpose, but it can also be powerful to understand the purpose of the people you're selling to. If you decide to do this exercise with a customer, remember it's important to proceed with caution so you don't come across as awkward or inappropriate by asking the wrong questions at the wrong time. (Once again, if you think you sound cheesy, you do, remember?) You must first build up enough of a relationship with someone to earn their (usually unspoken) permission to ask them these *why* questions. Once you have that permission, which normally comes after being vulnerable with them and establishing an authentic, trusting relationship, it can have a massive impact on your conversations.

For example, while working with an electric vehicle (EV) and energy services company, Colin was pitching a company with one of the largest delivery fleets in the world. His contact was on the fence about purchasing. As they talked, Colin asked why he was tasked with looking into adding EVs to their fleet (Why #1). The exec explained that his company needed to be an innovator in their space. When Colin asked why that was important (Why #2), he responded, "Because that's how we remain a leader in our industry." Colin then asked why his company remaining a leader was important to him *personally* (Why #3), and that's when the gold appeared: "We have thousands of employees. This is *my* project; it's my personal brand on the line, not just the company's. Innovative projects like this give me a chance to separate myself from being just another ant in the ant farm." By understanding that the exec's purpose was not just to be an innovator, or to make a meaningful impact on his entire industry, but to be a personally significant contributor, Colin was able to connect in a meaningful way and help him understand exactly how converting their fleet to electric could help him with all those things.

Remember, your job as a seller isn't just to reach your goals, it's to help your customers reach theirs.

Crafting a Purpose Statement

There's no one best way to craft a purpose statement. One person we know started by listing the happiest memories of her life and then identified what they all had in common. She realized that she was happiest when she was co-creating anything with people who had skills that complimented hers, which led her to her purpose: *to sur-round [herself] with interesting people and create products that change the world.* A sales manager we met asked his team members a series of deep questions like "What would you do for free?," "If you could change something about the world, what would it be?," and "If you only had a year left to live, what would you do?" He then used their answers to spot common themes. Using those same questions, he iden-tified his own purpose: *to live [his] life in a way that makes things better for the people around [him], and for the generations that will follow.*

When we work with teams, we love starting with a quick exercise to get people thinking about *why* they do what they do, and what brings the most meaning to their day. This exercise can help you de-velop a simple version of your purpose to start using right away:

1. First, list a couple of your unique qualities. Examples might be *enthusiasm* and *creativity*. The point here is to focus on traits that make you "you" and put them at the forefront of what you try to do every day. Are you friendly, charismatic, or intelligent? Do you exhibit strength, resilience, or calmness? If you're having trouble narrowing it down, think about times when you felt successful or accomplished something you were proud of. Ask friends what they most respect about you. If you were, hypothetically, a cou-ple of sales-mindset-advisors-slash-business-professors, you might end up with something like *passion* and *drive*.

2. Now list one or two ways that you enjoy expressing those qualities and interacting with other people. Examples here might be *sup-porting* and *inspiring*. Write them down as verbs ending in -ing. Do you look forward to deep conversations with people you've never met before? If so, you might say *connecting*. Do you love

seeing your name in lights? One of your verbs might be *achieving*. Would you rather spend your entire day interacting with executives who inspire you? You could put down *learning*. The two guys in our totally hypothetical example might say *teaching* and *inspiring*.

3. Next, think of a time you felt most joyous, fulfilled, and complete. What does it feel like? In our example, it might be: *Our interactions with people are authentic, vulnerable, and meaningful; we are learning as much from them as they are from us, and they believe in our mission so much that they can't wait to start living it themselves and teaching it to others.* Yours will almost certainly be completely different, and that's great! Try to think in detail about what you're saying, where you are, who you're with, how you're feeling, and any other details that come to mind until you can boil it down to something tangible.

4. Lastly, combine the three into a short statement that is motivating and inspiring to you. Using the above examples, these hypothetical-but-hopefully-somewhat-likable sales mindset guys might end up with: *Our purpose is using our passion and drive to teach and inspire people to have authentic, vulnerable, meaningful interactions, and to bring more authenticity and good into the world.*

To develop your purpose statement further, we recommend following the eight guidelines Mike Murphy lists in his book *The Creation Principle* in his discussion about what he calls Intention Statements:

1. Write in present tense
2. Use positive language
3. Make it emotionally powerful and authentic

4. Express gratitude within it
5. Really home in on what you truly desire
6. Make sure there is no judgment
7. Approach it as if there were infinite possibilities
8. Upgrade your purpose as you evolve

Doing these things makes it more likely that your purpose will resonate and that you'll internalize it to get maximum mileage out of it.

We know the process of creating a purpose statement works because we've done it with hundreds of people. One young entrepreneur, who owned a clothing company that catered to counterculture students, was struggling to keep his company alive. He was considering giving up on the business he'd been relentlessly building for two years. After doing this exercise, he ended up with a statement that changed the way he looked at his life and his business: *"My purpose is to use my compassion and passion to empower, inspire, and give a voice to outcasts who don't fit the cookie-cutter mold of collegiate apparel and to be an advocate for everyone who has earned the right to be proud of their university and accomplishments."* He typed this out, made it his screensaver on both his laptop and phone, and completely transformed the way he looked at his business. He decided to donate a percentage of his company's revenue to mental health causes that were important to him, which changed the way he spoke to his customers. He was no longer talking about clothing, he was talking about a means to having an impact on the world he'd always dreamed of. After making this shift, he tripled his company's revenue over the next three months! His actions and conversations started to have real meaning instead of just doing things because he felt like he was supposed to.

A student in our class was struggling to sell herself to interviewers and land her first job. She couldn't figure out where she was going wrong in the interview process. After working through her purpose statement exercise, she realized that her purpose was *to use my technical prowess and sense of humor to teach and guide people how to embrace technology and not fear it, by working together to take complex solutions and make them digestible for anyone to understand how technology can help their businesses change the world.* This led her to conclude that she was applying for the wrong kinds of jobs the whole time—no wonder she was striking out. She soon landed a job as a technical salesperson at one of the largest companies in the world (it rhymes with "shmamazon") and has been able to share her story with other students applying for jobs as part of a student outreach recruiting program.

One last note, as you reflect on your own purpose, it may help to talk with family and friends; they have often perceived things about us, and what we care most about, that we may have lost some sight of. Taking the time to do the work to identify and articulate your purpose will pay big dividends; it's one of the most eye-opening exercises you can do.

Crafting Your Purpose-Driven Goals

For most people we work with, once they've articulated a strong purpose statement, creating their own set of purpose-driven goals is easy. For any goal you set, or any goal that is set for you, use a bridging word to connect your goal to your purpose. The bridging word can be *because*: "My goal is to raise $100 million in new capital for my startup *because* it will create more jobs for people in low-income communities that otherwise wouldn't have access to those opportunities." Another bridging word is *so*: "My goal is to get hired at a Fortune 500 company *so* I can inspire a younger generation of diverse candidates that they belong wherever they choose to belong." Others might be *to, for,* or *since.*

In almost every case, even things that don't seem remotely related to your purpose can be tied to it in some way. One student we took through the purpose statement exercise came to us after class looking very concerned. "I loved this exercise," she told us, "but it's got me stressing out. I've been interviewing like crazy for what I thought was my dream job as a product manager, but that job has nothing to do with my purpose."

We asked her to share her purpose statement with us, and she promptly recited, "My purpose is to help others realize their potential by being supportive, caring, and inspirational and giving them a forum to be the best they can be." A beautiful purpose. Now she had to tie it to designing technology products for a living.

"What's a product manager's job?" Garrett asked her.

"Collecting information from customers, developers, and other stakeholders to help drive the direction of the software we build."

"And what happens if you do your job well?" Colin probed.

She was starting to see it now. "I guess we could end up building something that is valuable and useful for everyone who uses it. I see where you're going with this. If I help create a great product, the value the people using it get will help them do their best work, which hopefully will allow them to realize their potential!"

If you can't find a way to make a goal a purpose-driven goal, keep thinking it through. And if you truly get stuck, it might be time to set a new goal instead.

• • •

Since the early days of building Microsoft, Bill Gates has been guided by purpose. Immortalized in Microsoft's mission statement, his purpose is "to empower every person and every organization on the planet to achieve more." Looking at all he's accomplished in his career (and beyond), it seems clear his goals were all driven by this purpose. The goal to have "a computer on every desk, in every home" is certainly germane to helping everyone on Earth "achieve more." So are his current projects aimed at eradicating poverty, preventable diseases, and world hunger. Even Oprah is still thriving and striving for more. In an interview, she said her new goal was to figure out "how to get people to see that we are more alike than we are different." Talk about an audacious, and meaningful, goal, which couldn't be more in keeping with her original, core purpose to be a teacher and inspire others.

When you approach life with an Unsold Mindset, setting and achieving purpose-driven goals, you're no longer on the treadmill, you're climbing the mountain *you* chose, looking forward to scaling the next set of peaks you'll see from the summit. You won't be discouraged by the fact that as soon as you achieve one goal you're going to immediately get started on the next one. You'll *want* to keep going, testing your limits, using all your talents, learning what you're capable of. You'll feel the value and impact of your efforts every day, for you and for others. And when it comes to selling, you'll be constantly reminded that *for you*, the work is about so much more than closing deals and hitting numbers. When done the right way for the right reasons, selling can be one of the most powerful instruments for doing good in this world.

The Best Part of the Movie

When we first began sharing the Unsold Mindset with other people, we realized even minor shifts in thinking were having an outsized impact on how they approached the art and science of selling. Different elements of the mindset resonated with different people. Some would light up as we talked about something as simple as giving yourself permission to be imperfect by saying what you're really thinking in the moment or by *not* having all the answers all the time. Others fell in love with, well . . . falling in love, and gravitated toward the idea of looking for the good and finding it. Still others shared that they didn't understand why hitting goals didn't always equate to happiness until they understood the interplay between their goals and their purpose.

As we said at the start, there's no "right way" to do anything, and that includes practicing an Unsold Mindset. Use the ideas from this book in *your own way*. Focus on how you're going to think, rather than what you're going to say. Your thoughts will determine what being "unsold" means to you, but only if you're aware of them. Over time, we hope you'll try taking on *all* the shifts in perspective we've introduced. They reinforce one another, and the more we've been able to inhabit the Unsold Mindset, the more our lives have changed because of it. We found ourselves more engaged in our interactions, more certain things would work out in our favor, and more eager to learn. We started asking better questions and consciously looked for ways to be the realest versions of ourselves with our clients, our audiences, our students, and our families. We made decisions based on purpose, and reminded ourselves to celebrate the process, especially when it wasn't easy to do.

To say that learning from so many remarkable people with an Unsold Mindset had an impact on us would be the understatement of the century. The inspiration we took from our interactions with them encouraged us to pursue a goal we hadn't even really allowed ourselves to admit we had, launching us into one of the most improbable but thrilling sales cycles of our lives. The realization of how important that opportunity was came from one of the last interviews we conducted and an Impactful Question we weren't expecting . . .

• • •

DeeDee Gordon is one of the most successful branding experts on the planet. It's her job to help the world's biggest companies understand consumers, markets, and culture so they can meet their customers in the right places, with the right message, at the right time. She's so good at what she does, famed author and *New Yorker* columnist Malcolm Gladwell once called her the "cool hunter." We couldn't resist asking her for some advice.

"How do we create the biggest impact we can with this book?" we asked her at the very end of our conversation.

She didn't hesitate. "Your impact will be the greatest if readers believe in *you*. Which means they have to *know* you. How can you get as many people as possible to know who you really are so they want to buy the book and *then* get up and take action?"

Whoa, talk about an Impactful Question! How did she know to ask us that?

DeeDee had met us less than an hour earlier, yet, in true Unsold fashion, she locked straight in on our purpose. She had picked up on how important it is for us to not just write this book, but to influence actual change. By forcing us to think about our objective in a context we'd never considered before, she turned what could have been a transactional interaction into a transformational one. She grinned as we said our goodbyes, as if she already knew the new journey we were about to embark on.

As soon as the interview ended, we started trying to answer her question. For a short while, we tiptoed around admitting to ourselves what we truly believed would be the best way to communicate our take on selling to an audience at scale. Should we launch a podcast? A YouTube channel? A social media campaign? All great options, but once we decided to be brutally honest with ourselves we realized what we needed to do was bigger. Way bigger. Something we knew nothing about.

We were going to create a TV show.

Are we crazy? we asked ourselves. Maybe, but as we thought about it, we realized we'd both been manifesting the idea since we first started working on the book. It had snuck its way into our conversations with each other and friends when we discussed what we were writing. We'd asked our literary agent, Lisa, about TV rights when we were weighing options from publishers. We'd thought about what great TV the interviews we'd conducted and recorded for the book would make and commented more than a few times about how odd it is that there aren't really any sales-specific shows on TV. After all, there are shows about catching crabs, driving trucks on ice, working on a cruise ship . . . hell, there are even shows about watching other TV shows! We decided to go for it, and we started by practicing intentional ignorance.

It was tempting to learn everything we could about the process of developing a show, but we knew there were others with that expertise, and that it might serve us better to lean into what we didn't know, letting them own their dharma, so we could own ours. With this in mind, we asked our friend Josh Pearl, an agent at Creative Artists Agency (CAA), one of the top talent agencies in the world, if we could take him to lunch. We asked him if we were delusional for thinking we could pull this off and, to our surprise, he loved the idea! "Selling is something everyone, literally everyone, does in some capacity every day," he responded. "It's crazy that there's not more television programming that plays to that. It won't be easy, but with the right idea, you *could* do this."

We spent the rest of the meal as learners, asking about things that excited us, peppering him for advice. In true Unsold fashion, he was incredibly generous; he wasn't just adding value, he was being valuable to us in a way that took the conversation way beyond transactional. He told us how to think about creating show ideas, he laid out the process for getting a production deal, and he gave us a download of all the main players in the space—he even said he'd introduce us to people who could help once we were ready. Imagine that! The first person we told about our crazy idea not only didn't laugh us out of the building, he offered to help.

As we talked about next steps, we committed to one another that we would stay completely "us" throughout the entire process. We wanted to create something that was an authentic representation of the Unsold Mindset, and of each other. We vowed we wouldn't let the concept get hijacked and become something that ends up perpetuating the stigma we're trying to get rid of. The show would have to redefine what it meant to sell, revealing how great selling of all kinds can be when people think about it differently.

Next, we gave ourselves total, unadulterated creative freedom, meeting frequently over chips, salsa, and more than a few spicy margaritas, to throw all kinds of ideas around. Eventually, we narrowed our ideas down to four shows: a scripted comedy about people with different sales jobs living together in Los Angeles (think *Friends* but where the characters all have sales jobs); an unscripted show based on the greatest salespeople in the most stereotypical sales industries we could think of (used cars, insurance, timeshares, etc.) that would show just how unfounded the stereotypes could be when people sell with an Unsold Mindset; an interview show that would bring conversations like the ones we'd been having with amazing salespeople to the screen; and our favorite, a human interest reality show that would help people who desperately need to sell learn about the Unsold Mindset and change their lives forever. We had no idea if any of them would appeal to producers. All we knew for sure was that *we* would watch any one of them—like anyone with an Unsold Mindset, we believed in our product.

As we began fleshing out the ideas, we stayed anchored to the Unsold Mindset, focusing on the process and remaining detached from the outcome. Doing this kept us motivated, even when it seemed as if we weren't making any progress, and we had a blast figuring it out. We would come up with ideas, tweak the good ones, throw out the mediocre ones, and get right back at it the next day. We intentionally ignored advice from books or blogs on how people are "supposed" to develop shows; we were operating way outside the boundaries of what we knew, but one thing we did know was that we wanted to stay fresh. If we were truly going to practice what we teach, we couldn't allow ourselves to be inhibited by worries about meeting expectations, and we didn't want to copy what others had built.

We kept the research we'd done about everyday creativity in mind and used some of the techniques we'd learned from our interviews, like being present with ideas as they arose, not judging them right away, and reminding ourselves that our terrible ideas (which we had plenty of) were essential to learning when we had good ones.

When we were ready to try to sell our concepts, we consciously chose to remain pathological optimists, and when one of us needed to hear it (which was often), we reminded each other we had an abundance of opportunities everywhere, we just needed to look. TV has never been available through so many platforms. We were also hopeful people would want to help us once they understood our mission, so we told whoever would listen what we were trying to do. We asked for any advice they could give, or introductions they might make, no matter whether it seemed likely they could. What do you think happened? People wanted to help!

One of those people was Jason Ferguson, a friend, sales leader, and speaker we'd interviewed when we first started writing the book. As soon as we told him what we were up to, his eyes lit up. "I know exactly who you should talk to!" he exclaimed. An hour later we were trading texts with a senior vice president of development for a production company behind some of the biggest non-scripted TV shows in the world. A call was scheduled the next day, so we had an entire night to fall in love. Turns out we only needed a few seconds. The first thing that jumped out on his LinkedIn profile was his alma mater: *University of Southern California, B.A., Cinematic Arts*! The next day we told him about us, our class, and this book. He immediately got it. "Let's set up a meeting with my boss," he said. "I don't know what will come of it, but at the very least you can get some feedback on what you're trying to do." His boss turned out to be the chief creative officer of the company who spearheaded huge unscripted hit shows. When we looked him up to do our Love 3x3, we realized quickly he was the real deal. He'd won four Emmys!

We were nervous about the meeting. We expected the production company team would turn it over to us and we'd pitch while they scrutinized the idea like the panel of investors on *Shark Tank*. But it wasn't like that at all. Instead, they greeted us warmly and told us they were fans of our content and that they were excited to hear our ideas. That helped us resist the temptation to put on an act. "We're not exactly sure how this is supposed to go," we admitted, showing our work, "and we don't really know what you or the people you sell shows to are looking for. We've put together some ideas that we're really excited about and proud of and we'd love to know what you think."

Instead of making us feel like we were the sellers and they were the buyers, with all the power and knowledge, they made us feel like we were on the same team from the very beginning. They were genuinely interested in learning about us, our ideas, and our mission, and we felt like we were in a whiteboard session with the same shared goal: to come out of the conversation with something everyone believes in. They were authentic, too, making suggestions that made our ideas better and pointing out challenges we hadn't thought to address due to our lack of experience in the medium. They gave us a lot of advice and seemed genuinely interested in us, and in the shows.

In the weeks that followed, we found ourselves on both sides of the table, selling and being sold to every day. We were introduced to agents, and there was a vibe with one television agent at CAA (not Josh) who sold us on representing our interests by reaffirming our deepest belief: that we were valuable *because* we were unsold on who the entertainment industry wanted us to be. We decided to work with him, and he set up meetings with more production companies, ones he thought had the potential to be even better fits for one or more of our shows. In our meetings with those companies, we again sold our ideas as they sold us on their value(s). When one production company strongly suggested we consider being the on-screen hosts for a show, we had to sell our wives on the idea of us potentially being in front of the camera. (Those are stories for another book!) The production company we ultimately signed a term sheet with sold us on their vision by caring about ours. They saw more good in our ideas than we did, and it was obvious they didn't just have experience in looking for the good, they knew where to find it. Our ideas sounded better coming out of their mouths than they did from our own, and they brought new ideas to the table we never would have thought of ourselves.

In all these interactions, just as we'd found throughout the process of writing the book, the Unsold Mindset made the experience incredibly enjoyable and rewarding. We showed up as exactly who we are and never pretended to know things we didn't. We learned from mistakes we made, fell in love with so many people we'd never expected to meet, and truly felt like many of them were on our team. Yet another sales stereotype—that of greedy Hollywood types who are only out for themselves and their egos—proved to be BS. Giving ourselves permission to be creative gave us a daily injection of joy and allowed us to apply ourselves to a totally new way of living our purpose and furthering our mission to get rid of the stigma associated with selling.

We still don't know how this story ends, but ultimately it doesn't matter. In fact, that's the point. It's not about celebrating the ending, it's about celebrating the process. We're enjoying the wins *and* learning from the missteps along the way. Maybe the most valuable lesson we've learned from our entire journey to understanding the Unsold Mindset is that *this, here, today, is the best part of the movie.* We don't spend $72 for two movie tickets and some Sour Patch Kids just to see the ending, when the protagonist comes out on top. We go to see everything that happens in the middle. We go for the highs, the lows, the adventures, the mistakes, the lessons, the laughs. If we can remember that, we'll realize that we're *always* in the best part of the movie. When we look back at the good days, the bad days, and all the days in between, they'll *all* be the "good old days." Remembering that makes the drama of selling (and life) that much more fulfilling every day.

Selling is nothing to be ashamed of. It offers a unique opportunity to express ourselves, connect with people, be creative, learn about ourselves (and so much more), and grow from challenges. Best of all, it allows people to further their purpose, whether by gaining support for ideas, helping people solve problems in their lives, or being the catalyst for a transformational change.

At the beginning of this book, we told you we've asked a lot of hugely successful sellers the same question: *Who is the greatest salesperson you know?* Of all the answers we heard, two names came up more than any others: Steve Jobs and Dr. Martin Luther King Jr. Think about that. Two of the most influential figures of the last hundred years are remembered, at least by some, for how they were able to *sell*. Next time you feel a twinge of unease about selling, remember that. Be proud to sell. For some of you, selling will change your life. For others, selling will change other people's lives. And for a few of you, selling might just change the world.

Big love,

Colin & Garrett

Acknowledgments

Colin and Garrett:

It's been said the best way to learn is to teach, and this book is proof of that. Over the years, the students that have taken our class have supported us, challenged us, and made us better in just about every way. As they've made their way in the "real world," it's been inspiring to see them put the Unsold Mindset to work in their careers *and* in their lives. Without them, this book doesn't exist, and we are forever grateful.

One lesson we always try to impart on our students is that the answer is always *no* until you ask. When we first started the journey of writing this book, we were blown away by how many people were willing to help us when we asked, even though many of them had no idea who we were, and there certainly wasn't anything obvious in it for them. Specifically, we owe a HUGE thank you to everyone who was generous enough to sit down with us to be formally interviewed for the book. You were all brilliant and we wish we could have included stories and lessons from all of you. We promise to try to find another avenue for sharing your voices so others can benefit from your wisdom as we did.

To the people who helped us secure so many of those interviews, none of this happens without you! Thank you so much for introducing us to some of the most fascinating and hard-to-reach people on the planet. You didn't have to vouch for us, but you did, and we don't take that lightly.

It's not lost on us that the people you surround yourself with have as much to do with your success as anything you might do yourself. Somehow we got lucky and ended up with an amazing group of people on our book team who are not only legends at what they do, they're also great human beings. Our literary agent, Lisa DiMona, put us through the ringer for almost two years, challenging us when we needed to be challenged, giving us incredible advice, pushing us to make sure our ideas were "pithy," and making sure the things we say when we're speaking to classrooms or audiences translated to the page. Our developmental editor extraordinaire, Emily Loose, might have had the hardest job of all, taking two voices and tens of thousands of words (at least!) and helping us boil it all down to the book you just finished. And Hollis Heimbouch, our leader and champion at HarperCollins, took a chance on two first-time authors with nothing but a mission, a plan, and *way* too much pathological optimism. Thank you all for believing in us. You changed our lives.

Some people only joined us for part of the journey, but still had a huge impact on the outcome. Will Weisser and Nikki Katz, the influence you had on early versions of our concepts can still be felt in these pages. Wendy Wong, your career deservedly moved faster than the book writing process, but we're so grateful we got to benefit from your perspective while we could.

Lastly, thanks to *you* for taking a shot on us and reading our book. We hope you had as much fun reading it as we did writing it. If there's ever anything we can do to help you drive your own purpose forward, just reach out and let us know. We're easy to find, and if we can help, we're in!

Acknowledgments

Garrett:

Writing a book is no joke. Even when you're not sitting at your computer to write or edit, the book is on your mind. There's no off switch. Fortunately, my wife, Lauren, is a superhuman, juggling family, work, and a million other things to keep the ship running smoothly. Lo, thank you for being the best partner anyone could ask for, and for giving me the opportunity to chase all these crazy dreams.

My sons, Cooper and Brady, are *by far* the best salespeople I know. It's almost impossible to say no to them, and if you do, they'll find a way to change your mind anyway! Everything I do is for you boys. I love you.

My parents, Steve and Shelly Brown, are my heroes. I'm sure any decent therapist would tell me it's not a coincidence I started my career as a lawyer (like my dad) and have now become a teacher (like my mom). I couldn't have asked for better role models. Thanks, Mom and Dad.

To all of my family and friends, I appreciate all of you so much. I know you're mad I didn't thank you by name, but you can blame Harper Business for giving us a page limit for our acknowledgments, and Colin for demanding I give him his fair share of that allotment.

And speaking of Colin . . . Colin, thank you for seeing something in a slightly insecure, overly analytical introvert and deciding to throw in with me. I don't think many people are lucky enough to hang out every day with their best friend and call it "work," but I am, and I'm grateful for it. The adventure we've been on since we met is *insane*, and it's just getting started!

Colin:

Margot, you are the love of my life. This book doesn't exist without you. You gave me courage when it wasn't easy to feel courageous.

Acknowledgments

When I was flying, on stages, in hotels, and in the garage writing until the wee hours of the morning, you were packing lunches, changing diapers, making dinners, doing bedtime, and holding our family down day-in and day-out so I could pursue my dreams . . . all while having your own thriving career with a whole other group of people who depend on you to show up. You're such a boss, I love you, and I'm so proud to be your husband. Thank you.

Lambo (Liam) and Cale (Caleb), everything I do is for you. Daddy loves you both so much. The hardest part of this book process has been the time away from you two. You are the most compassionate and kind human beings I've ever met. Thank you for the lessons you teach me every day and proving that miracles exist. Always remember Rule #1!

My loving parents, Joyce and Vinton. I grew up thinking I was more special than I probably was, mainly because that's all you've ever told me my entire life. I have no idea why I believed you, but I am who I am because of it, and because of you. Ironically, you two are the actual special ones. Thank you for being delusional; I finally get it. I love you.

My brothers! No one will ever know how much you really mean to me. I've never had to look over my shoulder because you've always had my back. You inspire me daily and I'm so grateful to have you in my corner. You *are* the Unsold Mindset. Love you guys. Abbondanza!

Speaking of brothers, Garrett, I don't know how we got so lucky. Oh wait, I do know . . . because of you. I love you, brethren (Garrett *hates* when I say "brethren"). Me and you man . . . here's to the best part of the movie!

Jay-Z, Barack Obama, and Lenny Kravitz. Your authenticity has inspired me in the most meaningful of ways. Thank you for existing so people like me can look up to people like you.

Notes

INTRODUCTION Who Are the Unsold?

9 *two thirds of salespeople reported*: Serenity Gibbons, "Sales Teams are Experiencing a Burnout Epidemic," *Forbes*, December 8, 2020. https://www.forbes.com/sites/serenitygibbons/2020/12/08/sales -teams-are-experiencing-a-burnout-epidemic---heres-how-to-prioritize -your-teams-tasks/?sh=1e7ef2674f92.

CHAPTER ONE You Can't "Act" Authentic

15 *A person's name:* Dale Carnegie, *How to Win Friends and Influence People* (1936; rev. ed., 1981).

16 *named one of the most annoying characters*: Willa Paskin, Margaret Lyons, and Amanda Dobbins, "TV's Ten Most Annoying Characters," Vulture, December 5, 2011. https://www.vulture.com /2011/12/tvs-ten-most-annoying-characters.html.

16 *"The worst fault a salesman can commit"*: Kenneth Roman, *The King of Madison Avenue: David Ogilvy and the Making of Modern Advertising* (St. Martin's Griffin, 2010), 41.

17 *This is the awareness*: Marian Friestad and Peter Wright, "The Persuasion Knowledge Model: How People Cope with Persua- sion Attempts," *Journal of Consumer Research* 21, no. 1 (1994): 1–31. http://www.jstor.org/stable/2489738.

17 *Studies of consumer responses*: I. Silver, G. Newman, and D.A. Small, "Inauthenticity aversion: Moral reactance toward tainted actors, actions, and objects," *Consumer Psychology Review* 4 (2021): 70–82. https://doi.org/10.1002/arcp.1064.

17   *. . . just one piece of inconsistent information*: Ibid.

18   *in selling interactions*: Colleen Stanley, "Two Reasons Your Sales Team Lacks Authenticity," LinkedIn, November 15, 2018. https://www.linkedin.com/pulse/two-reasons-your-sales-team-lacks-authenticity-colleen-stanley-ceo/.

20   *One reason that's true*: George W. Dudley and Shannon L. Goodson, *The Psychology of Sales Call Reluctance: Earning What You're Worth in Sales* (Behavioral Science Research Press, Inc. 2007).

26   *One study was conducted*: Dan Cable, Francesca Gino, and Bradley Staats, "The Power Way Onboarding Can Encourage Authenticity," *Harvard Business Review*, November 26, 2015. https://hbr.org/2015/11/the-powerful-way-onboarding-can-encourage-authenticity.

26   *Similarly, research by Ernst & Young*: Henna Inam, "The Importance of Being Authentic," *Wharton Magazine*, Fall 2016. https://magazine.wharton.upenn.edu/issues/fall-2016/the-importance-of-being-authentic/.

26   *As for employee satisfaction*: Ante Glavas, "Corporate Social Responsibility and Employee Engagement . . . ," *Frontiers in Psychology*, May 31, 2016. https://doi.org/10.3389/fpsyg.2016.00796.

26   *In fact, psychologist Abraham Maslow*: A.H. Maslow, "A Theory of Human Motivation," *Psychological Review* 50, no 4 (1943): 370–96, esp. 382.

27   *In his book* Authentic: Stephen Joseph, *Authentic: How to Be Yourself and Why It Matters* (Piatkus, 2016), 15.

27   *Specific benefits he points to*: Ibid., 119, 125.

27   *Authenticity is also associated*: Ibid., 120.

28   *A final reason*: Ibid., 103.

31   *Sara tells how she interrupted*: Sara Blakely, "How a Pitch in a Nieman Marcus Ladies Room Changed Sara Blakely's Life," interview by Guy Raz, *How I Built This*, NPR, September 12, 2016. https://www.npr.org/transcripts/493312213.

32 *As psychologist and Wharton professor*: Adam Grant, "The Fine Line Between Helpful and Harmful Authenticity," *New York Times*, April 10, 2020. https://www.nytimes.com/2020/04/10/smarter -living/the-fine-line-between-helpful-and-harmful-authenticity.html.

32 *326 percent growth*: BBC News, "Zoom sees more growth after 'unprecedented' 2020," BBC News, March 1, 2021. https://www .bbc.com/news/business-56247489.

33 *as Susan Cain emphasized*: S. Cain, *Quiet: The Power of Introverts in a World That Can't Stop Talking* (Crown Publishers/Random House, 2012).

34 *As Adam Grant highlights*: Grant, "The Fine Line Between Helpful and Harmful Authenticity."

CHAPTER TWO Intentional Ignorance

42 *But research conducted*: Nicholas Toman, et al., "The New Sales Imperative," *Harvard Business Review*, March–April 2017. https:// hbr.org/2017/03/the-new-sales-imperative.

44 *This is a bias called* belief superiority: Michael P. Hall and Kaitlin T. Raimi, "Is belief superiority justified by superior knowledge?," *Journal of Experimental Social Psychology* 76 (May 2018): 290–306.

45 *One reason psychologists cite*: F. Diane Barth, "What's the Best Way to Handle a Know-It-All?," *Psychology Today*, December 21, 2013; Mark Banschick, "Narcissists and Other Know-It-Alls," *Psychology Today*, December 18, 2020.

46 *But people don't want to feel*: James W. Moore, "What Is the Sense of Agency and Why Does It Matter?," *Frontiers in Psychology*, August 29, 2016.

47 *Chip and Dan Heath*: Chip and Dan Heath, "The Curse of Knowledge," *Harvard Business Review,* December 2006.

48 *Economist George Loewenstein and colleagues*: Colin Camerer, University of Pennsylvania; George Loewenstein, University

of Chicago; Martin Weber, "The Curse of Knowledge in Economic Settings: An Experimental Analysis," *Journal of Political Economy* 97, no. 5 (1989).

48 *As profiled in the book* Blue Ocean Strategy: W. Chan Kim and Renee Mauborgne, *Blue Ocean Strategy*, Expanded Edition (Harvard Business Review Press, 2015), 33.

51 *This is a form of "job crafting"*: Justin M. Berg, Jane E. Dutton, and Amy Wrzesniewski, "What Is Job Crafting and Why Does It Matter?," University of Michigan Ross School of Business, Center for Positive Organizational Scholarship, Theory to Practice Briefing, revised August 2008.

51 *Research shows it also*: Timothy Butler and James Waldroop, "Job Sculpting: The Art of Retaining Your Best People," *Harvard Business Review*, September–October 1999.

59 *Dharma has been described*: Kitty Waters, "How to do your Dharma (and live your best life)," Thrive Global. https://thrive global.com/stories/how-to-do-your-dharma-and-live-your-best-life/.

60 *"You can know too much"*: Paul McCartney, interview by Howard Stern, *The Howard Stern Show*, November 10, 2021.

CHAPTER THREE Growing into an Unsold Mindset

61 *"I went to every single record label"*: Kyle Anderson, "Jay-Z Recalls How Record Labels Thought He Was 'Terrible,'" MTV News, August 27, 2009. http://www.mtv.com/news/1619696/jay-z-recalls-how -record-labels-thought-he-was-terrible/.

62 *"[The rejection] made me appreciate it . . ."*: Ibid.

63 *Stanford psychological researcher Carol Dweck*: Carol Dweck, *Mindset: The New Psychology of Success* (Random House, 2006).

65 *A growth mindset also inspires people*: Ibid., 48.

65 *She writes that some with a fixed mindset worry*: Ibid., 226.

66   *That begins, as Dweck writes*: Ibid., 10.

69   *Psychologist Rahav Gabay*: Scott Barry Kaufman, "Unraveling the Mindset of Victimhood," *Scientific American,* June 29, 2020. https://www.scientificamerican.com/article/unraveling-the-mindset-of -victimhood/.

69   *In his book* The Power of TED: David Emerald, *The Power of TED* (*the Empowerment Dynamic)* (Polaris Publishing, 2015).

72   *More than thirty years ago*: Stephen Covey, *The 7 Habits of Highly Effective People* (Free Press, revised edition 2004), 219–20.

74   *We want to cultivate* adaptive *resilience*: Mark Robinson, "Making Adaptive Resilience Real," Arts Council England, July 2010, 14. http://culturehive.co.uk/wp-content/uploads/2013/04/Making -adaptive-resilience-real.pdf.

74   *In her book* Bouncing Back: Linda Graham, *Bouncing Back: Rewiring Your Brain for Maximum Resilience and Well-Being* (New World Library, 2013), xxv.

74   *To drive home the point*: Ibid., 49.

75   *"we all have an innate capacity"*: Ibid., 120.

79   *Psychologist Tchiki Davis*: Tchiki Davis, "Positive Reappraisal," Berkeley Well-Being Institute. https://www.berkeleywellbeing .com/positive-reappraisal-activity.html.

80   *Linda Graham's "Finding the Gift in the Mistake" exercise*: Graham, "Bouncing Back," 243–44.

81   *He always recommended*: Trevor Moawad, *It Takes What It Takes* (HarperOne, 2020).

85   *As cognitive psychologists have shown*: Elaine Mead, "What is Positive Self-Talk?," PositivePsychology.com, March 22, 2022, version. https://positivepsychology.com/positive-self-talk/.

CHAPTER FOUR Pathological Optimism

89 *and helped Becky's family contend*: Christine Hall, "Exclusive: Preveta Raises $2M to Help Coordinate Care for Early Disease Detection," Crunchbase News, March 26, 2021; Breanna De Vera, "How Preveta Could Change the Game for Early Cancer Detection," Dot.la, March 31, 2021. https://dot.la/early-cancer-detection -2651298138.html.

91 *Barbara Ehrenreich, author of* Bright-Sided: Jia Tolentino, "Barbara Ehrenreich Is Not an Optimist: But She Has Hope for the Future," NewYorker.com, March 21, 2020. https://www.newyorker .com/culture/the-new-yorker-interview/barbara-ehrenreich-is-not-an -optimist-but-she-has-hope-for-the-future.

92 *Psychologist Kimberly Hershenson:* Brianna Steinhiler, "How to Train Your Brain to Be More Optimistic," NBCNews.com, August 24, 2017. https://www.nbcnews.com/better/health/how-train -your-brain-be-more-optimistic-ncna795231.

92 *It's described as an explanatory style*: "Optimism," *Psychology Today*. https://www.psychologytoday.com/us/basics/optimism.

92 *Research has determined*: Robert Plomin, Michael F. Scheier, et al., *Optimism, pessimism and mental health: A twin/adoption analysis, Personality and Individual Differences* 13, no. 8 (August 1992): 921–30.

93 *Martin Seligman*: Martin Seligman, *Learned Optimism* (Vintage, 2006 edition).

93 *In the 1980s*: Martin Seligman and Peter Schulman, "Explanatory Style as a Predictor of Productivity and Quitting Among Life Insurance Sales Agents," *Journal of Personality and Social Psychology* 50, no. 4 (1986): 834.

94 *The strong link*: Jack Singer, "The Important Link Between Optimism and Sales Success," Pressive Blog. https://develop themindsetofachampion.com/the-important-link-between-optimism -and-sales-success/.

Notes

95   *Business professor Scott B. Friend*: Scott Friend, et al.,
"Positive Psychology in Sales: Integrating Psychological Capital," *Journal of Marketing Theory and Practice* 24, no. 3 (2016): 306–27.

97   *Research has revealed that optimism*: Brianna Steinhiler,
"How to Train Your Brain to Be More Optimistic," NBCNews.com,
August 24, 2017. https://www.nbcnews.com/better/health/how-train
-your-brain-be-more-optimistic-ncna795231.

97   *An analysis of the results*: Eric S. Kim, et al., "Optimism
and Cause-Specific Mortality: A Prospective Cohort Study," *American
Journal of Epidemiology* 185, no. 1 (January 1, 2017): 21–29.

98   *This is called the negativity bias*: Amrisha Vaish, et al.,
"Not all emotions are created equal: The negativity bias in social-
emotional development," *Psychological Bulletin* 134, no. 3 (2008):
383–403. https://www.ncbi.nlm.nih.gov/pmc/articles/PMC3652533/.

98   *Psychologist Roy F. Baumeister*: Alina Tugend, "Praise Is
Fleeting, but Brickbats We Recall," *New York Times*, March 23, 2012.
https://www.nytimes.com/2012/03/24/your-money/why-people
-remember-negative-events-more-than-positive-ones.html.

98   *This explains*: Ibid.

99   *In his book* Flourish: Martin Seligman, *Flourish: A Visionary New Understanding of Happiness and Well-being* (Free Press,
2011), 33.

100   *They also include mental health conditions*: L. Rood, J.
Roelofs, S.M. Bögels, and L.B. Alloy, "Dimensions of negative thinking
and the relations with symptoms of depression and anxiety in children
and adolescents," *Cognitive Therapy and Research* 34, no. 4 (2010):
333–42.

100   *. . . as well as physical health effects*: J.B. Whitfield, G.
Zhu, J.G. Landers, et al.,"Pessimism is associated with greater all-cause
and cardiovascular mortality, but optimism is not protective," *Scientific
Reports* 10, no. 1 (July 2020): 12609.

103   *Positive psychology has shown*: Maike Neuhaus, "Self-

Coaching Model Explained: 56 Questions and Techniques for Self-Mastery," PositivePsychology.com. https://positivepsychology.com/self-coaching-model/.

104 *Seligman advocates*: Jeana Magyar-Moe, *Therapist's Guide to Positive Psychological Interventions* (Academic Press, 2009), 111.

108 *According to psychologist and gratitude expert*: Rick Hanson, "Taking in the Good," Greater Good Science Center, UC Berkeley, November 1, 2009. https://greatergood.berkeley.edu/article/item/taking_in_the_good.

109 "Life Orientation Test": M.F. Scheier, C.S. Carver, and M.W. Bridges, "Distinguishing optimism from neuroticism (and trait anxiety, self-mastery, and self-esteem): A re-evaluation of the Life Orientation Test," *Journal of Personality and Social Psychology* 67, no. 6 (December 1994): 1063–78.

110 *In the early 1990s*: A. Favaro, E. St. Philip, and A.M. Jones, " 'To be a scientist is a joy': How a Hungarian biochemist helped revolutionize mRNA," CTV News, November 14, 2021. https://www.ctvnews.ca/health/to-be-a-scientist-is-a-joy-how-a-hungarian-biochemist-helped-revolutionize-mrna-1.5666043.

CHAPTER FIVE Fall in Love, Actually

116 *For example, the body releases*: Katherine Wu, "Love, Actually: The science behind lust, attraction, and companionship," Harvard University Science in the News, February 14, 2017. https://sitn.hms.harvard.edu/flash/2017/love-actually-science-behind-lust-attraction-companionship/.

116 *But Fredrickson posits*: Barbara L. Fredrickson, *Love 2.0: Finding Happiness and Health in Moments of Connection* (Avery, 2013), 14.

116 *"Love blossoms virtually anytime"*: Ibid., 17.

117 *"Do I really need to call"*: Ibid., 36.

118 *In fact, Fredrickson writes*: Ibid., 10.

118 *as psychologist Marc Schoen writes*: Marc Shoen, *Your Survival Instinct Is Killing You* (Plume, 2014), 177.

119 *Research shows*: C. J. Price, "A review and synthesis of the first 20 years of PET and fMRI studies of heard speech, spoken language and reading," *NeuroImage* 62, no. 2 (August 2012): 816–47.

119 *Neuroscientist Uri Hasson*: Greg J. Stephens, Lauren J. Silbert, and Uri Hasson, "Speaker–listener neural coupling underlies successful communication," *Proceedings of the National Academy of Sciences* 107, no. 32 (August 2010): 14425–30.

119 *The brain activity*: Fredrickson, *Love 2.0,* 41.

119 *"a whopping 44 percent"*: Ibid., 48.

120 *Fredrickson even addresses this*: Ibid.

123 *In a study involving college students*: G.M. Walton, G.L. Cohen, D. Cwir, and S.J. Spencer, "Mere belonging: the power of social connections," *Journal of Personality and Social Psychology* 102, no. 3 (March 2010): 513–32.

127 *He once said about his interviewing style*: Larry King, interview by Cenk Uygur, "Soft Questions? Larry King Explains His Interview Style," https://www.youtube.com/watch?v=2YqNyfeIyNc.

132 *In an article written for* Psychology Today: Judith E. Glaser, "The Neuroscience of Conversations," *Psychology Today,* May 16, 2009. https://www.psychologytoday.com/us/blog/conversational -intelligence/201905/the-neuroscience-conversations.

CHAPTER SIX Be a Teammate, Not Just a Coach

141 *They often have clever little names*: "The Door in the Face Technique: Will It Backfire?," Harvard Law School Program on Negotiation, January 14, 2021. https://www.pon.harvard.edu/daily/dispute -resolution/the-door-in-the-face-technique-will-it-backfire-nb/.

Notes

142 *A side effect of this*: Zig Ziglar and John P. Hayes, *Network Marketing for Dummies* (John Wiley & Sons, 2011), 429.

142 *Many studies have proven this*: Simon Schindler and Stefan Pfattheicher, "The frame of the game: Loss-framing increases dishonest behavior," *Journal of Experimental Social Psychology* 69 (September 2017), 172–77. https://www.researchgate.net/publication/308697226 _The_frame_of_the_game_Loss-framing_increases_dishonest_behavior.

143 *One study found*: Brendan Nyhan and Jason Reifler, "Does correcting myths about the flu vaccine work? An experimental evaluation of the effects of corrective information," *Vaccine* 33, no. 3 (2015): 459–64.

143 *The negative response*: Paul Marsden, "The Backfire Effect—When Marketing Persuasion Backfires," digitalwellbeing.org, March 30, 2015. https://digitalwellbeing.org/the-backfire-effect-when -marketing-persuasion-backfires/.

143 *the tendency for people*: C. Steindl, E. Jonas, S. Sittenthaler, E. Traut-Mattausch, and J. Greenberg, "Understanding Psychological Reactance: New Developments and Findings," *Zeitschrift für Psychologie* 223, no. 4 (2015): 205–14. doi:10.1027/2151-2604/a000222.

144 *As Simon Sinek wrote*: Simon Sinek, *Start with Why: How Great Leaders Inspire Everyone to Take Action* (Penguin, 2019), 19.

147 *One study found*: R.C. Barragan, R. Brooks, and A.N. Meltzoff, "Altruistic food sharing behavior by human infants after a hunger manipulation," *Scientific Reports* 10, no. 1 (February 2020): 1785.

148 *By the age of three to four*: Jane Chertoff, "The Toddler Years: What Is Associatie Play?," Healthline, July 22, 2019. https:// www.healthline.com/health/parenting/associative-play.

148 *An article in the* Harvard Business Review: David Mayer and Herbert M. Greenberg, "What Makes a Good Salesman?," *Harvard Business Review*, July–August 2006. https://hbr.org/2006/07 /what-makes-a-good-salesman.

149 *In* Unleash Your Primal Brain: Tim Ash, *Unleash Your Primal Brain: Demystifying how we think and why we act* (Morgan James Publishing, 2021), 136–37.

152 *Neil Young calls him*: Amy Wallace, "Steve Jobs' Doctor Wants to Teach You the Forumula for a Long Life," *Wired,* December 17, 2013. https://www.wired.com/2013/12/david-agus-rules-to-live-longer/.

152 *Salesforce.com CEO Mark Benioff*: Ibid.

152 *He's even credited*: Carrie Ghose, "CrossChx adds 'End of Illness' author David Agus to board," The Business Journals, October 12, 2016. https://www.bizjournals.com/columbus/news/2016/10/12/crosschx-adds-end-of-illness-author-david-agus-to.html.

153 *An added benefit*: Wayne Jonas, M.D., "Walking Meetings: The Future of Safely Collaborating," *Psychology Today*, March 22, 2021. https://www.psychologytoday.com/us/blog/how-healing-works/202103/walking-meetings-the-future-safely-collaborating.

155 *In* Think Again: Adam Grant, *Think Again: The Power of Knowing What You Don't Know* (Viking, 2021), 105.

157 *When Will Smith was first*: Will Smith and Mark Manson, *Will* (Penguin Press, 2021), 223.

163 *In his book* Wanting: Luke Burgis, *Wanting: The Power of Mimetic Desire in Everyday Life* (St. Martin's Press, 2021), 174.

CHAPTER SEVEN Transform, Don't Transact

171 *In* Give and Take: Adam Grant, *Give and Take: A Revolutionary Approach to Success* (Penguin Books, 2014), 4.

172 *As Daniel Pink showcased*: Daniel Pink, *Drive: The Surprising Truth About What Motivates Us* (Riverhead Books, 2011), 18.

172 *For example, a team from Harvard Business School*: Colleen Walsh, "Money spent on others can buy happiness," *Harvard Gazette,*

April 17, 2008. https://news.harvard.edu/gazette/story/2008/04
/money-spent-on-others-can-buy-happiness/.

172 *In another experiment*: J. Moll, F. Krueger, R. Zahn,
M. Pardini, R. de Oliveira-Souza, and J. Grafman, "Human fronto-
mesolimbic networks guide decisions about charitable donation,"
Proceedings of the National Academy of Sciences 103, no. 42 (October
2006): 15623–38.

173 *The positive feeling that stems*: Project Helping, "Helper's
High: Why Doing Good Makes Us Feel Good," ProjectHelping.org,
August 9, 2017. https://projecthelping.org/helpers-high.

175 *But according to a* Business Insider *article*: "Rising Stars
of Real Estate: Christine Wendell," *Business Insider*, December 2021.
https://www.businessinsider.com/rising-stars-real-estate-commercial
-residential-proptech-industry-leaders-2021-12#christine-wendell-pronto
-housing-8.

176 *In creating Rock the Vote*: https://www.rockthevote.org
/about-rock-the-vote/.

188 *"A mitzvah," the rabbi wrote*: Rabbi Seinfeld, "What's a
Mitzvah and What's the Difference?," June 6, 2007. https://jewcy.com
/religion-and-beliefs/whats_a_mitzvah.

CHAPTER EIGHT Creative Selling

193 *One study found that cold calling*: Brett A. Hathaway,
Seyed M. Emadi, and Vinayak Deshpande, "Don't Call Us, We'll Call
You: An Empirical Study of Caller Behavior Under a Callback Op-
tion," *Management Science* 67, no. 3 (2020): 1508–26.

193 *You've got to make fifty calls a day*: Kosti Lepojarvi, "Cold
Calling Is Dead? Not So Fast," Leadfeeder.com Blog, February 29,
2021. https://www.leadfeeder.com/blog/cold-calling-is-dead/.

193 *Einstein said, "The greatest scientists"*: P.H. Bucksbaum
and S. J. Gates Jr., "The Scientist as Artist," APS News, December

2020. https://www.aps.org/publications/apsnews/202012/backpage .cfm.

194 *It keeps them engaged*: Falon Fatemi, "Why Creativity Is a Secret Weapon in Sales," Forbes.com, July 27, 2018. https://www .forbes.com/sites/falonfatemi/2018/07/27/why-creativity-is-a-secret -weapon-in-sales/.

194 *Research has shown*: Ieva Martinaityte and Claudia A. Sacramento, "When creativity enhances sales effectiveness: The moderating role of leader-member exchange," *Journal of Organizational Behavior* 34, no. 7 (October 2012). https://www.academia.edu/4718609 /When_creativity_enhances_sales_effectiveness_The_moderating_role _of_leader_member_exchange.

194 *According to leading creativity researcher*: Scott Barry Kaufman, *Wired to Create: Unraveling the Mysteries of the Creative Mind* (TarcherPerigee, 2015), 23.

194 *As psychologist Peggy Orenstein writes*: Peggy Orenstein, "How to Unleash Your Creativity," Oprah.com. https://oprah.com /spirit/how-to-unleash-your-creativity/.

195 *Psychologist Ruth Richards*: R. Richards, "Everyday creativity: Our hidden potential." In R. Richards, ed., *Everyday creativity and new views of human nature: Psychological, social, and spiritual perspectives* (American Psychological Association, 2007), 25–53.

195 *"Our creativity helps us cope"*: Ibid., 3.

195 *"Immediately after the days"*: Tamlin S. Conner, Colin G. DeYoung, and Paul J. Silvia (2018), "Everyday creative activity as a path to flourishing," *Journal of Positive Psychology* 13, no. 2 (2018): 181–89.

196 *Happiness expert*: Mihaly Csikszentmihalyi, "Happiness and Creativity," *The Futurist* 31, no. 5 (September–October 1997): S8–S12.

196 *No wonder, as one researcher writes*: Scott Redick, "Surprise Is Still the Most Powerful Marketing Tool," *Harvard Business*

Review, May 10, 2013. https://hbr.org/2013/05/surprise-is-still-the
-most-powerful.

196 ... *more sexual partners*: M.L. Beaussart, S.B. Kaufman,
and J.C. Kaufman, "Creative Activity, Personality, Mental Illness, and
Short-Term Mating Success," *Journal of Creative Behavior* 46, no. 3
(2012): 151–67. https://scottbarrykaufman.com/wp-content/uploads
/2012/12/Beaussart-Kaufman-Kaufman-2012.pdf.

197 *But as psychologist*: Ken Robinson, "Do schools kill creativity?," TED Talk, January 6, 2007.

197 *Education specialist*: R.A. Beghetto, "Creative mortification: An initial exploration," *Psychology of Aesthetics, Creativity, and the
Arts* 8, no. 3 (2014): 266–76.

198 *Harvard specialist on creativity*: Teresa M. Amabile, "How
to Kill Creativity," *Harvard Business Review*, September–October 1998.

198 *Csikszentmihalyi backs that up*: Csikszentmihalyi, "Happiness and Creativity."

204 *One of Teresa Amabile's*: Teresa Amabile, "Necessity, Not
Scarcity, Is the Mother of Invention," *Harvard Business Review*, March
25, 2011. https://hbr.org/2011/03/necessity-not-scarcity-is-the.

204 *Even seemingly daunting impediments*: Matthew E. May,
"How Intelligent Constraints Drive Creativity," *Harvard Business Review*, January 30, 2013. https://hbr.org/2013/01/how-intelligent
-constraints-dr.

209 *Mind-wandering is so good*: Nate Klemp, "Harvard
Psychologists Reveal the Reasons We're All So Distracted," Inc.com.
https://www.inc.com/nate-klemp/harvard-psychologists-reveal-real
-reason-were-all-so-distracted.html.

209 *Scott Barry Kaufman*: Scott Barry Kaufman, "The Real
Neuroscience of Creativity," *Scientific American*, August 19, 2013.
https://blogs.scientificamerican.com/beautiful-minds/the-real-neuro
science-of-creativity/.

209 *Ruth Richards also commends*: Richards, "Everyday creativity: Our hidden potential," 48.

210 *. . . as introduced by Dr. Edwin de Bono*: Edwin de Bono, *Six Thinking Hats* (Back Bay Books, 1999).

210 *Huge companies like Prudential Insurance*: https://www.debonogroup.com/services/roi-reports-and-testimonials/.

211 *Ruth Richards points out*: Richards, *Everyday Creativity and the Healthy Mind*, 3.

CHAPTER NINE Set Goals on Purpose

213 *the Oprah Effect*: Clay Halton, "The Oprah Effect," Investopedia, September 14, 2021. https://www.investopedia.com/terms/o/oprah-effect.asp.

214 *Oprah has said*: "Every Person Has a Purpose," *O, the Oprah Magazine*, November 2009. https://www.oprah.com/spirit/how-oprah-winfrey-found-her-purpose.

214 *It wasn't until she was thirty*: Sara McCord, "In Very Exciting News, Oprah Just Shared Her Secret to Success," TheMuse.com. https://www.themuse.com/advice/in-very-exciting-news-oprah-just-shared-her-secret-to-success.

217 *The authors of a* Harvard Business Review *article*: Andrew Zoltners, et al., "Five Ways That Higher Sales Goals Lead to Lower Sales," *Harvard Business Review*, September 12, 2011. https://hbr.org/2011/09/five-ways-that-higher-sales-go.

217 *Choosing to ignore*: Francesca Gino and Bradley Staats, "Your Desire to Get Things Done Can Undermine Your Effectiveness," *Harvard Business Review*, March 22, 2016. https://hbr.org/2016/03/your-desire-to-get-things-done-can-undermine-your-effectiveness.

218 *Researchers who studied this problem*: Ibid.

Notes

218 *In one newsworthy example*: Jack Kelly, "Wells Fargo Forced to Pay $3 Billion for the Bank's Fake Account Scandal," *Forbes*, February 24, 2020. https://www.forbes.com/sites/jackkelly/2020/02/24/wells-fargo-forced-to-pay-3-billion-for-the-banks-fake-account-scandal/?sh=48e2550542d2.

219 *Even if performance goals are realistic*: Lisa Ordóñez, Maurice Schweitzer, Adam Galinsky, and Max Bazerman, "Goals Gone Wild: The Systematic Side Effects of Over-Prescribing Goal Setting," *Academy of Management Perspectives* 23 (January 2020). https://www.hbs.edu/ris/Publication%20Files/09-083.pdf.

221 *In positive psychology*: "What to Know About the Hedonic Treadmill and Your Happiness," Healthline.com. https://www.healthline.com/health/hedonic-treadmill#what-is-it.

223 *A large study of top sales performers*: Lisa McLeod, interviewed by Jan Rutherford, "Selling with Noble Purpose," May 6, 2021. https://www.youtube.com/watch?v=DeYZURrIiEk.

226 *As Lisa Earl McLeod*: Ibid., at 16:57.

235 *To develop your purpose statement further*: Mike Murphy, "8 Steps to Living Intentionally," Thrive Global, 2018. https://thriveglobal.com/stories/8-steps-to-living-intentionally/.

239 *In an interview*: Oprah Winfrey, interview on VanityFair.com, January 25, 2018. https://www.vanityfair.com/video/watch/oprah-winfrey-on-her-new-goal-here-on-earth.

About the Authors

COLIN COGGINS and GARRETT BROWN are longtime sales leaders, practitioners, teachers, and best friends. They met at software startup Bitium, which they helped lead to an acquisition by Google. They teach the popular course they created, Sales Mindset for Entrepreneurs, at the University of Southern California's Marshall School of Business. They are also investors, corporate advisors, and cofounders of Agency18, a firm that helps mission-driven companies adopt the Unsold Mindset. Sought after as keynote speakers and guest lecturers, they love connecting with audiences from diverse industries, professions, and backgrounds and showing them that it's possible to successfully sell without being someone you're not.

Colin and Garrett live in Southern California with their families. To learn more, visit colinandgarrett.com.